The Old Testament

Part II

Professor Amy-Jill Levine

THE TEACHING COMPANY ®

PUBLISHED BY:

THE TEACHING COMPANY
4151 Lafayette Center Drive, Suite 100
Chantilly, Virginia 20151-1232
1-800-TEACH-12
Fax – 703-378-3819
www.teach12.com

Printed in the United States of America

ISBN 1-56585-615-5

Amy-Jill Levine, Ph.D.

E. Rhodes and Leona B. Carpenter Professor,
Vanderbilt University Divinity School/Graduate
Department of Religion

Amy-Jill Levine earned her B.A. with high honors in English and religion at Smith College, where she graduated magna cum laude and was a member of Phi Beta Kappa. Her M.A. and Ph.D. in religion are from Duke University, where she was a Gurney Harris Kearns Fellow and held the W. D. Davies Instructorship in Biblical Studies. Before moving to Vanderbilt, she was Sara Lawrence Lightfoot Associate Professor and chair of the Department of Religion at Swarthmore College.

Professor Levine's numerous books, articles, and essays address such topics as Second-Temple Judaism, Christian origins, and biblical women's roles and representations; she has written commentaries on Ruth, Esther, and Daniel, as well as on the Gospels of Matthew and Mark. She is currently completing a manuscript for Harvard University Press on Jewish narratives from the Hellenistic period and a major commentary on the Book of Esther for Walter de Gruyter Press (Berlin). Professor Levine has served on the editorial boards of the *Journal of Biblical Literature* and the *Catholic Biblical Quarterly*, among other publications, and has held office in the Society of Biblical Literature and the Association for Jewish Studies. Among her awards are grants from the Mellon Foundation, the National Endowment for the Humanities, and the American Council of Learned Societies.

A widely sought speaker, Levine has given lectures and workshops throughout the United States and Canada for universities, biblical associations, synagogues, temples, churches, and interfaith and civic groups, as well as two series of lectures at Chautauqua in the Hall of Philosophy.

As a graduate student at Duke, Levine was initially prevented from teaching New Testament in the Divinity School by an administrator who did not think it appropriate that a Jew would teach this material. "You can teach Old Testament," he told her. "I don't do Old Testament," she said; "You do now," was his response. Thus began her ever-growing fascination with the subject of these lectures.

Within a semester, the administrator was no longer at Duke and Levine's teaching opportunities broadened, but she chose to continue in the Old Testament classroom while adding courses in the New Testament. Completing coursework in both Old Testament/*Tanakh* and Christian origins, Levine has been studying and teaching both topics ever since.

Levine and her husband, Jay Geller, Ph.D. (who also teaches religion at Vanderbilt), live with their children, Sarah Elizabeth and Alexander David, in Nashville, Tennessee.

Table of Contents

The Old Testament
Part II

The Old Testament

Scope:

The Bible has been labeled, correctly, as the foundation document of Western thought. It is read in synagogues, temples, and churches; it is cited on the floor of the Senate and from the bench in the courtroom. Contemporary politics is inextricably intertwined with it, from conflict in the Middle East to the claim by many in the United States that a return to "biblical values" is warranted. The Bible influenced the Pilgrims to leave England in the seventeenth century; it inspired the founders of the new republic in the eighteenth; it roused both slave and abolitionist to seek a new Moses and sponsor a new Exodus in the nineteenth and the Jews to establish a homeland in the twentieth. Missionaries, with Bible in hand, journeyed to Asia, Africa, and South America, and among the indigenous populations they met, the Bible galvanized attempts to throw off the yoke of colonialism. Its influence permeates Western literature, from medieval plays to modern novels, art, music, theatre, film and dance; its prophetic calls for social justice challenge all readers to reevaluate their own behavior even as its Wisdom literature challenges our views of God. Replete with genres ranging from myth and saga to law and proverb, containing dry political history and erotic love poetry, informed by a world view much different than our own, these texts are a compendium of a people's sacred story. And that story is the foundation document of Judaism and the first part of the canon of the church.

These twenty-four lectures offer an introduction to the history, literature, and religion of ancient Israel and early Judaism as it is presented in the collection of texts called the Old Testament, the Hebrew Bible and the *Tanakh*. Not all books will, or even could, be covered; the content of certain books, such as Genesis, could easily fill twenty-four lectures alone, as could the stories of certain figures, such as the Patriarchs and Matriarchs, Moses, and David. Attention is given not only to the content of the biblical books but also to the debates over their meaning and the critical methods through which they have been interpreted. Often, a book will be examined by means of an analysis of a representative text or figure in it.

The lectures presuppose only a very general familiarity with the Bible's major figures and themes (e.g., Adam and Eve, Moses, the

Ten Commandments, David and Bathsheba); biblical literacy, as sociologists have noted, is on the wane in the West. Although students do not need to follow the lectures with an open Bible, reading the texts listed at the top of each of the outlines will enhance appreciation for the material.

Oriented toward historical context and literary import, the lectures do not avoid raising issues of religious concern. The goal of an academic course in biblical studies should not be to undermine religious faith. Rather, it should provide members of faith communities with richer insights into the literature that forms their bedrock. Even were one to argue that the text is divinely inspired or dictated by God, one might still want to know as much as possible about the particulars: Why these words? Why this order? Why this social context? Why this translation?

Lecture Thirteen

The Book of Judges, Part I (Judges 1–8)

Scope:

The Book of Judges is, as Mieke Bal describes, "a book about death." Repeating the type scene of apostasy, punishment, repentance, and rescue, the book ultimately spirals into idolatry, rape, and near-genocide. Yet the barbarity is broken by moments of delight. Judges plays on traditional definitions of the hero: tricksters like Ehud, mothers like Deborah, cowards like Gideon, tragic figures like Jephthah, even blockheads like Samson. Offering high comedy and profound tragedy, Judges continues to raise historical, theological, and moral challenges. After a brief note on the date of the volume, this lecture introduces, by means of the variations on type-scene conventions, the more capable judges, all of whom appear in the first part of the book: Othniel, Ehud, Deborah, and Gideon.

N.B.: Many scriptural quotations in the lectures are translated by Dr. Levine directly from the Hebrew and thus may vary slightly with the text of standard printed editions in English. In other cases she draws from the New Revised Standard Version (NRSV), the King James Version (KJV) and the New English Bible (NEB).

Outline

I. Date: Judges is set ca. 1200–1000, at the beginning of the Iron Age.

- **A.** The narrative suggests a long editorial process culminating shortly before or during Babylonian captivity in the sixth century.
- **B.** Individual tribal legends are combined in the Deuteronomic editorial framework: the view that fidelity is rewarded and apostasy punished.

II. The type scene guides all but the last several chapters.

- **A.** The basic pattern appears with the first judge, Othniel, in 3:7–11.
  - **1.** "The people of Israel did what was evil" (3:7).

2. YHWH gives them to Cushan-Rishathaim of Mesopotamia for eight years (3:8).
3. The people cry out to the Lord, and "the Lord raised up a deliverer for the people of Israel" (3:9).
4. Othniel receives the divine spirit, wages war, and prevails (3:10).
5. Othniel judges Israel forty years, then dies (3:11).
6. "And the people of Israel again did what was evil" (3:12).

B. Even this introductory pattern is broken by textual anecdotes.

1. Othniel is less stalwart than his betrothed, Caleb's daughter Acsah.
2. Acsah and Caleb function as ironic foils to Jephthah and his daughter (Jdg. 11).

III. The first variation, the account of Ehud, is so sexual and scatological that it was just as likely a favorite of ancient Israel even as it is rarely cited from pulpits and bimas today.

A. Ehud the trickster prevails by means of brains, not brawn.

1. Like cross-cultural tricksters (Pan, Loki, Hermes), he is left-handed.
2. This trait allows him to conceal his weapon: he "girded [the sword] on his right thigh under his clothes" (Jdg. 3:16).
3. A sexual undertone begins.

B. King Eglon, the enemy, also possesses an unusual characteristic: he is "very fat" (3:17).

1. Because kings are military leaders, Eglon is already shown to be unworthy.
2. That *eglon* means "fatted calf" hints that he will be sacrificed to that hidden sword.

C. The judge's victory is filled with sexual and scatological imagery common to folktales.

1. Ehud states (3:19), "I have a message for you, O king," and the king, stupidly, orders everyone except Ehud away.
2. "Ehud came to him, as [Eglon] was sitting alone in his cool roof chamber" (3:20).
3. "Ehud reached with his left hand" (the hand used for handling genitals; 3:21).

4. He "took his sword from his right thigh, and thrust it into Eglon's belly… the hilt went in after the blade, and the fat closed over the blade." The image is of perverse intercourse.
5. Reading 3:22 euphemistically: "And the dirt came out"; more directly, the king defecates—there is an emission, but the wrong kind.
6. Eglon's servants, believing that the king is relieving himself, avoid entering and, thus, permit Ehud to escape. "They waited until they were utterly at a loss; but when he still did not open the doors of the roof chamber, they took the key and opened them, and there lay their lord, dead on the floor" (3:25).

D. Shamgar is the next judge, though little is said of him. He provides a break between the account of Ehud and the Song of Deborah.

IV. The story of Deborah (Jdg. 4–5), told first in prose, then in poetry, plays on the themes of mothers, violence, and seduction.

A. Deborah's introduction challenges military, gendered, and maternal conventions.

1. Underneath her palm tree, the judge presides before the military problems arise.
2. Most translations render 4:1 "wife of Lappidoth," but no such character appears.
3. The phrase could be translated "woman of flames," which complements the name of her general, Barak ("lightning").
4. Her relationship to Barak complicates gender roles. Barak refuses initially to battle: "If you go with me, I will go; but if you will not go with me, I will not go" (4:8). This passage may be read, however, as Barak's testing of Deborah.
5. Deborah agrees, but at the price of his honor: "The road on which you are going will not lead to your glory, for the Lord will sell [the enemy] Sisera into the hand of a woman" (4:9).

B. This "woman" who claims the honor Barak loses is Jael, the second "mother."

1. Jael is married to the absent but frequently mentioned "Heber the Kenite [who] had separated from the Kenites, the descendants of Hobab the father-in-law of Moses." (In the next lecture, we shall see how far Moses's household has fallen.)
2. Sisera, the enemy general, fleeing Barak, goes "to the tent of Jael, the wife of Heber the Kenite, for there was peace between Jabin the King of Hazor and the house of Heber the Kenite."
3. But what of Jael: Is she Israelite, Kenite, Canaanite? To whom are her loyalties?
4. Are we to be reminded of Cain: a murderer, yet protected?

C. Jael inverts Near Eastern concerns for hospitality and conventions of motherhood.

1. Her invitation is more seduction than protection: "Jael came out to meet Sisera, and said to him, 'Turn aside, my lord, turn aside to me; have no fear'" (4:18).
2. Maternally: "She covered him with a rug. And he said to her, 'Pray, give me a little water to drink, for I am thirsty.' So she opened a skin of milk and gave him a drink and covered him" (4:19).
3. Then "the wife of Heber, took a tent peg, and went softly to him, and drove the peg into his temple, until it went down into the ground, as he was lying fast asleep from weariness. So he died."
4. The imagery evokes Eglon's death: sword and tent peg, trickster assassin, bedroom demise.

D. The Song of Deborah offers one of the oldest examples of Hebrew poetry.

1. The song restages Sisera's death: he is standing as he dies, and his unmanning becomes even more manifest:

   She struck Sisera a blow
   She crushed his head
   She shattered and pierced his temple.
   He sank, he fell.
   He lay still at her feet.
   At her feet he sank, he fell;
   Where he sank, there he fell, done to death.

2. The song also mentions a third mother. Unlike Deborah and Jael, Sisera's mother is inside a home, not under a tree or in a tent; she has all the luxuries of the city-state, yet she lacks peace:

   Out of the window she peered.
   The mother of Sisera gazed through the lattice.
   Why is his chariot so long in coming?
   Why tarry the hoofbeats of his chariots?

3. Before Deborah's song allows too much sympathy, Sisera's mother develops her own explanation.

   Are they not finding and dividing the spoil?
   A womb or two or every man?
   Spoil of dyed stuff for Sisera…?
   She will receive neither.

V. Gideon's story (Judges 6–8) reveals increasing problems with charismatic leaders who are less confident and less capable.

A. The convention expands description of the judge's appointment: In the modern idiom, "good men are becoming harder to find."

1. Gideon complains about the weakness of his tribe (Manasseh), family, and personal ability.
2. He also complains about divine inaction. As Gideon is beating wheat in the winepress to hide it from the Midianites, an angel announces, "The Lord is with you, you mighty man of valor" (6:11). Given Gideon's position, the sarcasm is palpable. Gideon responds: "Pray sir, if the Lord is with us, why then has all this befallen us? And where are all his wonderful deeds, which our ancestors recounted to us, saying, 'Did not the Lord bring us up out of Egypt?'"
3. Gideon risks trivializing divine ability by continually testing God. He taxes God's patience—and the reader's: "Let not your anger burn against me; let me speak but this once. Pray, let me make trial only this once with the fleece; pray let it be dry only this once on the fleece, and on all the ground let there be dew" (6:39).

B. This unpromising beginning matches his unpromising end.

1. Gideon's other name is "Jerubaal," "Let Baal contend," a Canaanite "Israel."
2. His final action, one of apostasy, confirms his fall: "Gideon made an ephod of [the gold captured from the Midianites] and put it in his city in Ophrah; all Israel whored after it there, and it became a snare to Gideon and his family" (8:27).

C. One of his sons, Abimelech ("my father is king"), will prove to be a false judge. With his tenure, the benefits of the charismatic leader become increasingly insecure. As we shall see in the next lecture, the role of the judge must eventually cede to that of the king.

Supplementary Reading:

Susan Ackerman, *Warrior, Dancer, Seductress, Queen: Women in Judges and Biblical Israel*, Anchor Bible Reference Library (New York: Doubleday, 1998).

Mieke Bal, *Death and Dissymmetry: The Politics of Coherence in the Book of Judges* (Chicago: University of Chicago Press, 1988).

Gail Yee (ed.), *Judges and Method: New Approaches in Biblical Studies* (Minneapolis: Fortress Press, 1995).

Questions to Consider:

1. Is Judges "funny"?
2. What are the functions of such motifs as scatology, perverse sexual humor, and reversed gender roles (military women, mothers who kill, generals who seek protection from women) in a community's national epic?
3. What is the "theology" of Judges?

Lecture Thirteen—Transcript
The Book of Judges, Part I
(Judges 1-8)

As we move from the Book of Joshua and into the Book of Judges, we change worlds. Gone is the time when the tribes are working in unity to gain the Promised Land. Gone is the time of miracles, the sun standing still, or the trumpets blaring and the walls of Jericho falling. In fact, gone is the time when you can tell the difference between the good guys and the bad guys. When we move to the Book of Judges, it is as if we are coming closer to our own world. There are fewer miracles, more divisions among the tribes, and individual charismatic leaders fighting individual battles with individual enemies. The tribes are no longer united. This is a new world.

It begins on an extremely promising note, but, by the time we get to the end of the Book of Judges, we find this covenant community spiraling out of control into chaos and into anarchy. So what ultimately happens in the Book of Judges is that we have an apology for the monarchy, an excuse to explain why the covenant community commissioned to be a nation independent and under God suddenly finds itself with King Saul and then King David pretty much like all the other nations of the world.

The Book of Judges is difficult to read. Scholar Mieke Bal refers to it as "a book about death," and that is, in fact, what it is, but, especially at the beginning of the text, the chaos and the anarchy and the tragedy are broken by moments of great humor, indeed, moments of farce. So we'll take two lectures to look at the Book of Judges. This first lecture will look at the initial judges, where we have a little bit more humor than we have tragedy.

We'll look at the judge Othniel to begin with, and Othniel actually establishes the pattern for the Book of Judges. We've already talked about type scenes, literary conventions such as the ancestress in danger or the annunciation to a woman that she will have a child. The Book of Judges can be looked at as an enormous type scene that fits a particular pattern where the people begin a form of apostasy. They begin worshipping foreign gods or idols. God punishes them by turning them over to a foreign nation, and they are enslaved or repressed. The people repent. God hears them and raises up a judge to rescue them. The judge rescues the people, defeats the foreign enemy, judges for a set number of years, and dies. Then the pattern begins again as the people sink into apostasy.

But this is not simply a repetition, over and over the same pattern. There are variations on the theme, which we'll notice, and we'll also see that each time the pattern is repeated it becomes more and more tragic, as if the people are ultimately spiraling out of control, so that at the end of the Book of Judges, in fact, there are no more judges—there is only chaos.

We start with the judge Othniel, we'll move to Ehud, and then to Deborah and then to Gideon. Things are pretty good at this point. Before we start with Othniel, just a brief mention of the setting of the Book of Judges. Judges is like Joshua set at the beginning of the Iron Age, but it's simply telling us what Joshua didn't. Joshua gives us a very positive notice, a full conquering. Judges says, not quite, not quite. We didn't quite conquer everything. The Book of Judges is, like Joshua, however, presented within a Deuteronomistic framework, which means that the editor, the Deuteronomic editor, is very concerned that people who behave properly, who worship God in the appropriate way, will be rewarded and people who sin will be punished. We will see some of that comeuppance that occurs to some of these judges who do not particularly behave well.

Here we go with the basic pattern. We're going to start with Othniel. This is Judges, Chapter 3. Othniel is the first judge. The pattern begins with apostasy: "The people of Israel did what was evil. Forgetting the Lord their God, they started to worship Baalim and Asherah," the Canaanite divinities. God gets upset. YHWH leaves the people to the consequences of their action and delivers them over into the hand of the enemy, the King of Cushan-Rishathaim—it's a Mesopotamian government—and the people are then oppressed. Israel repents, and God finally hears them and raises up a judge.

The judge here is Othniel, nephew of Caleb, and we will remember Caleb from his excursions into the Promised Land with Joshua. Caleb's line continues. But already we have a slight variation on the theme to begin with. It turns out that Othniel had actually been introduced to us a couple of chapters before—we already know he's on the scene. So here we have the book already letting us know we're going to have literary conventions but we're not going to be static about it.

Othniel comes on the scene because, the rulers of the community explain, we are under oppression. Caleb announces, I will give my daughter—her name is Acsah—to the ruler, to the judge, who was able to defeat the enemy. Othniel says, I'll take her. I will volunteer. And, in fact, Othniel winds up defeating the enemy. But here is another play. Othniel's wife Acsah winds up taking the lead. After their marriage she is the one who goes to her father and demands wells for water. She's the one who demands better land. So we see right at the beginning a judge who is capable of military conquest but not quite capable of getting what he specifically needs in order to thrive. That becomes his wife's job.

We'll also see even implanted in this very first story the problem of vows. Here is a story of a father who vows his daughter to a military leader pending conquest. In our next lecture we'll encounter the judge Jephthah, who vows to sacrifice to God the first person, the first being, who comes out of his house should he win the victory in battle. When fathers promise their daughters or make vows—this is a good example with Jephthah—we see the negative side. Themes are already implanted. Othniel judges for a set number of years; he dies. The people of Israel sink back into apostasy. The pattern will continue.

The next judge we find is the judge Ehud. I need to warn you that the story of the judge Ehud is both sexual and scatological. Most people who read the Bible do not assume that the Bible has such material in it. This is supposed to be, according to contemporary views, a holy book, a divine book. If we think back to Clement of Alexandria saying, "Moses would never have said that Noah got drunk," you can see the difficulty people might have. But the Book of Judges is like Israelites on the frontier. For people trying to establish a nation—the minority group within the major Mesopotamian area of numerous stronger kingdoms—people in such situations need to tell stories that will bolster them, that will serve to humiliate the enemy, that will serve to entertain. We might think of these as stories told by soldiers out in the encampment. They are not going to pull punches, and they are going to use whatever humor, earthy as it may be, in order to get their views across.

So now that you've been warned about the judge Ehud, let's watch his story. Here is the first variation on the scene. We are told that Ehud is left-handed, which, back then as well as today, does not encompass the majority of the population, and we've got to figure we're being told that for a particular reason. Ehud is not only left-handed, he makes himself an 18-inch-long sword that he straps onto the inside of his right thigh. You can picture where the sword is and how Ehud is functioning. When Ehud goes to the enemy king—his name is Eglon, which means, by the way, "fatted calf," not a great name for a king, and we're also told Eglon is very fat—when Ehud goes to Eglon, we might expect something tricky to occur, and that is precisely what happens. Ehud has his sword strapped onto his thigh. He is patted down by Eglon's soldiers. They do not find the sword. Ehud gets into the king's court, and he says to Eglon, "I have a message for you, O king, in secret."

Now, if I were an ancient Near Eastern king, I would have my entire army standing there (knowing anything about the Israelites) just for protection. Eglon the fatted calf has a brain like a cow. He immediately sends out all his soldiers, he retires to his upper roof chamber of his summer palace, and Ehud is invited in. The two men are alone, in private. Ehud comes to him as Eglon is sitting in his cool roof chamber, the text says. But, rather than receive the message that Ehud has promised him, Eglon receives death. Ehud reaches with his left hand—and the left hand, by the way, in the ancient world as well as, in fact, in the contemporary Middle East, is the hand that's normally used by men to handle genitalia—he reaches with his left hand underneath his clothes, he pulls out his sword, and he sticks the sword right into the fatted calf's stomach. We're told that the sword stayed in. It's an image of perverse intercourse.

To people in contemporary society, it sounds disgusting. I think, to people at the beginning of the Iron Age, people who are struggling to maintain a national identity and want to see their heroes succeeding, they would have loved—they would have loved—this story. Worse, the perversity of this intercourse continues with scatology. We have the Hebrew idiom, talking about Eglon, "and the dirt came out," which is simply an idiomatic expression for "he defecated." So not only do we have the sword penetrating him in front, we have an emission. It's sexual. It's scatological. The people in antiquity would have loved it.

What happens in the plotline? Eglon's soldiers are waiting outside the room, and they are expecting the king to call him and they are waiting, and they are waiting, and they are waiting, and he hasn't opened the door. They think to themselves, “Well, maybe he’s in the bathroom.” The text actually says this. Finally, when they can wait no longer, they break in the doors, and they find their king lying there with Ehud’s sword still stuck in him. Meanwhile, Ehud is able to escape. He rallies the Israelite troops. He gains his men, and they wind up killing 10,000 Moabites. That’s Chapter 3, verse 29. That’s the story of Ehud, the trickster judge who kills the king through secrecy, through beguiling him, and I think people would have laughed. That’s our second judge.

The third judge comes in only a verse or two. His name is Shamgar, son of Anath. Already we have a problem here because Anath is one of the Canaanite goddesses. So we might worry a little bit about Shamgar’s background. Shamgar offends the literary convention in a variety of different ways. There is no mention of public infidelity. There is no account of oppression by an enemy. There is no account of Shamgar’s judging or how long he judged or even his death. We’re simply told that Shamgar takes an oxgoad and kills 600 of the Philistines with it. That’s it.

Offending the plot line even more, in various early manuscripts of the Hebrew text, the story of Shamgar does not show up here at the end of the story of Ehud. It shows up well later in the Book of Judges, after the story of Samson—as if the biblical editor, the Deuteronomic editor, thought, “Well, we’ll put this story last because he, Shamgar, is so offensive to the pattern to the literary convention. It seemed like he might make the last judge.” This also tells us how unstable that early text is. The judges can, in fact, be interchanged to some extent.

I think the story of Shamgar might also be there to give us, in effect, a commercial break in between the long story of Ehud and the story we come to next, which is the Song of Deborah and the account of Deborah in prose narrative. This is Judges, Chapters 4 and 5. The thematics of this story, the prose narrative of Deborah and the Song of Deborah, play on the thematic of mothers: good mothers, dangerous mothers, honorary mothers, and biological mothers. The play on the type scene begins immediately, for we see Deborah sitting underneath her palm tree (Judges 4:4). She’s already there prior to any sort of need for military commission. But there does occur oppression. The people have gone into apostasy, and Deborah now, our only female judge—again a play on the convention—becomes the official who will commission the general to go into war.

We have problems with Deborah right from the beginning even before her commission, and we'll see this immediately in Chapter 4, verse 4, her introduction. She's called a prophetess. That's fine, although we don't really technically have prophets yet. She's also identified in Chapter 5, verse 7, as a mother in Israel, but it's not clear she actually has any children. Indeed, it's not clear she's actually married. Most English translations identify her as the "wife of Lappidoth." Mr. Lappidoth actually never shows up in this text. Husbands are a rare commodity in the Song of Deborah, as we'll see. Mr. Lappidoth is not there. Moreover, the expression "Lappidoth" can mean "of flames." So instead of looking at Deborah as "Deborah, wife of Lappidoth," we might just as well translate "Deborah, woman of flames;" which makes a good deal of sense, actually, because, when we come to her general, whose name is Barak, Barak in Hebrew means "lightning." So here is this war machine—flames and lightning going against the enemy. That may well be the case.

Deborah's relationship to Barak is also slightly problematic. Barak is the general. He is supposed to do all that military conquest, manly material. But when Deborah says to Barak, "Go into battle," Barak says, "I'm not going unless you come with me." Now, on the one hand, in a positive sense Barak might be thinking, "Well, put your money where your mouth is, lady. If you're going to send me into battle, you come, too." But I also have a sense that he's not quite ready to untie those apron strings. Deborah represents God, and she is going to go with him into the field. So Deborah says, "Yes, I will go with you. However, your honor will be lost here." As she puts it, "God will give the enemy into the hand of a woman." So because Barak is unwilling to go into battle without the woman by his side, the honor normally due to him as military leader will be taken away.

At first we might think that the woman to whom the honor will be given is Deborah. It turns out not to be the case. There is another woman in this story—her name is Jael. I really like Jael, but I find her very mysterious. Let's look at Jael for a minute. We are told that she is married. Her husband is identified as "Heber the Kenite," and this brings us back to those Kenites we've seen, already connected perhaps with Cain, connected with the Kenite hypothesis, the idea that the Kenites provided Israelites some knowledge of YHWH, the idea of the Kenites as resident aliens in the community but not fully absorbed. Heber the Kenite actually doesn't show up, and we're not technically told to what ethnic group Jael belongs. We don't know if she is Kenite or Israelite or Canaanite. She's already a mystery.

What we do know about the Kenites is they were in alliance with Israel, except that Heber the Kenite, Jael's husband, had made a treaty with the enemy. So here we have some disloyalty already shown, and then the question comes about: Whose side is Jael on? Will she fight for the Israelites? That's normally whom the Kenites would fight for. Will she fight for her husband's allies? Will she fight for herself? What are her motives? As we've already seen even back in Genesis, motives are frequently suppressed. I know what Jael does; I'm still not quite sure why.

In terms of what she does, here we go. Sisera, the enemy general, has been routed by Deborah and Barak and their troops. Sisera is using iron chariots—this is the beginning of the Iron Age—and his chariots have gotten stuck in the mud. His entire military effort is doomed. Sisera takes off on foot, and, as he is running away, he goes to the tent of Heber the Kenite because he knows Heber is loyal to his boss, the enemy. Coming out of the tent, coming out to meet him, is Jael. In the English, she says, "Turn aside, my Lord. Turn aside to me. Don't be afraid." But Hebrew has her purring like a cat coming out: "*Sura adoni, sura elai al tira*."

She entices him in, and he comes into her tent. In fact, he says to her, "I'm thirsty. Could I have some water?" And she gives him milk. Then he lies down, and she covers him with a rug. She's a good mom. She gives milk. She covers him. She tucks him into bed. Sisera then says to her, to the woman, "Stand by the door of the tent, and, if anybody comes by and asks, 'Is there a man here?' say no." No problem for Jael. She has already unmanned him. She's now standing guard; that should be the soldier's role. There is, in fact, no man in the tent because the manly activity is being accomplished by Jael.

Then we're told Jael, the "wife of Heber," took a tent peg and went softly to Sisera and drove the tent peg into his temple, and it went down into the ground, and he died. This is not the sort of mother most people would want. So here we go from Deborah, the mother in Israel, the battle leader who may not have any children of her own, to

Jael, the false mother, who gives you milk, tucks you in, and then takes a tent peg and kills you. Here again we have, of course, another inversion to the pattern. Normally it is the judge who dispatches the enemy. Here it is a second woman unexpected—neither Barak nor Deborah but Jael—and no motive is given. We do not know why Jael does this. Deborah says in her song it's out of loyalty to Israel. But the prose narrative never actually tells you.

At the end of the prose narrative, Jael, seeming to me much like a spider inviting a fly into her parlor, goes out to meet Barak, who has finally chased Sisera down, and she says to Barak, "Come into my tent and let me show you what I have." Barak comes into the tent as he is pursuing Sisera, and there lies Sisera dead, Barak finds, with the tent peg in his temple. And thereby Barak the general also becomes unmanned. His honor is usurped by this woman, Jael. Fascinating.

But that's just the prose narrative—let's go to the poem in Chapter 5. The poem in Chapter 5 may, in fact, be one of the oldest pieces of literature we have in the entire *Tanakh*. It's exceptionally ancient. In fact, before we look at the story of Deborah and Barak and Jael and Sisera in the poem, let's just do a little bit of background information. How early is this? Although it seems like in Deborah's Song she is calling all the tribes to unity, there are certain tribes who are missing. Simeon and Levi are not mentioned. Perhaps they had already been absorbed into some of the other tribes. More striking yet, the tribe of Judah is not there. Perhaps this is a song created by people up in the north originally, where Judah is the kingdom of the south, but his absence is conspicuous and problematic.

Now to the Song of Deborah. The poem restages Sisera's death. The prose narrative is nasty, it's problematic, but it's logical because we're told Sisera is lying down out of weariness. He's exhausted, which means it's very easy to plug him with a tent peg if he's lying down. In the Song he's standing up. Now, I don't think Jael went up to Sisera with a tent peg and said, "Hold still while I kill you." This has to be looked at on a metaphorical basis, and we can actually see him dying slowly, losing his honor, losing his ability, losing his manliness. Listen to the poem. "She struck Sisera a blow. She crushed his head. She shattered and pierced his temple." This is good Israelite poetry, to say the same thing several times: "He sank, he fell. He lay still at her feet. At her feet he sank, he fell. And where he sank, there he fell, done to death."

You can picture this being recited to a group of people who are perhaps losing a war, who need a little bit of bolstering, who want to see that enemy general really tent-pegged, as it were. And this actually works. The Song of Deborah then goes on to mention Sisera's mother, who never actually shows up in the prose narrative. Here is the third mother, and, in fact, the only biological mother of the three. Sisera's mother is pictured standing in a window behind the lattice. This idea of this woman framed in a window is a standard ancient Near Eastern artistic convention. We actually have ivory depictions of this. It's very, very common. We'll see it again, actually, with Jezebel, who meets her ending by—she puts on makeup first—and then she stands in a window, and she calls out to the people who will eventually engage her death.

But here's Sisera's mother behind the lattice, as if she's trapped. She's not like Deborah out in the field or Jael in her tent. She is comfortable, and she is there with her ladies-in-waiting, and she begins to ask, "Why is my son's chariot so long in coming? Why tarry the hoofbeats of his chariots?" But then she provides herself her own answer. She answers her question: "Are they not finding and dividing the spoils—a womb or two for every man?" Most texts read "a damsel or two," "a maiden or two," but this is a much more earthy text. What happens in war? Soldiers capture women—we've seen this in descriptions of holy war—and bring them back either for sexual objects or for servitude. This is what Sisera's mother is expecting, and that's, in fact, where she's left. She will not get stuffs, spoils, she will not get a servant from the women of Israel, and her son will never return to her. She is left in that window waiting, and that's the poet's part, the Song of Deborah in ancient text, but over the centuries I think it still has that power to grab.

After Sisera dies the land stays at rest for 40 years, and then the pattern continues, and we move on to Judges, Chapters 6 through 8. This is the story of Gideon, and here, in terms of the convention, the opening is substantially expanded because Gideon, like Moses before and like Saul later, typically rejects his commission. God calls him, and he's not too sure he wants to go. Here we go. Hesitant to accept his command when the angel calls him, he says, "Wait—my tribe, the tribe of Manasseh, is weak; my family is small; I'm not that able." It's as if he's saying, "Who, me? You want me? This is crazy." We actually see him at first when an angel comes to him, and we're told that the angel comes to him when he is hiding in a winepress beating wheat, but out of the eyes of the Midianites so that they can't see him.

There he is, hiding and beating this wheat, and the angel comes to him and announces, "The Lord is with you, you mighty man of valor." Now, if you were a military leader out in the camp, it makes a good deal of sense to say that. But the fact that he's hiding suggests that this opening might be a little bit more humorous than we would expect. The angel commissions him, but Gideon is not quite willing to go. He responds to the angel, "Pray, sir, if the Lord is with us, why has all this befallen us? Where are all his wonderful deeds which our ancestors recounted to us, saying, 'Did not the Lord bring us up out of Egypt?'" Gideon raises a good question. "Where are all those good miracles—what's happening? I'm stuck here in a winepress beating wheat." Something better has to happen.

He more or less accepts his commission, but he continues to put God to the test. He puts a fleece on the ground and says, "Tomorrow let it be dry," and then he says, "but tomorrow let it be wet." He continues to test God with these little petty miracles just to make sure that God will actually come through. Finally Gideon engages in battle, but, consistent with his hesitancy, just as he tested God, he will test his own men. He starts out with 22,000 men. He whittles it down to 10,000 and then finally to 300. And, by the way, for those of you familiar with the Gideon Bible, it's in this particular section that the Gideons from the Gideon Bible took their name. I actually looked it up in the Gideon Bible. This is what the opening passage says: They take their inspiration from Gideon, "who led a small band of men dedicated to the service of God." Those are those 300.

Gideon actually routs the enemy with his 300. Everything looks terrific. It's going great. Then problems begin again. Gideon's other name is "Jerubaal," which means "let Baal contend." There is a pagan background here, a Canaanite connection, and Gideon's final action is one of apostasy. We're told that Gideon made an *ephod*, some sort of idol, out of the gold captured from the Ishmaelites—a group of his enemies—in fact, from their earrings that they were wearing, that Gideon's men had taken in booty. From this gold he fashions an *ephod*, and we're told that this became a snare to Gideon and his family. Gideon and his family go astray.

The people come to Gideon, and they say, "Become a ruler after us, you and your sons and your sons following." In other words, establish a dynasty. Gideon says, "No, God is your ruler. God will be the one who will protect you." And that may be just as well, given his apostasy. But it turns out that Gideon has many sons. He has one son with the problematic name Abimelech, which translates "my father is king." One worries about a man who on the one hand denies dynastic rule but on the other hand names his child "my father is king." We will come to Abimelech in the next lecture. He will prove to be a false judge, and, with his tenure, the benefits of the charismatic leadership become increasingly insecure.

So we'll end this talk with just a brief mention of what happens with Gideon, and then we'll prepare for this downhill battle as we move from Abimelech, the false judge, to Jephthah, the judge who kills his daughter, to Samson, the judge who doesn't even realize his own commission to the people out of control. Here is the end of this section as we have it. After Gideon's death the Israelites again "whored after the Baalim and Baal-Berith." Most texts say "went astray;" the Hebrew actually says "whored after." This is a standard Hebrew idiom for apostasy. We'll see it especially in the prophets. And who are the people going after? The Canaanite gods, but, worse, not only Baalim, Canaanite gods, but a god called Baal-Berith, which translates "Lord of the Covenant"—a false god but with echoes of the Israelite deity. The text goes on, "They were unmindful of the Lord their God who had delivered them from all their enemies around them." What will then happen? We'll have to wait until the next lecture to see.

Lecture Fourteen

The Book of Judges, Part II
(Judges 8–21)

Scope:

Returning to Gideon's son Abimelech, then introducing the last two major judges, Jephthah and Samson, this lecture unveils the increasing instability of the judge as political leader and the descent of the tribal confederation into chaos. It concludes by observing how the apostasy and violence of the tribe of Dan, the rape of the Levite's concubine, and the ensuing civil war reflect a society symbolized by a dismembered corpse, a society out of moral control and—as the author of Judges strongly implies—in need of a centralized government.

Outline

I. Abimelech, the false judge, embodies the threat of dynasties.

- **A.** His usurpation of power highlights the inevitable dynastic problem: competition.
  1. Gideon rejected dynastic rule (8:22–23) in favor of rule by God.
  2. Abimelech, the child of Gideon's Shechemite concubine, convinces the Shechemites that he, rather than one of the seventy sons of Gideon's wives, would make their appropriate leader: nepotism triumphs over legitimacy and qualification.
  3. Abimelech kills all his seventy brothers save Jotham, the youngest (9:5). Throughout the Deuteronomic history, dynastic succession exists in tension with the traditions of charismatic leaders and the ambivalence concerning primogeniture.
  4. Although Gideon consistently receives divine aid, God sends an "evil spirit" between Abimelech and the Shechemite lords (9:23); rulers require divine as well as political support.

- **B.** Abimelech exacerbates his father's idolatry.
    1. Gideon (Jerubaal) made an *ephod*, likely an image of a local god (8:27).
    2. Abimelech, supported by his Shechemite mother's relatives, receives funding from the Shechemite temple of "*Ba'al Berit*" (ironically, "Lord of the Covenant" [9:4]).
    3. The scene evokes Gen. 34, the rape of Jacob's daughter by Shechem (the prince of the land and, symbolically, the entire city).
- **C.** Abimelech is killed when "some woman" (9:53) drops a millstone on his head.
    1. Horrified at this ignoble end, Abimelech orders his aide to kill him (9:50–57).
    2. The scene ends not with a reigning judge and peace, but a dead judge and a curse.

II. Jephthah (11:1–12:7), the tragic judge, shows the problems with appropriate selection.

- **A.** "Jephthah… the son of a prostitute, was a mighty warrior… When [Gilead's] wife's sons grew up, they drove Jephthah away, saying to him, 'You shall not inherit anything in our father's house, for you are the son of another woman'" (11:1–2).
    1. The opening recollects Ishmael and Isaac (Gen. 21:10).
    2. It anticipates David: Both rulers function initially as outlaws (Jdg. 11:3; 1 Sam. 25).
- **B.** Jephthah is commissioned not by God, but by his town's leaders: "Are you not the very ones who rejected me and drove me out of my father's house?" Yet he agrees: "*If you bring me home again*… I will be your head" (11:9).
    1. The reversal of the convention and the absence of divine involvement indicate the breakdown of the political system.
    2. The conditional response anticipates the rash vow Jephthah later makes.
    3. The desire for "home" increases Jephthah's tragedy.

C. Later (11:29), "the spirit of the Lord" comes upon Jephthah. He immediately vows: "If you will give the Ammonites into my hand, then whoever comes out of the doors of my house to meet me, when I return victorious from the Ammonites, shall be the Lord's, to be offered up by me as a burnt offering" (11:30–31).
   1. The lateness of the commission raises questions of divine culpability.
   2. The vow has no excuse.
   3. Jephthah appears incapable of accepting his own worth.

D. At the victory, Jephthah's daughter emerges—as is typical for women—in celebration: "She was his only child. He had no son or daughter except her" (11:34).
   1. The verse echoes the *Akedah*: "your son, your only son…"
   2. Jephthah blames his daughter: "Alas, my daughter, you have brought me very low. You have become the cause of great trouble to me…" (11:35).
   3. She supports him: "My father, you have opened your mouth to the Lord; do to me according to what has gone forth from your mouth…"
   4. The sacrifice is delayed while the daughter mourns her virginity. This becomes "a custom in Israel," perhaps a puberty or premarital rite.
   5. Or, as J. Cheryl Exum suggests, is "she" "an example" of daughters sacrificed to fathers' interests (cf. Othniel and Acsah; later, Saul and Michal)?

E. Jephthah's victory comes at the expense of tribal unity when Ephraim revolts.
   1. The problem is now internal to Israel, not external.
   2. His household tragedy assumes national implications.

III. Samson, Israel's Hercules (13:1–16:31), will eclipse, like the sun that is his leitmotif.

A. Samson's nativity spoofs conventional annunciations.
   1. His parents are childless, and there is no indication that they want children, unlike their Genesis counterparts.
   2. Mrs. Manoah meets an angel in the field who announces, "Behold, you are barren and have no child." This is news?
   3. The angel informs Mrs. Manoah that she will become pregnant, the child should be a Nazirite, and he will

deliver his people from the Philistines. She accepts this oracle without question; the same cannot be said for Manoah (13:6).

4. Manoah, after a ridiculous conversation with the angel, invites the angel to lunch (cf. Gen. 18:1–15); the angel suggests offering a sacrifice instead, which he does.
5. When the angel ascends in the flames, Manoah fears he and his wife will die, because they have "seen God." His wife retorts, "If the Lord had meant to kill us, he would not have accepted the burnt offering…" (13:23).

B. Samson's career spoofs, then tragically reverses, that of other judges.

1. Breaking his Nazirite vows, Samson consumes honey from a lion's carcass. He thus violates the commandment against eating (from) carrion.
2. He insists on marrying a Philistine, against his parents' objections.
3. Betrayed by his wife, his "military" action is against his bride's family.
4. Samson burns Philistine fields; the Philistines burn Samson's wife and her father.

C. Delilah, the woman "from Sorek" whom Samson loved, is a complex figure.

1. Viewed as Philistine, Delilah has a Hebrew name (cognate to *Layla*, "night"); she is the inverse of Samson, the symbol of sun and fire.
2. Viewed as immoral, she never lies to Samson, but she does betray him to the Philistines.
3. Viewed as mercenary, her motives are unexpressed: Might she fear Philistine reprisal? Is her cajoling a warning?

D. Samson's tragic end: the last of the judges.

1. Why does Samson reveal his secret to Delilah? She arranges to have his hair, the source of his power, shaved off.
2. Returned to a state of infancy—bald, sightless, and helpless—Samson eventually regains hair, strength, and a modicum of maturity.

3. He dies pulling down the Philistine temple. Thus ends the period of the judges. It is a tragedy akin to that of Oedipus.

IV. With the Danites, the type scene is fully broken; chaos follows.

A. Micah's story hints of Samson's and anticipates that of the Levite's concubine.

1. He is "in the hill country of Ephraim," the Levite's home (17:1; 19:1).
2. He obtains from his mother the "cursed" eleven hundred pieces of silver (17:1), the same amount received for Samson's betrayal.
3. Micah buys a Levite and procures Teraphim, but the Danites steal both.

B. The Danites represent the descent of the community into apostasy (18:1–31).

1. "Then the Danites set up the idol for themselves."
2. Jonathan, son of Gershom, son of Moses (some manuscripts read "Manasseh"), and his sons were priests to the Danites until the exile.
3. Dan and Beth-el held the Northern Kingdom's major shrines: perhaps this story and the next developed ca. 622, during Josiah's reform, which included disenfranchising Levites and centralizing sacrifice in Jerusalem.
4. The story is prefaced by "In those days there was no king in Israel" (18:1).

V. The story of the Levite's concubine reprises Sodom's destruction (Gen. 19), without divine intervention.

A. The narrative opens with a text-critical problem.

1. The Septuagint (19:2) reads that the concubine "became angry with [the Levite]." The Hebrew reads, "she played the whore" (anticipating prophetic metaphors).
2. The Levite follows her "to speak tenderly to her" (19:3). The expression recollects Shechem, Dinah's rapist, and, again, anticipates prophetic metaphors.

B. The story replaces Sodom with a Benjaminite city.

1. The Levite bypasses lodging in the non-Israelite city, Jebus; this is Jerusalem.

2. When they enter Gibeah, another Ephraimite gives them lodging.
3. The Benjaminites, "a perverse lot," demand of the stranger, "that we may know him."
4. The old man, like Lot, offers his own virgin daughter and Levite's concubine.
5. The Levite "seized his concubine and put her out to them. They wantonly raped her, and abused her all the night until the morning" (19:25).
6. In the morning, the Levite, seeing her "lying at the door of the house, with her hands on the threshold," commands: "Get up; we are going" (19:27–28). "She made no reply."

C. The concubine's body now summons, and symbolizes, broken Israel.
1. The Levite, in a perverse sacrifice, hacks her body into twelve pieces, which he distributes to the tribes.
2. The attendant message is: "Has such a thing ever happened since the day that the Israelites came up from the land of Egypt?" (19:30).
3. The tribes gather; the war leads to more loss as Benjamin's existence is threatened.
4. To preserve the tribe, hundreds of women are given to Benjamin; rapes escalate.
5. The text ends with the refrain "there was no king in Israel; every man did what was right in his own eyes" (21:25), and so sets the stage for the monarchy.

Supplementary Reading:

Phyllis Trible, *Texts of Terror: Literary-Feminist Readings of Biblical Narratives* (Philadelphia: Fortress Press, 1984).

See also works listed for Lecture Thirteen.

Questions to Consider:

1. Does the sacrifice of Jephthah's daughter provoke a reconsideration of the *Akedah*?
2. Why does Delilah, along with other women who trick men (such as Potiphar's wife in Gen. 39, a story we have not directly addressed) escape narrative judgment?

3. How does the story of Moses from Exodus through Deuteronomy contribute both to supporting the institution of the charismatic leader and undermining this system in favor of a dynastic monarchy?

Lecture Fourteen—
The Book of Judges, Part II
(Judges 8-21)

From the stories of Othniel and Ehud and Deborah and Gideon we can see that a judge is not simply someone who would sit in a courtroom and engage in decision making over land disputations or over whose ox gored whose. To the contrary, judges are charismatic leaders imbued by the spirit of God. The spirit actually enters into them. Then they function primarily as military leaders but also as public figures who can lead the land both into safety and then into peace. The problem is, in the second part of the Book of Judges, that the entire institution begins to break down as the judges don't immediately receive the spirit or don't receive it at all as they make rash vows, and, by the time we get up to Samson, as they are not even aware of what their divine commission is.

So in the second part of discussion on the Book of Judges we'll see how the community descends into chaos as the office of judge itself falls apart. We'll first meet Abimelech, whom we've already encountered in the last lecture, the false judge. We will move on to Jephthah, the tragic judge. Then we'll see Samson, judge as farce. Finally, at the end of the book where there are no judges, we'll see the apostasy of the tribe of Dan and then finally the rape of the Levite's concubine, a rape that signals finally the complete and total chaos into which the covenant community has sunk.

We begin here with Abimelech, Abimelech whose father is Gideon and Abimelech whose name is "my father is king"—that's what the Hebrew means. He is, however, a false judge, and we know he is set up right from the beginning to be a problem. Gideon has many, many wives and many sons. This will, of course, be a problem with Solomon and David and questions of dynastic succession. But here Abimelech is not the son of the legitimate wife; he is the son of a concubine. Concubinage was a perfectly normal category in ancient Israel. One took a wife to produce a legitimate heir, and, if one were a king, one would take a wife for alliance concerns. One takes a concubine for sexual pleasure, and, if the concubine happens to conceive a child, there is no guarantee that that child will inherit anything from the estate of the father.

So here is Gideon, the child of the concubine. He wants to inherit. He takes matters into his own hands. How is he going to get rid of all of his brothers? He winds up murdering them all. This is not a great way to start. What we're told in Judges 9, verse 4, is that he begins association with a group of reckless and worthless fellows, and he kills his brothers, the 70 sons of Jerubaal. That's Gideon. He butchers them all on the same stone block, with only his youngest brother Jotham escaping. Already this is abundantly evident: we have a false judge here.

Moreover, Abimelech, in order to ensure support, goes to his mother's family, and it turns out his mother is from Shechem, that location where Joshua engaged in covenant making but also the place back in Genesis, Chapter 34, where Jacob's daughter Dinah had been raped, and we'll encounter Shechem later on as well. It will become finally the capital of the northern kingdom of Israel, and, after the Israelite fall to Assyria, Shechem becomes renamed Samaria, one of the later enemies of Israel. So Shechem is a problem. And the god of Shechem is identified as Baal-Berith—we've encountered this before. The expression means "Lord of the covenant," but what we have here is a false judge and a false god. What we want is the Israelite God of the covenant, not this Shechemite god, false god. Abimelech gets money from his mother's family. He kills his brothers. God simply will not stand for this.

Finally, God, instead of sending a good spirit, a holy spirit, into Abimelech, sends an evil spirit into the people, and they revolt against Abimelech. The Shechemite Lord said, "We have had enough of this," and, as the text said, this was done in order that the violent murder of the 70 sons of Jerubaal might recoil on their brother, Abimelech, who committed the murder and might also recoil on the people of Shechem who encouraged him to do that. That's Judges 9:24.

A war occurs, and Abimelech is killed himself in the same sort of ignominious manner in which Sisera is dispatched. During the fight a woman from an upper apartment drops a millstone used for grinding bread on top of Abimelech's head and shatters his skull. Abimelech thinks with his dying breath and his dying thought, I can't have it be said that I was dispatched by a woman, so he calls one of his soldiers to run him through with a sword so it will not be said that Abimelech was killed by a woman. But Abimelech has died, and at this point

YHWH is getting annoyed with these people, upset with these people. The convention continues—apostasy, apostasy. And YHWH says, "I am not going to raise up any more judges for you." We can hear his anger in Chapter 10. YHWH states, "Did I not deliver you from the Egyptians and the Amorites and the Ammonites and from the Philistines and from the Sidonians and from the Amalekites?" and he goes on and on and on—"There will be no other judge."

But the people again sink into apostasy, and then they repent, and they need a judge, and nothing is happening. So here, in a variation on the scene, the people raise up their own judge. They call a fellow named Jephthah, and he becomes our tragic judge in a story of enormous pathos. This is Judges, Chapter 11. Jephthah also has ignominious beginnings. Abimelech is a child of a concubine. Jephthah is the child of a prostitute. So obviously he's not going to inherit anything from his father. It turns out that his father has numerous other legitimate sons, and they want to drive Jephthah away. As the text said, "They drove him away, saying, 'You shall not inherit anything in our father's house for you are the son of another woman.'" We might be reminded here back in Genesis of Sarah saying to Abraham, "Drive out the slave girl and her son, Hagar and Ishmael, because the son of the slave woman will not inherit with my son, Isaac." We'll see this over and over again, Judges replaying scenes in Genesis. But whereas in Genesis God almost invariably comes to the rescue, in Judges he rarely does.

Jephthah is driven away, and he gathers about himself reckless and worthless fellows just like Abimelech, indeed, just like King David. But all three have different fates. Abimelech is the false judge: his reckless and worthless companions are of no help to him. Jephthah is the tragic judge: his reckless and worthless companions become part of his army. David is the ideal king: he takes over. There is no worthlessness, there is no tragedy, in his companions.

Jephthah has, in effect, an army of brigands with him, and the townspeople come to him, and they say, "Be our ruler, be our judge. Help us remove the oppressive forces which are pushing us down, oppressing us." Jephthah says to the townspeople, "Aren't you the very ones who rejected me and drove me out of my father's house?" But Jephthah, the tragic judge, is yearning for a home, yearning for some stability, and he responds finally, "Yes, I will lead you if you bring me back home." In fact, they agree to that.

So Jephthah becomes the leader, and he turns out to be the most faithful Yahwist of all, the most faithful in terms of the covenant community's religious basis. Instead of immediately going to war he goes to the enemy, and he actually begins by pursuing peace. He says, "What have we done against you? We don't want to go to war with you. We simply want to inherit and settle in the land that God has promised us." He recites Israel's salvation history, and only after that are we told he received the spirit of the Lord. God relents on his thought, "I will not raise up a judge," and actually gives the Holy Spirit to Jephthah.

But then we here have a problem because immediately after Jephthah receives this Holy Spirit he makes a vow. He vows to God, "If you will give the Ammonites into my hand, then whoever comes out of the doors of my house to meet me when I return victorious from the Ammonites shall be the Lord's to be offered up by me as a burnt offering." One wonders already about the culpability of God here sending the Holy Spirit and then finding this rash vow. I also wonder about many biblical scholars who have commented on this particular verse. One frequently finds in Bible notations or in textbooks the idea that Jephthah was really expecting a puppy dog to come out of the house. I think this is a cop-out on the part of scholars. The vow is rash. There is no excuse. We don't even know if he has a dog. The fact is, Jephthah simply cannot believe that good things will happen to him. He sets himself up for failure.

And indeed that is precisely what happens. Jephthah has a victory, and, coming out of the house, as we might expect, is his daughter, because whenever the men have a victory the women always come out in celebration with dancing and tambourines. We've seen it with Miriam; we will see it again with the women celebrating David's victories. But we're told about this particular celebration, his daughter comes out and, the text reads, "She was his only child. He had no son or daughter except her." Here are the parallels with Isaac—we recall from the *Akedah*—"your only son, the son whom you love." Jephthah realizes the result of his vow, what will have to happen, and Jephthah simply can't deal with it, and he does the only thing that he possibly can. He strikes out at his daughter. He says, "Alas, my daughter, you have brought me very low. You have become the cause of great trouble for me." Or, as one biblical paraphrase puts it, "You have broken my heart." It's not exactly what the text says, but I think that captures the meaning.

The daughter, ensuring his compliance with the vow and providing him solace at the same time, responds, "My father, you have opened your mouth to the Lord. Do to me according to what has gone forth from your mouth." It's as if she can't bring herself to use the word "sacrifice." Before her death, however, the daughter requests two months to mourn her virginity, as the text says, with her friends, and they go up to the mountain. This may be an etiology for a woman's festival, perhaps a puberty rite or prenuptial rite, and it became a custom in Israel, so we are told, that the daughters of Israel went year by year to lament the daughter of Jephthah, the Gileadite, four days during the year. This becomes a custom.

Jephthah does to her as he had promised. We do not see the daughter again. Biblical scholar J. Cheryl Exum suggests that "not only did Jephthah's daughter's mourning become a custom in Israel, but in fact Jephthah's daughter is for the Book of Judges a custom in Israel." We've already seen this with the story of Othniel, with parents like Caleb vowing their daughters for military victory. But, whereas for Caleb's daughter Acsah it worked out well, for Jephthah's unnamed daughter tragedy accrues, and indeed the tragedy will continue to accrue. The chaos continues. Jephthah has won the battle, but suddenly the difficulties come from inside Israel rather than from outside. The tribe of Ephraim revolts against Jephthah. They say to him, "Why did you cross over to fight the Ammonites and did not call us to go with you? We will burn your house over you with fire." Who knew? People wanted to go to war, they didn't get summoned, and now they revolt.

The Gileadites, Jephthah's group, arranged to fight the Ephraimites, and they wound up killing 42,000 of them. Indeed, they guarded a river, the Gileadites did, and whenever the Ephraimites attempted to cross they put a test to them. They said, "Say the word 'shibboleth.'" It has come into English as a code word or a password. It turns out the Ephraimites could not pronounce the word. They wound up saying "sibboleth." So the Gileadites could tell by their accent, again signaling a break in the community, who were their friends and who were their enemies. Forty-two thousand dead Ephraimites: the problem is now violence internal to the community rather than violence on the outside. We can see Israel spiraling down.

And so we come to the next judge, Samson. Samson is like Hercules, only stupid. He's also like the sun, which is his leitmotif. Indeed, ultimately we will see that Samson, like the sun, burns himself out. We begin, actually, the story of Samson with yet another type scene, yet another literary convention. This is the annunciation type scene, the model of an angel or priest or seer explaining or promising to a woman that she will have a child who will go on to do great things. Indeed, the beginning of the Samson story starts out pretty much the way several of those stories in Genesis started.

We find out that there is an Israelite couple, and they have no children. We have an infertile wife. Except in this type scene, which seems to be a parody, this Israelite couple does not much seem to care that they are infertile. The wife is not saying to the husband, "Give me children or I shall die." There is no indication that they want children at all. Samson's father's name is Manoah. His wife is not named. We will call her Mrs. Manoah for lack of a better term. Mrs. Manoah is out in the field one day, and an angel appears to her and announces, "Behold, you are barren and have no child." This is news? But then he says to her, "You will become pregnant and you will have a son. You will make him to be a Nazirite," a particular holy person within Israel known for not cutting their hair and also from refraining from any sort of wine or strong drink. Nazirite vows are usually taken for a set period of time. Samson is to be a Nazirite from the day of his birth. The mother says this is fine.

She goes back home, and she announces to Manoah, "I met an angel in the field. He told me I'm going to get pregnant. I'm going to have a son." Manoah is a little concerned about this and starts asking his wife lots of questions. Finally he says, "Listen, the next time you are out in the field and the angel appears to you, come get me so I can see what's happening." And lo and behold the next day she is out in the field, and an angel appears, and Manoah comes out. Manoah says to the angel, "What have you been saying to my wife?" and the angel, who is getting somewhat frustrated here—you can see how this is a play on the original annunciation type scenes—said, "Look, your wife has already told you everything. I've already told her. Why do you need for me to repeat it?" But the angel does.

Manoah, then, after listening to all this, invites the angel to lunch. We've already seen this back in Genesis when the three men representing God come to Abraham and Abraham invites them to a meal and they predict that Abraham will have a son. But the angel says, "Well, lunch is not really quite what is needed. Perhaps"—hint,

hint—"you might offer a sacrifice to God." Manoah picks up on the hint and offers a sacrifice to God, and the angel goes into the flames and ascends into heaven, at which point Manoah thinks, "We've just seen God. We'll die." Mrs. Manoah has to explain to him, "Look, dear, it's unlikely we're going to die because I'm supposed to have this baby. If we die right now I will not have this child and this child will not redeem his people. Therefore, don't worry about it." Samson, as we'll see, very much takes after his father.

Samson's career, like his nativity scene, basically spoofs that of the other judges, at least at the beginning. Samson's play on the convention is that he has long hair. That would have meant something to people in the ancient Near East, where we have lots of inscriptions and artistic depictions of rulers with long hair, usually seven long locks. They are what used to be called "banana curls" for those of you of a certain age. Gilgamesh is usually depicted with these seven long locks. This is where Samson's strength resides—it's the sign of his Nazirite vow.

But it's not entirely clear that Samson realizes he's a Nazirite. Nazerites are supposed to keep themselves in states of ritual purity, but one of the first adventures Samson has is to encounter a lion and kill it and later on notice that bees have taken up residence in the lion's carcass. Samson eats some of the honey that the bees have produced. One is not supposed to eat anything dealing with blood. One is not supposed to deal with an animal which is carrion. That is entirely unkosher, and Samson eats it. Either he doesn't know his vow, or he doesn't take it seriously. Then next he insists on marrying a Philistine woman, and his parents say, sounding like many parents even today, "Look, can't you find a girl from your own family, from your own tribe?" But Samson insists, "She pleases me. Get her for me," and the parents yield, and he marries this Philistine woman.

As part of the wedding ceremony, Samson tells a riddle, and the answer to the riddle is, in fact, this lion with the honey in its carcass. Part of the riddle is, whoever guesses it gets riches from the riddle's teller. So the wife's relatives come to the wife and they say, "Get the answer for it so we can obtain from Samson his wealth." And the wife goes up to Samson and she starts cajoling him, day after day after day, "Tell me the answer to your riddle." Finally Samson gives in, and it's a good thing, too, for the wife, because the Philistines had said to her, "If you don't get the answer we're going to burn you and your father and your household." Good thing for the wife.

So she gets the answer, and she tells the Philistines, and the Philistines, on the last night of the wedding feast, say to Samson, "We have the answer to your riddle." Samson responds in good idiomatic Hebrew, "If you had not plowed with my heifer you never would have come up with the answer to this riddle." He is furious. He's absolutely furious because he has been betrayed. He winds up setting fire to the Philistine fields, and the Philistines, of course, are simply furious as well, and they wind up burning alive Samson's Philistine wife and her father. For the wife there is no way she can win, and she represents the tragedies of women in this book to come.

And poor Samson, he's now without a wife. He encounters a prostitute in the next scene. That's not going to get him anywhere. Finally he comes to a woman whose name has become legendary—Delilah. We don't actually know very much about Delilah. She's usually identified as a Philistine, but her ethnic background is never given. She may well be an Israelite. She's entirely independent. She is not somebody's daughter. She is not somebody's wife. She's on her own. She seems to own her own house, and she hobnobs with the rich and famous in the Valley of Sorek, where she lives. The Philistine leaders know all about her. We are told that Samson loves her, but we are never told that she loves him. One can hear echoes of Isaac and Rebecca back here.

The Philistines come up to Delilah, and they say, "We will give you a huge sum of money if you give Samson over into our hands," and Delilah proceeds to do precisely that. But, again, what's her motive? Is it to betray Samson to the Philistines because she is loyal to the Philistines, or does she know what the Philistines are capable of? They've already killed one of Samson's wives. Perhaps they will now kill her, Samson's lover. I'm not sure why she acts, but she does it quite well. She needs to find out from Samson the secret of his hair, and she starts cajoling him and cajoling him and cajoling him, and we readers, recognizing Samson's general dimwittedness, realize that the poor schlemiel is going to tell her the secret to his strength in any case, and finally he does.

The irony here is that Delilah signals to Samson time after time what she's doing. The first several times Samson lies to her, and she responds, "Samson, the Philistines are upon you," and he breaks his bonds and fights them off. He knows exactly what she's doing. She never lies to him. She never withholds the truth. And he's experienced these Philistines coming at him. Why he finally tells her the truth remains an open question. Is he trying to find some woman whom he can finally trust? He couldn't trust the Philistine wife to begin with. He can't trust the prostitute. Is he looking for trust here?

The Philistines actually capture him because he gives Delilah the secret: "My strength lies in my hair." So Delilah shaves his head, and, as he's resting on her knees, like an infant, bald and helpless, the Philistines come, and they attack him, and they put out his eyes, and they take him in chains, and they bring him to the city of Gaza. Here is Samson, like an infant, totally helpless, sightless. But slowly and inexorably his hair starts growing back, and his strength starts coming back. Finally his fidelity comes, and he prays to God, "Oh, Lord God, remember me, I pray you, and strengthen me." And through God's response and his long hair, Samson finally is able to accomplish what he was meant to accomplish. Chained to pillars holding up a Philistine temple, he pulls the pillars down, and the Philistines die all around him, and Samson dies in the rubble. He brings to death more Philistines during his death than he ever did at his life.

The story can be read at its end as if it is a tragedy like the story of Oedipus. The hero, blinded, finally comes to some sort of self-awakening, but it is a tragedy, and Samson, like the sun, is finally and totally eclipsed.

From the story of Samson we move on to the account of the shrine of Micah, which begins with a refrain that will echo again in Judges: "In those days there was no king in Israel." Here the type scene is fully broken. We will have no more judges. What we have is a guy named Micah living in the hills of Ephraim, and the first thing he does, we are told, is he steals a substantial amount of money, silver, from his mother—1,100 pieces of silver—and that turns out to be precisely the amount of money that the Philistines paid Delilah. Is Micah's mother Delilah? We don't know because we never actually find out what happens to Delilah.

But Micah admits to his mother he has stolen the silver, and the mother says, "Dear, it's all right. We'll use some of the silver to make an idol." You can see how downhill this tribe is going. So they make an idol, a pagan image, a molten image, and Micah sets up the shrine in his home, and first he has one of his sons become the priest, but later he encounters a Levite, and he says to the Levite, "I will give you 10 pieces of silver a year and a suit of clothes and your living. The priesthood is up for sale." And the priest becomes the priest to Micah's house.

Meanwhile, the tribe of Dan, who, as we have seen before, is looking for an inheritance in the land, stops by Micah's house to check with the Levite to find out if he's got any information on this. It turns out, they think to themselves, perhaps having a Levite is not a bad idea. So they say to the Levite, we're going to take you away, and, when the Levite complains, the tribe of Dan responds, "Keep quiet. Put your hand to your mouth and come with us and be to us a father and a priest. Is it better for you to be a priest in the house of one man or to be a priest to a tribe of a family in Israel?" In other words, it's a bigger job, it's an advancement in his career. We're told the priest's heart was glad, and he took Micah's *ephod*, his idol, as well as his *teraphim*, his family tribal signatories, perhaps gods, as well as a graven image, and he went in the midst of the Danites.

The Danites, of course, represent the descent of the community into apostasy, for, in their new city which they named Dan, the Danites set up the graven image for themselves, and we're told Jonathan the son of Gershom the son of Moses and his sons were priests to the tribe of Dan until the day of the captivity of the land. Moses' grandson, Moses' children, are also sinking into apostasy. Not surprisingly, there are some manuscripts which, instead of reading "Moses" read "Manasseh," as if certain scribes could not bear the idea that Moses's descendants would sink so low. The pagan encroachment has gone from one family to an entire tribe, and it will get worse because the final episode of the Book of Judges, beginning again, "There was no king in Israel, and every man did what was right in his own eyes" starts out with a man, again from the hill country of Ephraim, and he has a concubine, and we already know concubines are dangerous.

The concubine becomes angry with this man. The man is a Levite, a priest. The Hebrew actually reads, "She played the whore against him." The Greek simply says, "She became angry." I think the Hebrew might have been added on later, somehow to justify what happens to this woman. But in fact nothing justifies her fate. The concubine runs away to her father's house, but we already know the father's house is no place of safety for women in Judges. The Levite comes after her to speak tenderly to her. It's the same expression Shechem uses to Dinah, the girl he has already raped. And the father finally says, "Take my daughter and go," and they begin to go back home.

They bypass the town that will eventually become Jerusalem because they want to stay in a city that is an Israelite city—they think they will be safe. They enter the town of Gibeah, which is a Benjaminite city—it should have been okay—where another Ephraimite provides them lodging. Here we have a replay of Lot and Sodom, with visitors coming in to find lodging, but here the scene is worse than Sodom because these are not pagans. These are Benjaminites; they are in the family. The Benjaminites come out to the house of the man who has taken in the Levite and his concubine, and they say, "Send out the stranger that we may know him." Lot in Genesis 19 offered his two virgin daughters to the Sodomites. But Lot and his daughters were protected by the angels who had come to lodge with him. There is no angelic protection here.

The Levite seizes his concubine and pushes her out the door, and they wantonly rape her all night long and abuse her until the dawn. In the morning the Levite opens the door, and the text says, "He sees her lying at the door of the house with her hands on the threshold." He commands her, commands her, "Get up, we're going." And the text again says, "She made no reply." It's not even clear she's dead yet, but she is certainly dying. The Levite puts her on his donkey and brings her home and, in the most perverse sacrifice of all, hacks her body into 12 pieces and sends the pieces off to the 12 tribes of Israel with the attendant message, "Has such a thing ever happened since the days that the Israelites came up from the land of Egypt?"

The tribes gather, and they go to war against Benjamin, and the Benjaminites are almost wiped out. But then the tribes realize, we are a 12-tribe league. We cannot have genocide of one particular tribe. How does one repopulate Benjamin? They go find other women, other virgins, and give them to the Benjaminites, so one rape leads to more rapes and leads to more rapes after that. And the book ends in Chapter 21, verse 25, "In those days there was no king in Israel. Every man did what was right in his own eyes." Clearly a monarchy will be the only solution.

Lecture Fifteen

Samuel and Saul
(1 Samuel)

Scope:

The tribal confederacy under the leadership of judges had disintegrated, but the increasing threat of Philistine power made a centralized government desirable. This lecture begins with Samuel, who represents the transition from charismatic leader to prophet, then turns to the tragedy of King Saul to reveal the benefits and liabilities of monarchy.

N.B.: The Book of Ruth appears between Judges and 1 Samuel in Christian canons. Both because most scholars date the book's composition to a period later than these texts and because in the MT, it appears in the Ketuvim (Writings), discussion of Ruth is reserved for a later lecture.

Outline

I. Samuel combines the roles of priest, prophet, and judge.

- **A.** Hannah's personal emptiness symbolizes the problems of the nation.
  1. Unable to have a child, she recollects Sarah, Rebecca, and Rachel.
  2. Mocked by her fertile co-wife, she resembles Sarah.
  3. So distressed about her infertility, when her husband asks, "Am I not more to you than ten sons?" (1 Sam. 1:8), she can make no answer.
- **B.** At Shiloh, her encounter with the priest Eli anticipates the fall of Eli's house and implies the rejection of the priest as national leader at this stage of Israel's history.
  1. Hannah prays passionately for a child; Eli, seeing her lips move but hearing no words, assumes she is drunk and berates her.
  2. Eli cannot control his sons, who take the best portions of the sacrifices (1 Sam. 2:12–17) and have intercourse with women at the sanctuary (2:22).

3. When Hannah relates the truth, Eli prophesies her pregnancy and, thereby, evokes the annunciation type scene.
4. She promises to dedicate her son to God; he will, therefore, replace Eli's sons.

C. Hannah's hymn, "The Song of Hannah" (the model for Mary's Magnificat [Luke 1:46–55]), introduces extensive political concerns.
   1. It predicts social upheaval: the mighty brought down; the weak uplifted.
   2. It predicts Hannah's own changing circumstance: the barren made fertile.
   3. It locates the monarchy under divine support and direction.

D. Samuel's commission comes while he is under Eli's care.
   1. Weaning Samuel, Hannah brings him to Shiloh; each year, she returns, bringing him a knitted coat (2:19).
   2. The "word of the Lord" (3:1), "rare in those days," comes to Samuel when he is "lying down in the temple, where the ark of God was" (3:3).
   3. Eli's promise of a dynasty, offered in 2:30, is revoked, and Samuel becomes God's agent: "All Israel from Dan to Beersheva knew that Samuel was established as a prophet of the Lord… for the Lord revealed himself to Samuel at Shiloh…" (3:19–4:1).
   4. Samuel combines the strengths of Israel's earlier leaders: Like Moses, God speaks to him; like Aaron, he has priestly duties; like Joshua, he unites the people and sets up a witness-stone (called "Ebenezer," stone of help, 7:12), like Deborah, he "judged Israel all the days of his life" (7:15).

II. That Samuel and his role as judge, prophet, and priest will not prevail is foreshadowed by the capture of the ark, the first event to occur under his leadership (1 Sam. 4–7)

A. The ark's peripatetic journey adds unexpected humor.
   1. When the ark is brought to the Philistine temple at Ashdod, Dagon the idol keeps bowing to it. Re-erected, the idol falls apart. Ashdod's residents ship the ark to Gath, the home of Goliath.

2. Breaking out in "tumors" (RSV) or "hemorrhoids" (JB), the Gathites ship the ark to Ekron.
3. The people of Ekron cry, "They have brought around to us the ark of the God of Israel, to slay us and our people" (5:10).
4. Finally, the Philistines tie the ark to two cows, which head to Beth Shemesh. There, the Levites detach the ark and sacrifice the cows. The ark remains in Keriath-Je'arim for twenty years, until David establishes his capital in Jerusalem (2 Sam. 6).

B. Samuel's history frames the ark narrative: It begins when he takes office; it ends with a mention of his latter years.
1. "When Samuel became old, he made his sons judges over Israel… his sons did not walk in his ways, but turned aside after gain; they took bribes and perverted justice" (1 Sam. 8:1–3).
2. The "unworthy son" motif (Moses, Gideon, Eli) continues the polemic against dynastic succession.
3. Given that the judge, priest, and prophet cannot establish permanent leadership, government must derive from a new source.

III. 1 Samuel 8–11 offers arguments for and against kingship.

A. The people want a king "to govern us like all the nations" (8:5).
1. Their request undermines YHWH's kingship and compromises the tradition's egalitarian impulse.
2. Samuel notes: kings take sons to populate armies; daughters, for the palace staff.
3. "He will take a tenth of your flocks….
4. "And you shall be his slaves" (8:17).

B. 1 Samuel 9 offers a pro-monarchical perspective.
1. Samuel appears not as the national prophet but as a local "seer."
2. The Deity appears to favor not a king, but a prince: "I will send you a man from Benjamin, and you shall anoint him to be a prince over my people Israel."
3. The impetus is practical: "He shall save my people from… the Philistines" (9:16–17).

IV. Ambivalence about kingship is complemented by ambivalence about Saul.

A. His introduction implies that his qualifications are looks and wealth.

1. "There was a man of Benjamin whose name was Kish…a man of wealth.

2. And he had a son whose name was Saul, a handsome young man.

3. There was not a man among the people of Israel more handsome than he; from his shoulders upward he was taller than any of his people" (9:1–2).

B. Saul's first action is his failure to fulfill a type scene.

1. He "meets young maidens coming out to draw water" (9:11), but his mind is set on finding Kish's lost donkeys.

2. He finds, not donkeys, but royal anointing.

C. Like Moses and Gideon, Saul is a reluctant leader; he is also reluctantly anointed.

1. He is only "a Benjaminite, from the least of the tribes of Israel: "And is not my family the humblest of all the families of the tribes of Benjamin?" (9:21).

2. Samuel first anoints Saul in secret, as if God only minimally accedes to the people's demand.

3. When Samuel makes a public announcement, the process makes the choice of Saul anticlimactic: Lots are cast to see whom God will choose for the king.

4. The lots fall on Saul, but "when they sought him he could not be found. So they inquired again of the Lord… and the Lord said, 'Behold, he has hidden himself among the baggage'" (10:22).

5. Samuel asserts: "Do you see him whom the Lord has chosen? There is none like him among all the people."

V. As Israel struggles to harmonize traditional egalitarianism with a centralized monarch, Saul also has difficulty negotiating his role.

A. Samuel may have plotted his failure.

1. "Samuel did not come to Gilgal, and the people were scattering. So Saul said, 'Bring the burnt offerings here to me, and the peace offerings'" (13:8–9). The king usurps the priestly role.

2. As Saul completes the sacrifice, Samuel arrives to pronounce condemnation: "Your kingdom shall not continue" (13:14).
3. Instead of sacrificing the spoils of the Amalekite raid, "Saul and the people spared Agag [the king], and the best of the sheep and the oxen and the fatlings, and the lambs, and all that was good, and would not utterly destroy them" (15:9).
4. God "repents" of making Saul king.
5. Condemned by Samuel, Saul repents, but too late: "Samuel hewed Agag to pieces before the Lord at Gilgal" (15:33).
6. "Samuel did not see Saul again until the day of his death" (15:35).

B. Saul's untenable political position culminates in his final tragedy.

1. Suffering when the "evil spirit from God" (16:23) overtakes him, Saul is comforted only by his harp player.
2. His torment is divinely caused.
3. His harp player will usurp his throne
4. Saul's son and daughter will betray him.

C. His death confirms the fragility of his rule.

1. Facing Philistine onslaught, Saul finds himself needing Samuel's advice. Yet Samuel is dead, and "Saul had put the mediums and wizards out of the land" (28:3).
2. Saul, contravening his own law, seeks a medium.
3. Attesting to the ineffectuality of Saul's national policies, his soldiers quickly find one in Endor.

D. Samuel's return.

1. The medium tells Saul, "I see a god coming up out of the earth" (28:13). When he inquires about its appearance, she responds: "An old man is coming up, and he is wrapped in a cloak." The term matches that used for the coats Hannah had made, and Saul knew that the man was Samuel.
2. Told by Samuel that he will lose the battle, the king refuses to eat; the medium—whose livelihood and life were threatened by Saul's policies—feeds him dinner.

VI. The next morning, Saul and his son Jonathan die in battle. Making lament for them is their rival, the next king, David, to whose story we turn in the next lecture.

Supplementary Reading:

David Jobling, *First Samuel* (Collegeville, MN: Liturgical Press, 1998).

Questions to Consider:

1. Why is Saul made a sympathetic character?
2. Considering the previous seven biblical books, what model of political leadership would appear most beneficial for Israel?
3. What is compromised in the egalitarian (if androcentric) nature of Israelite religion, under the covenant, by the monarchy?

Lecture Fifteen—Transcript
Samuel and Saul
(1 Samuel)

The very loosely knit tribal confederacy under the charismatic leaders called judges has now completely disintegrated, but some need for a government still remains because the Philistine threat is still there. Consequently, when we move into First Samuel we will find the need for the monarchy recited over and over again. But First Samuel does not begin with a monarchy. To the contrary, it begins with the birth of Samuel and what looks like a very calm and pleasant society, as if somehow we're back to the good old days when people were not being raped or chopped into bits.

The beginning of the story of Samuel portends good things for Israel. We have an account of a married couple, and we haven't seen them in a while. But here is a married couple who actually seem to love each other—Hannah, a woman, and her husband Elkanah—and every year they go up to the local shrine at Shiloh to offer sacrifices. Nobody attacks them on the way. It looks quite good. But it turns out that Hannah is distressed because Hannah has no children. We've seen this before, and not only does Hannah replay the literary convention, the type scene of a barren woman to whom an annunciation will be given, but it may well be that Hannah in her loneliness, in her barrenness, represents the loss that the community still feels, that somehow she embodies a sense of hope, a sense of needing to be fulfilled. She represents the community here on a very positive level.

She also resembles all those infertile women from Genesis. Like Sarah and like Rachel, there is a fertile co-wife there; her name is Peninnah. Hannah simply cannot bear the fact that her husband has children with a co-wife. So every year when they go up to the shrine at Shiloh, Hannah prays for a child. Her husband simply can't understand why Hannah is so desperate, and he says to her at one point, "Am I not more to you than ten sons?" And she answers not, because, for a woman who can't have a child, in Hannah's case, the answer is "No, you're not."

Hannah goes up to the shrine and prays passionately for a child, and she actually offers a vow, but here a positive one, unlike Jephthah's. She prays, "Lord of hosts, if you will only take notice of my trouble and you will remember me, if you will not forget me but grant me offspring, then I shall give the child to the Lord for the whole of his life, and no razor shall ever touch his head." He, like Samson, will be a Nazirite. Samson the Nazirite is a fool. Samuel the Nazirite is a genius.

She prays her prayer, and Eli the priest at Shiloh looks at her and notices that her lips are moving and her eyes are closed and she is fervently praying, and he thinks she's drunk. He says to her, "Put away your wine, woman. This is not the way you should behave at the house of God." And she explains to him, "No, I've been praying for a child," and Eli recognizes the depth and concern that she shows, and here's another annunciation. He tells her, "Yes, you will have a child." Eli is ready to recognize true piety. The lives of Eli and Hannah and Hannah's child, Samuel, will be intertwined because, just as Eli originally is unable to realize the depth of Hannah's prayer, so, too, there are gaps in his own life.

It turns out he has two sons who were also priests, but he simply cannot control them. We learn as early as Chapter 2 that his sons are serving at the sacrifices, and they are taking the best cuts of meat for themselves, and, worse, they are actually having sex with some of the women who are coming up to the shrine. This simply cannot stay. And we learn that, although God had promised Eli that his children would always, the expression goes, "Go in and out before me forever, always serve as priests at YHWH's altar," God simply cannot stand this apostasy in which the priests are engaged, and he says, "That promise is now revoked." So God's loyalties will shift to Samuel.

In celebration of her motherhood, because Hannah does, in fact, become pregnant and does, in fact, have a child, she sings a magnificent hymn called the "Song of Hannah." This is a staple, the woman making celebration not only over victory but also over pregnancy. We've seen women's victory songs with Deborah. We've seen a short victory song with Miriam at the Song of the Sea. And for those within the Christian tradition, Hannah's song becomes the model for Mary's Magnificat at the beginning of Luke, when Mary celebrates the birth of Jesus. This song is, however, less a paean into childbirth, it's less thanking God for the fact that Hannah herself has had a child, than it is, well, a political manifesto. Hannah is expressing national yearnings. She predicts in her song social upheaval where the mighty are brought down and the weaker raised up. She also speaks about her own changing circumstances, but in broader terms. The barren are made fertile. And that will finally be what will happen to the kingdom of Israel.

Hannah bears her son, Samuel. She nurses him, and when she weans him she makes good on her vow. She takes him up to the shrine at Shiloh and puts him in trust to Eli the priest, and Samuel begins to serve at God's altar. That's where his call comes from. As he's there serving for God, and, by the way, his mother never actually leaves him. We're told in this very, very delicate note that every year Hannah would come up to the shrine at Shiloh with a little coat, a little cloak that she had made for him. The mother's love continues. Hannah has not forgotten Samuel and neither has God.

Finally, "the word of the Lord," we're told, "was rare in those days," but it comes to Samuel when he is lying down in the temple where the ark of God is. We're now in First Samuel, Chapter 3. Samuel hears a voice. He thinks it's Eli the priest calling, so he runs into Eli's room and says, "What can I do for you?" and Eli says, "Go back to sleep. I didn't call." By the third time Eli realizes, "Ah, it's God calling," and he tells Samuel to be prepared and to tell God that he, Samuel, is ready. God commissions Samuel to be his messenger, and, by the end of Chapter 3, we're told Samuel grew, and the Lord was with him. As the expression goes, "Let none of his words fall to the ground." In other words, everything that Samuel said was heeded by the people, and everything that Samuel said was given to him by God. "All Israel from Dan to Beersheba, from top to bottom, north to south, knew that Samuel was established as a prophet of the Lord," as the text continues, "for the Lord revealed himself to Samuel at Shiloh."

This portends great things for Israel. It looks really good. Samuel combines the strength of Israel's earlier leaders like Moses: God speaks to him and the people listen. Like Aaron, he's got priestly duties because he's serving at the shrine. Like Joshua, he is able to unite the people from Dan to Beersheba, and they listen to him. Samuel, indeed, sets up a witness stone in testimony to his truth, just like Joshua did at the covenant ceremony at Shechem. And, like Deborah, we're told about Samuel, Chapter 7, he judged Israel all the days of his life. He looks like the perfect leader. He's got the ear of the people, and God loves him. But there is still no centralized government, and the Philistines are still out there, and somebody has got to help out. We actually find out that a need for a centralized government and a standing military is not only just a need but it's essential.

The story of Samuel, his birth, and then his death notice provides the frame for what's called the ark narrative. Samuel, as we know, had been at the shrine of Shiloh with the ark, but, when the Israelites go into battle, the ark goes with them. What happens in Chapter 4 is that the ark is captured by the Philistines, and, during that capture, the two sons of Eli, those wicked, apostatizing priests, are slain. When the ark is captured, a Benjaminite who happened to be fighting on Israel's side comes to Eli, who is 98 years old at the time and blind, and he tells Eli, "The ark of the Lord has been captured. Your sons are slain." Eli, who is sitting on a stool— and we're told he's very heavy—falls over and he dies. The news also comes to his daughter-in-law, the wife of Phinehas, one of his children. She's pregnant, and she gives birth prematurely, and in her last moment she names her child. She calls him Ichabod, which means "the glory has departed from Israel." So here again a child represents the community's fate.

At this point the Deuteronomic historian, whom actually we've already seen in the Book of Judges, can move from farce to pathos and farce very quickly. The historian actually moves from this highly emotional scene of a dead priest and a dead daughter-in-law and a premature baby to a farce, and we have the ark narrative, the story of the peripatetic ark being dragged from Philistine city to Philistine city. In fact, some biblical scholars have suggested this, too, is a literary convention. We have, from the ancient Near East, stories of gods represented by their statues being moved from town to town to town, either being in exile because of war or deserting their people because they don't like the way their people are behaving.

Here is the ark representing God. The Philistines bring the ark to the Philistine temple at Ashdod, and there is an idol there called Dagon. Unfortunately, Dagon the idol keeps bowing down to the ark, so the Philistines have to upright Dagon again, and then Dagon bows down again and falls to pieces. The citizens of Ashdod say, "We better get rid of this ark," so they ship the ark off to Gath, which is where Goliath is from. We'll meet Goliath when we finally meet King David.

What exactly happens to the people in Gath is not quite clear. It depends upon how you want to translate the Hebrew. They either broke out into tumors, or they broke out into hemorrhoids. Either way, it's not a good scene. So the Gathites ship the ark to Ekron. The people in Ekron cry out, "They have brought around to us the ark of the God of Israel to slay us and our people." So the people of Ekron don't want it either, and they finally, after consulting with their own priest, come to the conclusion that they will leave it up to some god, either theirs or the one of Israel, to determine what to do with the ark. They tie the ark to two cows that have just calved, two milk cows.

The idea is, if you are a cow—unlikely to happen—and you have just had a calf, you need that calf to nurse because otherwise you, the cow, will simply explode with built-up milk. The idea is the cows would probably stay in Philistine territory to be near their calves. But what we're told is the two cows, looking neither left nor right, mooing as they go, head back toward Israelite territory and bring the ark back home. They head to Beth Shemesh, where the Levites pick up the ark and dispatch the cows as a sacrifice to God, and the ark remains in Israelite territory for 20 years until David establishes his capital in Jerusalem in Second Samuel 6 and brings the ark up there.

But God will not always rescue the people quite as easily with tumors and falling down idols. We need a king to help out, and that's what we get next. When Samuel became old, we're told at the end of the ark narrative, he made his sons judges over Israel, "but his sons did not walk in his ways. They turned aside after gain, they took bribes, and they perverted justice." Well, the story of Samuel is not done. He will continue up through the rest of this book. But we're already told early on that Samuel cannot establish his dynasty. Some other sort of ruler is needed. The judge isn't going to work—we've seen that from the Book of Judges. Charismatic leaders cannot hold. Samuel the prophet and priest cannot hold. A new type of leadership is needed. In First Samuel, Chapters 8 through 11, we have a compromised view of the monarchy. The upshot is, kingship is to be granted to these people, but the king must be subservient to God. God will still be the people's ruler; it will be God who chooses the king.

It used to be thought that these particular chapters were the combination of two different sources, one a pro-monarchical source and one an anti-monarchical source. That may be the case, but these days biblical scholars think that, in fact, both views are written by the same Deuteronomic historian, expressing the historian's own ambivalence about the kingship. It's necessary, but it's not quite what Israel was founded to be, and we can see that ambivalence even in Samuel's own discussion with the people. The people come up to Samuel, and they say, "Give us a king to govern us like all the nations." Samuel responds, "Look, God is your king. If you take a king like all the other nations you'll be undermining YHWH's rule."

Moreover, what happened to the egalitarian impulse of Yahwism that we saw underneath the covenant, where everybody is equal? A king establishes class distinctions, and a monarchy thereby entails Israel's loss of unique status. Under YHWH they are not like all the other nations; they are a nation holy and distinct apart. And, if the theological explanations were not sufficient, Samuel gives the people practical explanations for why they shouldn't want a king. Kings will take your sons, he says, to populate their armies, and they'll take your daughters for the palace staff. They'll take a tenth of your flock. They'll take the best of your cattle. They'll take your donkeys. And you shall be, Samuel says, the king's slaves. The conclusion at this point is, kingship is not good for the people, and it's an offense to God, but, despite what Samuel says, the people are resolved.

The irony is, by the way, that everything Samuel said actually came true. By the time we get up to King Solomon we find all of these predictions have come true. King Solomon has a corvée, forced labor. We already saw that with slavery in Egypt. He has a major capital center with a temple, with a palace, with the entire infrastructure that a capital center requires, both to work for the monarchy and to work for the centralized cult. He's got a royal priesthood. He's got a royal harem with international gods. He's got an overextended economy—too much importing, too little exporting. He's got a heavily taxed and increasingly frustrated peasant class, and there will be a revolt after he dies. In the Bible, like everything else, be careful what you ask for, right?

Nevertheless, although tepid, the Bible also offers a somewhat pro-monarchical condition. This is First Samuel 9. We see already the change in the perspective and the change in the description of Samuel. Here he's no longer the one who has the ear of the people from north to south. He's simply a country seer. He's a local fortune-teller, a finder of lost objects. And here the deity actually seems to favor some sort of monarchical rule. But God doesn't quite ask for a king yet. God says, "it's okay if you have a prince," and this brings us to the story of the prince who becomes King Saul. Here is the description: "I will send you a man from Benjamin, and you shall anoint him to be prince over my people Israel. He shall save my people from the hand of the Philistines, for I have seen the affliction of my people because their cry has come out to me." We've seen this before. A new leader will be raised up—but a different type of leader.

Saul's introduction is a tad on the problematic side. I get the feeling, when looking at it, that his primary job qualifications are good looks and wealth. Here is how we meet Saul: "There was a man of Benjamin whose name was Kish, a man of wealth, and he had a son whose name was Saul, a handsome young man. There was not a man among the people more handsome than he. From his shoulders upward he was taller than any of the people." He's rich, and he's drop-dead gorgeous. Other than that it's not clear what his qualifications are to lead the people. Nor are we sure he will make a good leader when we finally see him in action, and, indeed, we already have.

Think back to the type scene of men who meet women at wells. This is where we first see King Saul. He meets some young women coming up to draw water in Chapter 9, verse 11. But he's not looking for a bride. He is, as you will recall, looking for his father's lost donkeys. And the women sent him on his way, "Go to the local seer;"—and that turns out to be the prophet Samuel— "perhaps he will help you." The type scene, as you know, was aborted. Saul will not marry these women in the same way that he will not complete his kingship.

He goes to Samuel, and Samuel says to him, "You're going to be king." Saul, in typical fashion—you might think of Gideon or Moses in the background—is reluctant. He says, "I'm a Benjaminite. It's the least of the tribes of Israel," and he goes on, "Is not my family the humblest of all the families of the tribe of Benjamin?" Fat chance. We already know that his father is wealthy. Perhaps given both Saul's own doubts and Samuel's as well, Samuel anoints Saul in secret. It's not time for the public inauguration yet. When Samuel finally does make a public announcement regarding Saul's anointing, the events are not really auspicious. The tribes are collected, and lots are cast to determine whom God will choose to be king. The lots fall upon the tribe of Benjamin and then to a particular clan and then to Saul's household, and finally the lots fall upon Saul.

The people looked for Saul, "but when they sought him he could not be found, so they inquired of the Lord." I'm citing Chapter 10 here. And the Lord said, "Behold, he has hidden himself among the baggage." When Samuel then asserts, "Do you see him whom the Lord has chosen? There is none like him among all the people," I wonder about the tone that he would have used because kings do not usually hang out among the baggage. Some of the assembled crowd immediately shout out, "Long live the king!" It's in the Bible; we didn't invent it from the British monarchy. But some fellows called "worthless" by the narrator ask, "How can this man save us?" and it seems to me that the question is, in fact, not without merit.

So as Israel struggles to harmonize its original egalitarian tradition underneath the covenant with this centralized monarchy, we also find Saul trying to deal with this new change, not only in Israel's status but within his own. Saul is in a very difficult spot because Samuel himself is quite ambivalent about this kingship idea. It seems almost as if Samuel is setting Saul up for failure. Saul does go to war against the Philistines, and for the most part he is winning. But at one point in the midst of a military campaign he and Samuel had agreed to meet for Samuel to offer sacrifice, and Saul waits, and he waits, and he waits, and the people are beginning to leave, and he needs them to be gathered together. But Samuel has not shown up.

We're told Saul waited seven days, the time appointed by Samuel, but Samuel did not come to Gilgal, which is where they were, and the people were scattering from him, so Saul finally said, "Bring the burnt offerings here to me and the peace offerings" (First Samuel 13). Thereby the king usurps Samuel's role. The king is not supposed to be the one to offer sacrifice. That's the job of the priest. As Saul completes his sacrifice, Samuel arrives but only to pronounce condemnation. He says to Saul, "Your kingdom will not continue," which is not what you need to hear when you're a military leader, right?

The account of Saul's transgression is, in fact, given a different spin in Chapter 15, where his culpability, his guilt, and the situation of his rejection are even worse. There is a raid against the Amalekites, but this is holy war, and within holy war one is supposed to take every bit of that booty and dedicate it to God, and the men who are captured are supposed to be killed. We've seen this already. But Saul preserves some of the booty, and Saul and the people spare the king of the Amalekites—his name is Agag—as well as the best of the sheep and the oxen and the fatlings and the lands and all that is good and refuse utterly to destroy them. This is totally against the rules of holy war. Saul is here in violation of divine commands. We're told at this point God repents of making Saul king.

Samuel arrives and accuses Saul of transgressing the dictates of holy war and of failing to honor God, and Saul repents, but it's too late. We're told, "Samuel hewed Agag to pieces before the Lord at Gilgal"—Samuel's sacrifice to God. We're also told at that point that Samuel did not see Saul again until the day of his death. Saul's untenable position culminates in his final tragedy. God causes an evil spirit to come upon Saul. He can't get rest. He has no peace. We'll see in the next lecture that it's only through David's playing his harp that Saul gains any sense of serenity. His torment is divinely caused. His people are not entirely loyal. We discover that his harp player, the young David, will usurp his popularity and then usurp his throne. His daughter, Michal, who is in love with David, will betray him. His son Jonathan will also betray him because Jonathan's loyalty is to David. His remaining children and grandchildren will either be killed or stripped of their power. Saul will be left a solitary tragic figure, and his death confirms the tragedy as well as the fragility of his role.

Again, facing Philistine onslaught, Saul realizes he needs Samuel's support, Samuel's help, but not only has Samuel not spoken with him since the incident at Gilgal, Samuel is dead. Saul is stuck; he needs to speak to Samuel. What's he going to do? Worse, the one way you can speak to somebody who is dead is you get a medium to cause the ghost to come out of the ground. But we're also told that Saul, in one of his executive orders, had put all the mediums and wizards out of the land. So Saul, contravening his own law, seeks a medium. He goes to his servants, and he says, "Seek out for me a woman who is a medium, that I may go to her and inquire of her." Attesting to the total inability of Saul to rule and the inefficacy of his laws, the servants find a medium. Nobody was paying much attention to what Saul says.

They go to the land of Endor, and for those of you who know that old TVshow *Bewitched* and Endora, that's where the name comes from. The witch there, the medium of Endor, conjures up the spirit of Samuel, and the medium tells Saul, "I see a god coming up out of the earth," and when Saul inquires, "What is his appearance?" she responds, "He is an old man coming up, and he is wrapped in a cloak." It's the same word used for the cloak that Samuel's mother, Hannah, used to bring to him when he was at the temple in Shiloh. It's an odd word, so, in fact, we know this is Samuel. And Saul knows it is Samuel, and Samuel says to Saul, "You will lose the battle." Saul then refuses to eat, and ironically and graciously, the medium whose life had been put in danger by Saul's executive order kills a fatted calf and gives him dinner and says, basically, "You need your strength because you've got a battle on the morrow." The next morning Saul and his son Jonathan die in battle.

Here is the tragedy. The next day when the Philistines came to strip the slain they took armor and jewelry. They found Saul and his three sons lying dead on Mount Gilboa. They cut off his head, they stripped him of his armor, and they sent messengers through the length and breadth of their land to carry the good news to idols, to their gods, and to the people alike, because here they have prevailed over Israel. They have killed Israel's king. They deposit his armor in the temple of Ashtoreth as a sign that they have won, and they nail his body on the wall of Beth Shan. So even in death Saul is humiliated.

But when the inhabitants of Jabesh Gilead, a town Saul had protected, hear what the Philistines have done to Saul, all of the warriors among them set out, and they journey to recover the bodies of Saul and his sons from the wall of Beth Shan. They bring him back to Jabesh, they burn the bodies, and they take the bones and they bury them underneath the tamarisk tree in Jabesh Gilead, and for seven days they fast. That's the end of the story of King Saul, but it's not the end of the story of the monarchy—the pro-monarchical forces, the pro-monarchical voices, actually, right?

The Philistines are on the horizon. Somebody needs to help out. Somebody needs to retain the kingship. And thereby we come to King David. But, as we'll see, King David will replace some of these same conventions that we saw back with the judges and back even with Saul. An inauspicious beginning, association with worthless and reckless fellows—King David will even make an alliance with the Philistines. In the same way that the Israelites had to fight their way into Canaan, David is going to have to fight his way into the kingship. Will he succeed? Yes. And why? Because finally, for one more time, God has changed his mind, and he will establish his kingdom.

The final scene that we'll see that guarantees this kingdom is that royal grant covenant that we already know God will give. So David gets what Saul never had, the covenant with God, the royal grant like Noah had and like Abraham had, the promise of eternal kingship. In the next lecture we will meet King David hanging about with worthless fellows—beloved of God, a player of the harp, a slayer of Goliath, and a man who finally loses his role again by committing adultery, by having his sons go to war against him, and finally by dying a lonely, cold, old man alone in his bed.

Lecture Sixteen

King David
(1 Samuel 16–31, 2 Samuel, 1 Kings 1–2)

Scope:

David's accession anticipates a period of tribal unification, prosperity, and peace with neighboring kingdoms; the royal grant by which the Deity adopts David and guarantees that his descendants will hold the throne of Israel in perpetuity (1 Sam. 7) appears to confirm his promise. However, David's own failures lead to familial strife, civil war, and the bloody route to Solomon's throne. This lecture begins with a quick overview of David's status in history, then concentrates on his relationship with Bathsheba, a complex story that combines the personal and political as it reveals the king's own complexity: his charm, his ruthlessness, and his faith.

Outline

I. The story of David is worthy of an entire course.

- **A.** His story encompasses myriad roles, including:
  1. The erstwhile shepherd whose music soothes King Saul's spirit (1 Sam. 16).
  2. The armor-bearer whose shot kills the Philistine champion Goliath (1 Sam. 17).
  3. The enemy of Saul, but the intimate of Saul's son Jonathan and husband to Saul's daughter Michal (1 Sam. 18 *passim*).
  4. The leader of a gang of malcontents and the Philistine vassal (1 Sam. 22–27).
  5. The king granted an eternal covenant (2 Sam. 7).
  6. The adulterer who arranges the death of his lover's husband (2 Sam. 12).
  7. The father whose beloved son, Absalom, wars against him (2 Sam. 13–20).
  8. The old man who cannot find warmth (1 Kings 1).

B. David can be viewed as a culture hero, similar to King Arthur.

1. David's history receives no uncontested support from external evidence. An inscription possibly reading "house of David" has been found among fragments of Iron Age pottery. Some archaeologists claim that the inscription testifies to David's existence; others question both its date and its age.
2. The attribution to him of Goliath's death may be an example of form criticism at work: The story remains the same, but the characters change. Second Sam. 21:19 attributes Goliath's death to David's soldier, Elhanan.

II. David and Bathsheba (2 Sam. 11–13).

A. The opening verses signal political and personal deficiencies; David's domestic failures foreshadow and serve as a microcosm of the ensuing civil war.

1. "In the spring of the year, the time when kings go out to battle, David sent Joab with his officers and all Israel with him, and they ravaged the Ammonites…but David remained in Jerusalem." Clearly, he was not attending to his duties.
2. "It happened, late one afternoon, when David rose from his couch and was walking about on the roof of the king's house, that he saw from the roof a woman bathing; the woman was very beautiful."
3. Is this David, described as "skilled in music, a man of valor and a warrior, sensible in speech and handsome in appearance, and the lord is with him" (1 Sam. 16:18)?

B. Interpreters question Bathsheba's complicity in David's downfall.

1. Does she see him as he sees her?
2. Had she planned to be seen?
3. Does she know the king's movements?

III. David's relationship with Bathsheba is premeditated: "David sent for messengers and inquired and said, 'Isn't this Bathsheba... the wife of Uriah the Hittite?'"

A. The scene recollects David's other relationships, including:

1. His marriage to the clever Abigail, after complicity in causing her first husband's death (1 Sam. 16:1–25).
2. His marriage to Michal, who loves, then despises him, and "who had no child to the day of her death" (2 Sam. 23).

B. Whether David can "love" is an open question.

1. Jonathan loves David, to such an extent that he, Saul's son and heir, betrays his own father and king.
2. David makes public lament over the prince's dead body: "I am distressed for you, my brother Jonathan/greatly beloved were you to me. Your love to me was wonderful/passing the love of women" (2 Sam. 1:26).
3. David even orders the song to be "taught to the people of Judah" (2 Sam.1:18).
4. But David does not say he *loved* Jonathan.
5. The more cynical reader would see the lament as opportunistic.

IV. "So David sent messengers to get her, and she came to him and he lay with her. (Now she was purifying herself after her period)" (2 Sam. 11:4).

A. Did David abuse his power?

1. Had Bathsheba a choice when the "messengers" arrived? Is this rape?
2. Is this the "romance" of popular legend?
3. Had David read Deut. 22:22 on the punishment for adultery?

B. What of Bathsheba?

1. Is this the fulfillment of her plans?
2. Why does the text explicitly note that "she came to him"?
3. Is she depicted as faithful in her ritual practices, or simply as not pregnant?

V. "The woman conceived, and she sent and told David, 'I am pregnant'" (11:5).

   A. David is the father, because Bathsheba was introduced as purifying herself at the completion of her menstrual cycle.

   B. What does Bathsheba want David to do with this information?

      1. Pray she miscarries?
      2. Procure an abortion?
      3. Recall her husband?
      4. Kill her husband?

VI. First, the coveting of the neighbor's wife, then adultery, then murder.

   A. David recalls Uriah and encourages him to "go down to your house and wash your feet."

      1. This is an invitation to connubiality, because "feet"—Hebrew: *reglayim*—is a euphemism for genitalia.
      2. Uriah refuses: "The ark and Israel and Judah remain in booths... shall I then go to my house, to eat and to drink and to lie with my wife? As you live, and as your soul lives, I shall not do such a thing."
      3. David even gets Uriah drunk, but still he demurs.
      4. Finally, David sends him back with a sealed letter to Joab: Place Uriah "in the forefront of the hardest fighting, and then draw back from him, so that he may be struck down and die" (2 Sam. 11:15).

   B. Why does David want Uriah to return home to Bathsheba?

      1. To mask the matter of the child's paternity?
      2. To discover the pregnancy and divorce his wife?
      3. To kill Bathsheba in a fit of jealousy?
      4. To kill Bathsheba legally under the charge of adultery?
      5. To have intercourse with Bathsheba, violating the laws of holy war?
      6. Divorce Bathsheba?

   C. How is Uriah to be assessed?

      1. Do his fidelity and innocence make David's decadence even more monstrous?
      2. Does he so dislike his wife that he could not visit her?

3. Does he love her so much that he refuses to lead himself into temptation?
4. Does he respect Israel's Torah so much that he, a Hittite, is faithful where God's anointed is not?
5. Does he know what David did? Does he recognize that his fate is sealed?

VII. Bathsheba—after a time of mourning—marries David and bears a son. But "the thing David had done displeased the Lord" (11:27).

- **A.** Initially, it is not clear what the "thing" is: Rape? Adultery? Uriah's murder? Marriage to Bathsheba? Sinning against God?
  1. How can one atone for voyeurism, adultery, murder, and cover-up?
  2. Does David recognize his protection under the royal grant?
- **B.** God speaks to David through Nathan: "You have struck down Uriah the Hittite with the sword, and have taken his wife to be your wife… now therefore the sword shall never depart from your house… I will take your wives from before your eyes, and give them to your neighbor, and he shall lie with your wives in the sight of this very sun. For you did it secretly, but I will do this before all Israel" (2 Sam. 12: 10-12).
  1. Adultery is never private: It involves messengers, co-workers, confidants.
  2. It affects even one's children: Amnon rapes Tamar, and Absalom—leading a civil war against his father—will rape David's concubines on the palace rooftop.
- **C.** David admits his sin, and Nathan tells him that his sin has been passed over… at least in God's purview.
  1. Psalm 51 is titled "A Psalm of David, when the prophet Nathan came to him after he had gone in to Bathsheba."
  2. Despite David's repenting, Nathan predicts, "the child that is born to you shall die" (12:14).
  3. David and Bathsheba have a second child who, with the machinations of his mother and the prophet, obtains the throne. His name is Solomon.

Supplementary Reading:

J. Cheryl Exum, *Fragmented Women: Feminist Subversions of Biblical Narratives* (Sheffield: JSOT Press, 1993).

Stephen L. McKenzie, *King David: A Biography* (Oxford and New York: Oxford University Press, 2000).

Marti J. Steussy, *David: Biblical Portraits of Power* (Columbia, SC: University of South Carolina Press, 1999).

Questions to Consider:

1. How might the story of David function as later propaganda for the monarchy?
2. Should rulers' personal lives enter the assessment of their governing capabilities?
3. Is David admirable despite his (major) failings? If so, how? If not, what does one make of the royal grant?

Lecture Sixteen—Transcript
King David
(1 Samuel 16-31, 2 Samuel, 1 Kings 1-2)

With the introduction of David, soon to become king in Israel, the Deuteronomic historian provides us a hint of prosperity to come, tribal unification, and the royal grant covenant finally put into play. Israel, after all those disasters in the period of judges and the difficulties between Samuel and Saul, will finally have a time of fulfillment of those promises made to the patriarchs Abraham, Isaac, and Jacob. Indeed, David captures the imagination so much I suggest he's actually worthy of a course in and of himself.

How best then to look at King David, this magnificent hero, this charmer, this rogue, this scoundrel? Let's take a quick look at some of the various characterizations by which the Deuteronomic historian portrays David. Then what I'd like to do is look very, very closely at one particular scene, the very well-known story of David and Bathsheba, because in this one story one finds an epitome of everything that makes David so compelling: his charm, his fidelity, his conniving, his trickery, and ultimately his piety to God and God's love for him but also God's refusal to let him get away with murder and with apostasy.

So here we go with the story of King David. In effect, who is he? He begins as an erstwhile shepherd, the youngest son of a man named Jesse, who is called to the royal court to soothe King Saul's spirit when Saul's spirit is troubling him. In this sense he's also the psalmist whose hymns to God reach the heights of poetic artistry. When one looks through the psalms one finds numerous of these psalms ascribed to King David. Could he have actually written them? If there were a King David, it's possible.

He's also the King's armor bearer. He is a warrior. But in this wonderful story, the stuff of legend, I fear, we're told that he eschews Saul's armor—it's simply too big for him—and he will go up against the Philistine champion, Goliath of Gath, with only a slingshot, and with that slingshot he brings down the giant and thereby the Philistine forces.

He's also the enemy of King Saul, the reigning monarch. David is fighting for his own throne. He wants to take over, and he will do so with the aid of Saul's daughter, Michal, who loves him—we're never told he loves her—and Saul's son, Jonathan. He's the roguish leader of a gang of malcontents. He's a political opportunist who usurps Israel's throne, and, in order to do so, actually becomes a Philistine vassal for a while. David will take help from anywhere he can get it. But he's also a king granted a royal eternal covenant by God, indeed, adopted by God. And he's an adulterer who arranges the death of his adulterous partner's husband. He's a parent who allows one of his children to rape another and does nothing about it, and he's a parent who watches yet another son engage in a civil war against him. This is a son David actually loves, Absalom. Finally, he's an old man, bedridden, unable to rule, who cannot find warmth.

These roles and more contribute, in fact, to the scholarly quest of David, so we must raise the question, is David a real person? It would be lovely if archaeological investigation around Jerusalem from the period circa 1000 B.C.E.—Before the Common Era—when we normally date David, showed the great city of Jerusalem, but it doesn't. It would be lovely if we had external sources—archaeological, inscriptional, epigraphic—attesting to David's evidence, but we don't. Some biblical scholars say no David ever existed; he's much like King Arthur, the stuff of legends, inventions passed down from parent to child, glorified here, ambivalent here, always developed, always ongoing. If there is a real King David, and frankly I want there to be—I want there to be somebody who is this rich—there is no way we're ever going to get back to him. There is no way we can penetrate back behind the legends. All we can do at this point, until archaeology discovers something new, is look at the story.

One final point on archaeology. Some archaeologists have claimed to have discovered an inscription on a potshard entitled or read "House of David"—"*Bet David*." By this, they attest, because the potsherd seems to date from the right time period, "Aha, we have evidence of King David, House of David." The problem is the date of the shard is not entirely clear, and the meaning of the inscription itself is also not entirely clear. Archaeology is sometimes as much a discipline of believing rather than actually scientifically proving. If one wants to believe this is testimony to David, by all means, but the proof is not yet finally in.

We also have a problem with the historicity of David, at least of some of his stories, when we look to the Bible itself. One of the best-known stories, we've already mentioned it, is the death of Goliath, the Philistine giant, the Philistine hero. The problem is when we look at the book of Second Samuel, Chapter 21, verse 19, we also find a reference to the death of Goliath, except this death is attributed to David's soldier, one Elhanan. Did David kill Goliath? I suspect not. It's part of the stuff of legendary development that major stories accrue to heroes. Here is a major story of the death of a particular figure. The person who killed him, this Elhanan, is not well-known. "Ah," said the later legendary developers, "we'll give that one to David, too." We actually find similar stories in United States history. Did George Washington do everything we actually think he did? Actually, no. Sometimes some of those things were done by his generals. Did the pilgrims coming over on the Mayflower do everything we attribute to them? No, in fact, they didn't. Much is the stuff of later legendary development. And so, I fear, it is with David.

We can even see the development of David's legends when we look to later sources in the Bible. Not only are the records in the books of Samuel material of legend, but the legend continues. When we look, for example, at the books of Chronicles, which are basically post-exilic, much later replays of the Deuteronomic history—First and Second Samuel, First and Second Kings—we do find references to David, but when we go to First Chronicles, Chapter 20, we find that First Chronicles will tell us the story of Second Samuel, Chapter 11, about the siege of the Ammonites at Rabbah and the defeat of the Ammonite king. Left out is what happens in between. That's the story of David and Bathsheba. The Chronicler simply bypasses it. Here David's reputation will not be sullied at all. Indeed, whitewashing political peccadilloes is not a modern invention. The Chronicler does it before the Common Era.

It's also, I think, to be expected that David's story would be developed by southern scribes, those people down in Judah, in Jerusalem, who believe that their city Jerusalem, their kingdom Judah, is there by divine right, and they believe it in part because of this royal grant which they claim David to have received. As we'll see later when we get to the prophetic text, people like Isaiah and Jeremiah have a very difficult time convincing the population of Judah and Jerusalem that their kingdoms actually are in danger. They are convinced God will protect them because God is under contract. David is therefore very, very important for people in the south.

Where does this idea come from? In Second Samuel, Chapter 7, spoken to David by the court prophet Nathan, we find God's words: "When your days are complete and you lie with your fathers, I will raise up your seed, your posterity. I will make his throne secure forever. I will be a father to him, and he will be a son to me. When he errs I will chastise him with the rod of people and the lashes of men, but my steadfast love, my *hesed*, my deep abiding love, I will not remove from him. Your house and your kingship shall be secure before me forever, and your throne will be established permanently." Not only do we find this from the pen of the Deuteronomic historian, we also find it in the psalms. In Psalm 89, the poet Ethan the Ezrahite exults that God has promised, "I have made a covenant with my chosen one. I have sworn to my servant David, I will establish your descendants forever and build you a throne for all generations." You can see with material like this why David is so important to Israelite history.

Now let's look closely at one of these stories of David. Although David is exceptionally important, although he has a royal grant, although he is God's beloved, that does not make him a perfect person. Consistent with the way the ancient Hebrews and Israelites told their stories, their heroes are shown, pardon the cliché, warts and all. That's what, in fact, makes them human. That's I think in part what makes them so compelling as literary figures. Our test case here is David and Bathsheba. As we go on you might think to yourselves, "Do I still like David? Do I want him to win? Does he somehow retain my affection? What do I want to happen to him?"

One other point. There is no way we can look at this story without bringing to bear on it our own cultural concerns. I have difficulty looking at some of these biblical stories without thinking about movies. I can't think about King David without thinking about Gregory Peck, and Bathsheba will always be Susan Hayward. But the movies always add on to the text material that the text itself does not say. If you know these films, if you know the stories from popular culture, see if you can bracket them from your mind and just follow along in the text.

Second Samuel, Chapter 11. Here is the opening verse. "In the spring of the year, the time when kings go out to battle, David sent Joab and his officers and all Israel with him and they ravaged the Ammonites." So far, so good. "But David remained in Jerusalem."

Already the narrator is cueing us in that something has gone wrong. David is not doing what he is supposed to do. If this is the time when all kings go to battle and David is a king, he should not be home. He should be out at the front; that's where kings belong. David's deficiencies are beginning to show. And not merely has he removed himself from battle, he's sent his soldiers out there. People will die on his behalf. The least he could do is put in an appearance in the field, and he will not do that.

I suspect that this failure right in the first verse simply foreshadows the increasing failures. First David fails on the political front. He fails to become the general he is, to be the king that he is and lead his troops. We'll see subsequent failures in his monarchy simply as we go along in the story, which continues, "It happened late one afternoon when David rose from his couch and was walking about on the roof of the king's house that he saw from the roof a woman bathing, and the woman was very beautiful." This is David, that skilled musician, that man of valor, that warrior sensible of speech and handsome in appearance, whom the Lord favors. This is David our hero who's taking a nap late one afternoon, rising from his couch while his troops are in the field. What sort of warrior is this?

And what of this woman he sees, this luscious Bathsheba in her bath? Bathsheba really doesn't mean "bath." "Bath" is really the Hebrew *bat*—"daughter of," "daughter of Sheba." Interpreters frequently question Bathsheba's complicity in her relationship with David. Does she know he's there? If you see the movie, Susan Hayward knows exactly what she's doing, but Bathsheba the character, I don't know. Does she know that the king hasn't gone to the front? Does she know that he normally walks on his roof at this time of day? Is her bath time a convenience? Had she planned to be seen? Does she know he sees her? Whatever we answer to any of these questions, all of which are legitimate, whatever our answers will be, those answers will influence how we interpret the rest of the story and how we interpret Bathsheba, because once again the woman's motives are never given.

Now, David's relationship with Bathsheba is no simple spur-of-the-moment lust. He's got to plan this out; it's premeditated. Next verse: "David sent for messengers and inquired and said, 'Isn't this Bathsheba, the wife of Uriah the Hittite?'" That's one translation. Another one reads, "It was reported, 'This is Bathsheba the wife of

Uriah the Hittite.'" The ambiguity is telling. Does David actually know who she is, or does he have to find out? If he does know, how long has he had his eye on her? Readers familiar with the David story to this point might recollect his other relationships with women because David has been around the block a time or two.

For example, he marries the very, very clever Abigail after being, I think, complicit in causing the death of Abigail's husband. A woman's marital state will not stand in David's way if she can provide him something that he wants or something that he needs. Indeed, by marrying Abigail— the story is in First Samuel, Chapter 25—David is able to consolidate his base with the Calebite tribes. So marrying Abigail functions in terms of political opportunity. But here with Bathsheba there is no political opportunity. This is simply lust.

In terms of political opportunity, one could also note how David can manipulate women throughout his life. Michal, Saul's daughter, loves David. It's not clear David ever loves her, but he uses her as a pawn, and, finally, after years of being used by David, Michal finally turns against him. We find this in Second Samuel 6. This is David bringing the ark of the Lord to Jerusalem. "As the ark came into the city of David, Michal, daughter of Saul"—the narrator wants to tell us exactly who she is—"looked out the window [like Sisera's mother, the woman in the window] and saw King David leaping and dancing before the Lord, and she despised him in her heart." So she comes to David, and she berates him for uncovering himself before the eyes of maids and servants, as she puts it, as any vulgar fellow might uncover himself. David retorts to her, "It was the Lord who made me king over your father Saul."

Then we're told Michal, the daughter of Saul, had no child until the day of her death. This is narrative artistry. Did she have no child because God condemned her to barrenness because of her berating of God's beloved David, or did she have no child because David refused again to come into her bed? If that's the case, why? Because he hated her or because he was afraid that if she had a child that child would also be Saul's heir and that child eventually would raise up an army against David? It's narrative artistry all the way through. In fact, whether David can actually love or not, I think, remains an open question. We know people love David, but it's not clear David loves anyone.

The only time David actually seems to show love is his public lament over Jonathan's dead body. He says, "I am distressed for you, my brother Jonathan. Greatly beloved were you to me. Your love was wonderful, passing the love of women." But it's easy for David to say that then. Jonathan is dead; Saul is dead. David knows his throne is secure. Indeed, he even orders that this song be taught to the people of Judah, but does he actually love Jonathan or is this simply political opportunism—Jonathan's love was passing the love of women; Jonathan is dead? I see David as opportunist. You all can make up your own minds.

Moving back to the story of Bathsheba, David sent messengers to get her. Here is the line, "She came to him; he lay with her. Now she was purifying herself after her period." All this great romance: wine, flower, champagne, a bath—nothing. She came to him; he lay with her—boom. This verse is loaded with questions. Did David abuse his power? If somebody sends soldiers to your house, the king's messengers, and says, "The king wants to see you," it's very difficult to say no. This is a royal summons. Is this a rape? Had Bathsheba any choice? The king wants you. What do are you going to do—say no? Did David recognize by his actions that he's committing adultery? We might look to something like, oh, Deuteronomy, Chapter 22, which says, "Both the man and the woman who in town commit adultery should be put to death." Does he care that he's making Bathsheba an adulteress?

In turn, what about Bathsheba? Could she have said no? Could she have said, "I will come tomorrow"? Was she expecting the invitation, thinking, "Finally I've gotten what I wanted. I've trapped him, and he's risen to my bait"? What of the notice that she came to him, not that they took her? Is this simply an expression, or is there willingness involved? And what about the statement she was purifying herself? It's true, according to the Levitical law codes, after a woman is done with her menstrual cycle, she is supposed to bathe, ritual immersion, and that puts her back in a state of purity, which means she can then have sexual intercourse without incurring being in a state of impurity. Are we told this to be told that Bathsheba is faithful to the laws of God? Or are we being told this to let us know, on the more biological level, here is a woman who was not pregnant, and therefore we know that when Bathsheba conceives, the child is not her husband Uriah's; the child is King David's?

Well, the great romance of Hollywood legend is simply one verse: "He lay with her; she returned to her house." But then events move very quickly. The next verse: "The woman conceived, and she sent to David and she told him, 'I am pregnant.'" My question is, what does she want David to do? It's clearly David's child—he admits that—but what should he do? Does she want him to pray to God that she miscarry so the evidence will be wiped away? Does she want him to procure for her an abortion? Might he know someone who can do this? Does she want him to recall her husband from the front to cover up the adultery—get Uriah home and into her bed quickly? Does she want David to kill her husband and marry her himself so that she could give birth to a child who might at some point be the royal heir? All we know is she tells him she is pregnant, and then he needs to do something.

Questions continue to abound. From coveting his neighbor's wife to adultery, David will next turn to murder. The king recalls Bathsheba's husband from the front. His name is Uriah. He is identified as a Hittite; therefore, he is not an Israelite. He's a mercenary. He's a soldier for hire working on behalf of King David. David recalls Uriah, and, after meeting with him, encourages him, "Go down to your house and wash your feet." This is not simply an invitation to clean up. This is an invitation to connubiality because "feet" in biblical Hebrew, *reglayim*, is a euphemism for genitals. David is simply saying, go home and sleep with your wife. You're back from the front—take leave. Uriah actually knows what David is asking, and he the Hittite, the non-Israelite, responds finally with fidelity.

He says to David, "The ark and Israel and Judah remain in booths. They are in tents in the encampment. Shall I then go to my house to eat and to drink and to lie with my wife?" He knows exactly what David wants, but he goes on, "As you live and your soul lives, I shall not do such a thing." There's loyalty. The next night he gets Uriah drunk, hoping to send him home, and Uriah grabs a blanket and sleeps with the soldiers at the door of the king's house; he still demurs. Finally, David, knowing he's not going to get Uriah home, sends him back with a sealed letter to Joab the general, saying, "Place Uriah in the forefront of the hardest fighting and then draw back from him so that he may be struck down and die." Now the plot is very clear here. We know what David wants ultimately to happen.

But why exactly did David want Uriah to go home? Most of the time when people think about this the answer seems obvious: Go home so Uriah can sleep with his wife and thereby everyone can pass off the baby as Uriah's. David is not going to tell anybody. Bathsheba is not going to tell anybody. And Uriah will never know the difference. That's possible, but there are other possibilities as well. I think we tend not to think about them because we want David to be the good guy, and that's the most benign of all chances.

Might he have wanted Uriah to discover that Bathsheba was pregnant and kill her? That solves David's problem. Might he have wanted Uriah to find Bathsheba pregnant and agree to divorce her? Again, it solves David's problem. Might he have wanted Uriah to kill Bathsheba in a fit of jealousy? And again, David's problem is resolved. Or might he have wanted Uriah to sleep with Bathsheba and thereby violate the conventions of holy war because, as we've seen, soldiers in holy war must keep themselves pure; they are not allowed to have intercourse with women? What happens if they do? The idea would be God would strike them dead because they've violated a divine command, or, if their fellow soldiers found out about it, their fellow soldiers would have to remove that impurity from the camp, and the fellow soldiers would thereby kill him. Again, David is off; he is free. I don't know what his motives are. Some of them are more difficult to believe than others.

And how indeed is Uriah to be assessed here? In the movies Uriah is usually pretty awful, and there are some novels about David and Bathsheba in which Uriah is an abusive wife-beater and David is simply the kind, gentle man who comes to the rescue and provides Bathsheba the love and the tenderness that she had never known. But that's not what we have in the Bible. That makes the story easier, but the Bible doesn't let us off the hook that easily. Do his fidelity and his innocence make David's decadence even more monstrous? Here the Hittite is the faithful one. David, God's beloved, the Israelite king, is not. Or should we conclude that he has no relationship with his wife whatsoever? Certainly he could have gone home and at least said, "Hello, Bathsheba. How are you?" Nothing required that he sleep with her.

Why does he avoid her? Or is he so in love with her that he knew he could not resist the temptation, because he knew the minute he set foot in that door he would grab his beloved wife and kiss her and, before you know it, the conventions of holy war would be violated? Or does he respect Israel's Torah so much that he, a Hittite, is faithful to what God wants when God's beloved is not? Does he finally realize, after David keeps saying, "Go home, go home, go home," that his fate is sealed? Does he realize what David has done? Because adultery can never stay hidden. The news is going to get out. What exactly does Uriah know? When he is handed the sealed letter signing his death warrant, does he actually know that he is bringing that warrant to the commander and that he will die, and he dies bravely, accepting his fate, because what other choice did he have? Again, the text does not tell us, and this is what makes it so rich.

I can picture people in the ancient world listening to this text and debating it. It may be that the way we answer these questions tells us more about ourselves and our values than the text itself. The text raises the questions; the answers are ours to provide.

Well, Bathsheba, after a time of mourning, marries David and bears him a son. But then we're told, "The thing David had done had displeased the Lord." We've already seen David mourning in public grief for Saul and Jonathan. Here again I question the sincerity of that public grief because I question David's sincerity about Bathsheba all the way through. She mourns. What about him? And by the way, as long as we're here, what about Bathsheba's mourning? Does she do it because it's the socially polite thing to do—if she didn't mourn her husband people would talk? Or does she do it because she really loved him and now she knows her fate is doomed? Or did she do it because she thought, "Good riddance, and I've now got what I wanted—I'm going to marry the king and have his child"?

As for David, what do we do with him? He's gone from voyeurism to adultery to possible rape to murder and then cover-up, and this is the man who has a royal grant. Where is God going to come in? The news of the adultery gets out. God speaks to David through the prophet Nathan, the same one who gave him the royal grant, and Nathan says to him, "You have struck down Uriah the Hittite with a sword, and you have taken his wife to be your wife." What offends God here is less the adultery than the murder. "You have struck down Uriah. Therefore the sword will never again depart from your house. I will take your wives from before your eyes and give them to your neighbor." It turns out that neighbor is David's son, Absalom.

Nathan goes on, "He shall lie with your wives in the sight of this very sun. For what you did in secret, this I will do before all Israel." During the civil war, David's son Absalom, who revolts against him, takes David's concubines up to the roof of the palace and sleeps with them in the sight of all of Israel. Adultery is never private. It involves messengers, Nathan knows, and coworkers and confidants, and it even affects one's children because this adultery will lead to disasters in David's house: the rape of his daughter by his son, the murder of that son by another son, and defeat all around. David doesn't admit his sin regarding Bathsheba, and Nathan tells him that at least this particular sin has been passed over in God's purview. We have Psalm 51, which is entitled, "A Psalm of David when the prophet Nathan came to him after he had gone into Bathsheba."

Despite this repenting, Nathan tells him, "The child that is born to you shall die." And, as we know, older sons do not inherit. David and Bathsheba do have a second child, who, with the machinations of his mother, Bathsheba—who discovers how to work the harem to her advantage—and the prophet Nathan, is put on the throne. This is Solomon. So this is the end of her story, at least. Bathsheba makes her own fate, and Solomon will become the ideal and quite typical Near Eastern king and so fulfill the pro- and the anti-monarchical predictions made back when by the prophet Samuel. What happened to David regarding a woman will ultimately happen to Solomon, because, we're told in First Kings, "Solomon had 300 wives and 700 concubines, and they led his heart astray after idols." We'll see this in the next lecture.

Lecture Seventeen

From King Solomon to Pre-classical Prophecy (1 Kings 3—2 Kings 17)

Scope:

The biblical prophet (*Nabi*; plural: *Nevi'im*) is known less for predicting the future than for communicating divine will, usually through poetry, and often in debate with kings and priests. Prophecy thus can be separated neither from politics nor from the concern for social justice. Although Abraham, Aaron, Moses, and Miriam are all called "prophets," biblical scholarship traditionally speaks of the formal role of the prophet as beginning with the monarchy and gradually ending with the rise of the theocratic state. This lecture looks at divine human communication first, briefly, through implements, turns to the phenomenon of "ecstatic prophecy," and comes to focus on the "pre-classical" or non-writing prophet, with particular attention to Elijah. But we begin with Solomon, to establish a picture of the type of king against which the prophets inveighed.

Outline

I. Solomon becomes an ideal, and quite typical, Near Eastern king; thus, he fulfills both the pro- and anti-monarchical views expressed by Samuel.

A. On the positive side:

1. Solomon solidifies David's political basis and geographical holdings.
2. He builds the Jerusalem Temple.
3. He establishes enormous treasury reserves.
4. He develops a positive international reputation, as witnessed by the Queen of Sheba's embassy (1 Kings 10).
5. His court becomes known as a center of learning, such that much of Israelite wisdom literature (the Song of Songs, Proverbs, Ecclesiastes) is attributed to him.
6. Thus, 1 Kings 4:29: "God gave Solomon wisdom and understanding beyond measure, and largeness of mind like the sand on the seashore."

B. On the negative side:

1. His rule is marked by *corvées* (the extrication of unpaid labor from the population).
2. He creates an overextended economy marked by the importation of luxury items.
3. He consequently has a heavily taxed peasantry; the "golden age" of Solomon was likely golden only for the elite.
4. He disobeys Deut. 17:14–20 concerning not only the build-up of capital, but also: "he must not acquire many wives for himself, or else his heart will turn away."
5. "Solomon has three hundred wives and seven hundred concubines," who "lead his heart astray" after idols (1 Kings 11:1–8).

II. The end of centralized government.

A. The inflated government, in conflict with the Yahwistic premise of social egalitarianism, could not survive.

B. Under Solomon's heir, Rehoboam, the northern tribes secede. David's kingdom will remain divided—Israel in the North; Judah in the South—for the next two hundred years.

C. Israel, lacking the Davidic grant and always in a precarious situation with leaders, develops a strong counter to the power of the king: the prophet.

III. Divine/human communication.

A. The Urim and Thummim, interpreted by the priests, were likely forms of lots.

1. The King James Version of 1 Sam. 28:8 reads, "Divine for me by a familiar."
2. The Hebrew reads *ob*, the Hittite/Akkadian cognate to which is "hole in the ground."

B. Necromancy, consulting the dead, involves pouring wine or oil into a hole in the ground, although, because of a translation error, it has been misunderstood.

C. Astrology is indicated in Isa. 47:13: "those who 'divide' [the meaning of the Hebrew here is uncertain] the heavens, who gaze at the stars, who at the new moons predict what will befall you."

D. Hepatoscopy, the reading of liver omens, is the best-attested Near Eastern divinatory practice.

1. Archaeologists have located clay livers from Hazor.
2. The technique is noted in Ezek. 21:21: "The King of Babylon stands at the parting of the way, at the head of the two ways to use divination. He shakes the arrows, he consults the teraphim, he looks at the liver."

IV. The division of functions. One theory argues that the office of prophet in its uniquely Hebrew sense was born when the office of judge—with its theological and gubernatorial elements—evolved into two distinct branches: prophets and kings.

V. An alternative, and complementary, view relates prophesy to ecstatic possession.

A. Etymology.

1. The Hebrew *nabi* has no clear ancient Near Eastern cognates. Its closest linguistic relation, the same root with different vowels, means "to rave like one insane" (cf. 1 Sam. 18:10, on Saul who "raved").
2. Prophetic ecstasy (literally, "to stand outside, or be beside, oneself") involves possession and, sometimes, an accompanying message.

B. Ecstatic prophecy is particularly, and problematically, associated with King Saul.

1. Saul meets a band of prophets "coming down from the high place with harp, tambourine, lyre, and flute before them, prophesying." He is told: "The spirit of the Lord will come mightily upon you, and you shall prophecy with them and be turned into another man" (1 Sam. 10:6–7). The account ends: "Therefore it became a proverb, 'Is Saul also among the prophets?'"
2. Saul sends messengers to take David, but "When they saw the company of prophets prophesying, and Samuel standing as head over them, the Spirit of God came over the messengers… and they also prophesied."
3. Saul's next two groups are similarly affected.
4. Finally, Saul goes himself, "and he too stripped off his clothes, and he too prophesied before Samuel, and lay naked all that day and all that night. Hence it is said: 'Is Saul also among the prophets?'" (1 Sam. 19:24).

C. Cross-cultural components.

1. Ecstatic prophecy, unlike classical (literary) prophecy, is widely attested cross-culturally. For example, the Egyptian "Travels of Wen-Amon" notes that "while he was making offering to his gods, the god seized one of his youths and made him possessed."
2. Num. 24:16 introduces Balaam by saying that the spirit of God possessed him and by describing his position: "falling down but having his eyes uncovered."

D. This type of prophecy can be and was artificially induced.

1. From a shrine in Anatolia dating to the fifth millennium B.C.E., archaeologists have recovered an opium pipe.
2. In Ugarit, wine was used.
3. In South America, psylocibin, toad skins, and so on.
4. At Delphi, noxious fumes.

VI. The shift from ecstatic to pre-classical prophecy.

A. The "sons of the prophets" who travel in bands (1 Sam. 10:5) and prophesy with one voice (1 Kings 22:12) may have served as the transition group.

1. These prophetic bands may be directed by a teacher (cf. 1 Sam. 19–20, in which the leader is Samuel). Elijah's band apparently preserved the traditions of their teacher.
2. The prophetic guilds may have worn external signs of office, such as shaved heads; Cf. 2 Kings 2:23–25: "Some small boys came out of the city and jeered at [Elisha], saying: 'go up, you baldhead. Go up, you baldhead.' And he turned around, and when he saw them he cursed them in the name of the Lord. And two she-bears came out of the wood and tore up forty-two of the boys."

B. Separation from the group: When an individual prophesies apart from the group, pre-classical prophecy formally begins. This is the case with Micaiah, the son of Imlah, of whom Ahab, the king of Israel, states: "I hate him, for he never prophesies good concerning me, but evil," (1 Kings 22).

VII. Elijah, the major pre-classical prophet, is cast as a new Moses.

A. Like Moses and Joshua, he parts water (the Jordan, in 2 Kings 2:7).

B. Like Moses, he experiences a theophany at Horeb (1 Kings 19:8ff.).

C. Elijah builds an altar with twelve stones (1Kings 18:30); Moses constructs an altar flanked by twelve pillars (Exod. 24:4).

D. Elijah performs a sacrifice, the altar is consumed by fire, and the people bow (1 Kings 18:38ff.); Moses offers a sacrifice after consecrating his altar, the fire consumes the offering, and the people bow (Lev. 9:24).

E. Like Moses, Elijah has no tomb.
   1. He is carried to heaven in a fiery chariot (hence the spiritual; see 2 Kings 2:11).
   2. In later legend, Elijah associated with Enoch, who also never "dies."
   3. The prophet Malachi, the last of the canon's classical prophets, predicts his return "before the great and terrible 'day of the Lord' comes" (Mal. 4:5 [3:23]).

VIII. Elijah's task is to prevent the people from succumbing to Baalism, sponsored by King Ahab of Israel and, especially, by his Sidonian wife, Jezebel.

A. The predominant Canaanite deity is Baal, often accompanied by his consort(s) Anath, Ashtoreth/ Ishtar/Astarte.

B. Against their worship not only Elijah but also the classical prophets Amos and Hosea struggle, as we shall see in the next lecture.

Supplementary Reading:

Commentaries in series listed in the bibliography.

Michael D. Coogan (ed.), *The Oxford History of the Biblical World* (New York: Oxford University Press, 1998).

Questions to Consider:

1. What is the most effective way of overcoming temptations to syncretism: incorporation of competing language (the psalms), prophetic polemic, political persecution, or other?

2. In what way is madness culturally constructed? Is according a prophetic role to one who "raves" a helpful means of giving people who behave in nontraditional ways a place in society?

Lecture Seventeen—
From King Solomon to Pre-classical Prophecy
(1 Kings 3–2 Kings 17)

At the end of our last lecture we met David's heir—Bathsheba's son—King Solomon, and that begins, at least according to the biblical description, the golden age of ancient Israel, fulfilling some of the pro-monarchical comments already found in First Samuel. We find that King Solomon builds a gorgeous court and constructs a magnificent temple. It would be nice if we actually had some archaeological evidence of that temple; we do not.

But, at least according to the biblical tradition, Solomon was a spectacular king. He establishes enormous treasury reserves. His court becomes a center of wisdom and learning. Many people are familiar with the story of the Queen of Sheba who comes from Africa to Solomon's court because she had heard about his great wisdom. Solomon is so wise that the biblical tradition attributes to him wisdom literature, a genre we will encounter later. Attributed to Solomon, in addition to the love poem, Song of Songs, are also the Proverbs and Ecclesiastes—wonderful wisdom literature. We're told in First Kings, Chapter 4, "God gave Solomon wisdom and understanding beyond measure, the largeness of mind like the sand of the seashore." This is a smart guy.

But there is a downside to the centralized monarchy under King Solomon, and in this sense Solomon also fulfills the anti-monarchical material that we saw voiced by the prophet Samuel. For example, he engages in forced labor, not all that distinct from what the Israelites faced when they were in slavery in Egypt. Solomon creates corvées, laborers forced to work on his temple for him. He has an over-extended economy marked by the importing of luxury items. He's got a very, very heavily taxed peasantry. The golden age of Solomon was golden, I suspect, only for the elite. The vast majority of people were unable to participate in the glories of the kingdom, the wisdom of Solomon, or, in fact, any of the economic benefits.

As we already know, the reign of Solomon will at some point come to an ignominious end, because we're told about Solomon's many, many wives and many, many concubines. In addition to signaling Solomon's apostasy, these various wives lead his heart astray after idols. Why? Because many of them are daughters or sisters or relatives of other ancient Near Eastern kings, and therefore Solomon married these women in order to create political alliances. But it's also the case that, given the over-extended economy and these various international treaties, the center could not hold, and indeed it didn't. After Solomon's reign, his son Rehoboam was unable to retain the throne, and we will return to him in a little bit.

But think right now about the difficulties of a united monarchy, a king who has all power. He's controlling the temple; he built it. He's establishing who the priests will be. He's setting economic and political policy. For governments to stand there needs to be some sort of system of checks and balances, and it may be, given that need, that we can find therein the origins of Israelite prophecy. So it's to Israelite prophecy we will now turn.

In terms of prophecy, we've, in fact, already seen prophets. We've encountered the prophetess Deborah, who's actually a judge in Israel but called a prophetess. We've seen Nathan, David's court prophet who excoriates him for the adultery he commits with Bathsheba and the subsequent murder of Bathsheba's husband, Uriah. And we've seen, of course, Samuel, who epitomizes early prophecy. Indeed, he is the major character in the book that bears his name, First Samuel.

One can already see with this listing of three—Deborah and Nathan and Samuel—that the definition of prophet encompasses a variety of different roles. We have, for example, Deborah the military judge. We have Nathan functioning as the court conscience, and we have Samuel engaged both in priestly activities, engaging in animal sacrifice, for example, as well as in very political activities like anointing kings and, indeed, dispatching kings when he decides they are not good enough.

Today when we think of prophets, at least I typically think about people who predict the far-flung future, folks like Nostradamus or, for more contemporary concerns, Jeanne Dixon or Edgar Cayce. These are people who are interested in what's going to happen five years from now, centuries from now. For the most part the prophets in the Bible are not interested in predicting the far-flung future, in foretelling. As the saying goes, they are much more interested in forthtelling: taking a look at the current climate; how the royal house is functioning; how the economy is going; how the poor, the orphaned, the strangers are being treated; and then speaking to the people who can make a difference—the priests in the cult, the upper classes, the king—and telling them, "Folks, straighten up." The prophets will engage in both political critique, telling kings whether to engage in international treaties or not, and they will engage in cultic critique if they think that the cults are running improperly, as if, for example, people are offering animal sacrifice because they think it's the thing to do without being repentant in their hearts. And they will offer moral critique if they see the ethics of the country going to *she'ol*, their ancient version of hell.

We start with the biblical prophets from the very earliest period—Samuel, Deborah, even farther back. They are all called prophets, but here the term is so vague, like the term "judge," we really can't get a handle on it. When biblical scholars typically talk about prophets, we typically divide them into two categories. We have the pre-classical prophet, epitomized by the prophet Elijah. Pre-classical prophets are known not for writing, so we don't have any written oracles from them, but they are known for engaging in substantial political concerns. Indeed, Elijah is involved with the court of Ahab and Jezebel, and Elijah's successor, Elisha, is actually one of the people who prompts Jehu's very, very bloody coup over against the house represented by Ahab and Jezebel. Those are pre-classical prophets, and we will return to Elijah later in this lecture.

The classical prophets, on the other hand, are those prophets known for their written oracles, prophets who probably had followers who preserved what they said, prophets such as Amos, Josiah, Isaiah, and Jeremiah, and we will turn to them in subsequent lectures.

In terms of these early pre-classical prophets, we can see here perhaps the beginning of true Israelite prophecy, and here is why I want to make a distinction between Moses and Miriam and Deborah and even Samuel, on the one hand, and people like Elijah and Elisha on the other. Prophets ideally in the traditional Israelite sense are there to complain against the system. They are there to provide checks on the system. The problem with classifying someone like Moses or Deborah or even Samuel as a prophet is, in fact, they are the system. They are not engaged in critique; they are engaged in actually telling Israel what to do. They are in charge. By the time we get down to Nathan, we've now got people who are critiquing the system, and, again, Elijah becomes the ideal example of a pre-classical prophet who argues against the king, both for moral reasons as well as for cultic reasons and, indeed, international reasons.

Let's back up a little bit and talk about how prophecy functions in the ancient Near East as a means of conveying information between God and the covenant community and, indeed, the covenant community and God, because both classical prophets and their pre-classical predecessors actually have two jobs when it comes to God. On the one hand, God speaks to them and tells them information that they need to convey to the covenant community, to the kings, to the priests, to the laity, to the elite, to the poor. On the other hand, since the people frequently repent of their crimes—their apostasies—and since God frequently gets very angry at these crimes and apostasies, the prophet is also in the business of mediating back the people's repentance to God. So we might think of prophets as conduits between God and the community. But it's not simply by divine oracle or Holy Spirit that one can get information from God and convey it to the people. There are actually numerous techniques found throughout the ancient Near East, both in the Bible and external biblical sources by which people are able to get information about the divine. Most of these techniques would, in fact, be looked at, at least from current standards, as forms of technology or forms of science. They are learned arts. Priests would study how to figure out what the gods or, indeed, God, wanted.

The process here is known as divination, to determine what the divine has to say, and there are a series of techniques. Let's look at a couple of them because, in fact, we've seen them already. We simply haven't classified them in these terms. One particular divinatory technique we've already seen is called necromancy. Necromancy is the calling up of somebody who is dead to get information about the future. We saw that with King Saul, who sought out a medium, the medium of Endor, to call up the spirit of Samuel. That is actually a form of divination.

The technique we know from ancient Near Eastern sources goes like this. In the ancient Near East early on, during the First Temple Period, there is no sense of dead people living in a glorious heaven. Dead people, at least according to the biblical source, go to a place called *she'ol*. It's non-place; not much happens there. The dead are like shades floating through without much sense of consciousness, but they do have some clue as to what might happen in the future.

Now, if you decide you wanted to become a medium or a witch in the ancient world, how would you facilitate your art? You would dig a hole in the ground and into that hole you would pour wine or oil or milk, and that would cause the shades of the dead to come up because, in fact, they are thirsty; nobody is feeding them. That's probably what the witch of Endor did. She dug a hole in the ground, poured something into it, and thereby allowed the shade of Samuel to come up.

We have, however, an interesting translation problem. When the King James Version of the Bible was translating this particular material at the end of First Samuel, the King James translators translated the Hebrew term for "hole in the ground" as "familiar." That's where we get the idea that witches have familiar spirits, often cats or newts or some sort of reptile, some animal that conveys to them what the devil wants. But that's not at all what's happening in the ancient Near East. The problem is they translated "familiar spirit" rather than "hole in the ground." Necromancy is one form of divination.

The priests in ancient Israel had another form called Urim and Thummim. These are actually lots. We might think of dice that they would cast, and, depending upon whether the dice or the lots came up positive or negative, they would be able to determine what God's will was. We actually see this in the inauguration ceremony for King Saul, where the prophet cast lots and first the lot fell on the tribe of Benjamin, and then the lot fell on Saul's family and ultimately on Saul himself. Divination by casting lots or by casting dice was very common.

Astrology, of course, was common. People always looked at the stars, and, if the stars fell into a certain pattern, or if the planets came up in a certain way, one could make predictions. If it was noticed that the planet Mars was on the ascent at a particular time, that, for example, a king died, the next time Mars showed up at exactly the same place astrologers might tell the king, "You better watch out this month; it does not bode well."

My favorite example of ancient Near Eastern divinatory techniques is called hepatoscopy. You actually know what this is because you've heard the term hepatitis. Hepatitis is liver disease. Hepatoscopy is divining by livers. We have from the ancient Near East, both in Israelite territory and beyond, thousands of clay livers with various spots and shapes that priests would consult. They would sacrifice a sheep, and then they would look at the liver, match that particular sheep's liver up with their models, and determine from the connections what the king ought to do, whether the queen would give birth to a son, or whether the nation should go to war. This is called hepatoscopy; it's an ancient science. We have this, in fact, cited in Ezekiel, the prophet Ezekiel, Chapter 21, where Ezekiel describes "the king of Babylon standing at the parting of the ways." He consults his *teraphim* (his family idols); he looks at the liver. Fascinating.

Other forms of divinatory techniques are mentioned in the Bible. I'll give you two more because we will see them when we get to the Joseph saga, which, as you know, we bypassed just slightly. Joseph is in Egypt; his brothers have sold him into slavery. He has risen to a position second in command to Pharaoh, and he needs some way of bringing his brothers to greater consciousness to get them to apologize to him, to repent of their evil deeds. At one point he actually plays a trick on them. He takes his cup and arranges his cup to be put in a sack of grain that his youngest brother, Benjamin, is taking back home. Then he sends out his soldiers to grab Benjamin, and the soldiers find the cup, and they respond, in Genesis 44, verse 5, "Is this not my Lord's cup from which he drinks and by which he divines?" This is probably a form of lecanomancy, the ancient technique of pouring oil onto water and watching the patterns.

Then, finally, and you should expect this, we have interpretation of dreams, particularly associated with Joseph and also associated with Daniel, two of the Jews we find in foreign courts. So we'll come back to dream interpretation later.

Now most of these forms of divination were frowned upon, at least by the official scribes, the writers of the Bible. I suspect that the average person in the ancient Near East—Israelite, Canaanite, Babylonian—would have thought all this stuff was perfectly okay in the same way today that people who would consider themselves faithful and religious and good churchgoers or synagoguegoers might, in fact, consult their horoscopes first thing in the morning. I actually do that myself, but I still consider myself quite religiously faithful. I think biblical figures would have done the same thing.

Now let's move from the question of divination to the question of actual prophecy and where prophecy in its uniquely Israelite sense came about. One explanation, which brings us back to that overextended economy of King Solomon, is that the prophet came about when the office of the judge split into two, one being the king and one being the conscience of the king. Judges are the system, but, by the time we come down to the end of the book of First Samuel, we now have kings, and we wind up with Samuel as that king's conscience. As we move on, we have David as king and Nathan as conscience.

Here the prophet is not so much engaging in divinatory practices, and the prophet is not ruling the country. The prophet is telling the king how to rule both in terms of military function as well as in terms of personal morality. But there is also an alternative view to the separation of the office of the judge, and here we move to etymology, word origins. We've already seen how biblical scholars, when they search for the origins of Yahwism, ask where that tetragrammaton, those four letters, came from. If you look at the letters that spell out the Hebrew word for prophet, the word is *nabi*. There are two possible etymological origins. One is from the Akkadian "to announce," but it's quite vague as to whether this actually works or not. The one that I think probably has the closest meaning is from another Akkadian cognate, meaning, in fact, "to rave like a mad person."

The origin here might be that the prophets in Israel began in terms of ecstatic prophesy, people who were considered possessed by the God and, in that possession, either spoke words that were intelligible, political concerns or moral concerns, or spoke words that were completely unintelligible and then other folks would come along and provide the interpretation. That is, in fact, what happens at the Greek shrine of Delphi, the Delphic oracle. The priestess would sit on a little tripod, and noxious fumes would come up, and she would simply babble. The Greek word *prophetes,* whence we get the English prophet, is actually the man who would interpret her unintelligible utterings.

We do have forms of ecstatic prophecy already in the Bible, and, in fact, we find them most commonly associated with King Saul, so let's go back to Saul for a minute. In First Samuel, Chapter 10, Saul has just been secretly anointed by Samuel, and Samuel says to him, "You're going to meet a band of prophets," and this is what happens. The band of prophets "is coming down from the high places with harps and tambourines and lyres and flutes," a lot of musical instruments, and they are "prophesying." We are not told what their prophecies are. We do not even know if these prophecies have content. They simply may be singing or making unintelligible sounds to the rhythm of the music.

Then we're told—in fact, Saul is told—"the spirit of the Lord," the *ruakh* that we already saw back in Genesis, Chapter 1, the spirit of God that hovers over the deep, the *ruakh*, "the spirit of the Lord will come upon you and you shall prophesy with them," says Samuel to Saul, "and you will be turned into another man." In other words, your own personality will become submerged, and a different person will arise. This is exactly what happens. Saul begins prophesying with this band of prophets—no content here but prophecy, and therefore the account ends. It became, in fact, a proverb: "Is Saul also among the prophets?" This is very positive. It's a sign that God approves of Saul's anointing.

When we get to First Samuel 19, we actually find the same saying, "Is Saul among the prophets?" but here in a very negative way. Saul has by now decided that David is his enemy, and Saul is right because David wants the throne. Saul at one point sends messengers to try to capture David. This is what happens to the messengers: "When they saw the company of prophets prophesying and Samuel standing as head over them, the spirit of God [here, *ruakh elohim*] overtook them and they also prophesied." Now, if you're engaging in this type of ecstatic prophecy you are in no position to be able to capture somebody who is about to usurp the throne.

Saul's messengers can't do what he wants, so Saul appropriately sends another band of messengers. They hook up with the prophets; they start prophesying. Things are not working out too well. A third group goes, and then finally Saul himself goes, and this is how the Bible describes him, speaking of Saul: "He too stripped naked of his clothes, and he too prophesied before Samuel and lay naked all that night and all that day; hence it is said, 'Is Saul also among the prophets?'" It's the same statement, but these are two very different contexts within which that statement is placed. That is, in fact, very, very common in oral traditions, oral cultures. People may well remember a particular phrase but not remember the content that gave rise to that phrase to begin with. For those of you familiar with the New Testament, we have Jesus quoted as saying, "Take up your palette and walk," but Matthew, Mark, and Luke give one particular context for that and the Gospel of John another. But, as you know, that's a very different lecture series.

In terms of ecstatic prophecy, the following example, I think, epitomizes the problem with King Saul. First Samuel 18:10 describes Saul as "one who raved within his house" or "engaged in frenzy within his house." This is why David is called upon to play the harp for him, to play the lyre, "to soothe his spirit." The Hebrew term for "raving" here is *vaet nabe,* which has the root *nabi*, the root for the Hebrew word "prophet." So instead of translating, "Saul raved within his house," we could even say, "Saul prophesied within his house." But this is ecstatic prophecy; Saul is uncontrolled.

We have examples of ecstatic prophecy elsewhere in the Bible as well as through the ancient Near East. The Egyptian "Travels of Wen-Amon," a very well-known and multiply-copied tale, talks about God seizing youths and causing them to prophesy. Among non-Hebrews in the biblical text, if we go back to the Book of Numbers, we find a spectacular prophet. He is not a Hebrew; he's a prophet for hire. His name is Balaam, and the King of Moab actually hires him to curse the Israelites because prophets have connections with the divine. Balaam, however, is possessed by God, and, instead of cursing the Israelite community in the wilderness, he winds up blessing them. The King of Moab complains, "I didn't hire you for this," and Balaam says, "Well, I'm sorry. I can only say the words that God puts into my mouth." Indeed, the irony of ironies here is that Balaam's prophecy is now part of Jewish liturgy. For those of you in the Jewish tradition you might know the song, "*Matovu Ohalekha Ya'akov.*" This is "How Goodly Are Your Tents, O Jacob, Your Encampments, O Israel." That's Balaam's blessing, possessed by the God.

Ecstatic prophecy could be accomplished not only by divine possession, it could also be accomplished by technology. From a shrine in Anatolia dating to the fifth millennium, B.C.E., archaeologists have recovered opium pipes, and I don't think those priests were smoking just because they enjoyed it. I think they used their opium haze in order to divine, to get the words of the gods. In Ugarit, wine was used, and in South and Central America, psilocybin, mushrooms, and toad skins. It was ecstatic prophecy at Delphi, as we've already seen, and perhaps even through transfer mutilation. When Elijah fights the prophets of Baal on Mt. Carmel, we are told that the prophets of Baal "cried aloud and cut themselves after their custom with swords and lances until the blood gushed out." They are beside themselves. They are, in fact, in ecstasy. If you think about the root of ecstasy, it simply means "ecstasis," "to stand outside yourself." That's ecstatic prophecy.

Where are we when it comes to biblical prophecy? I suspect that both explanations—the separation of the role of judge into king and prophet and also ecstatic prophesy—I suspect they are already combined in Samuel, whom we've seen is not only the conscience of the king and not only a political functionary but also the head of a band of prophets. Prophetic bands continued in Israel. We have a very good example of them, not only with the prophet Elijah but also with Elisha, who, along with many other prophets, follows Elijah in his jobs, in his travels. It's even been suggested that the bands of prophets had particular *sigla* such as bald heads.

That may explain Second Kings, Chapter 2, where we are told, "some small boys came out of the city, and they jeered at the prophet Elisha, saying, 'Go up, you baldhead! Go up, you baldhead!" and "go up" then more or less meant what the English equivalent means now. Elisha "turned around and when he saw them he cursed them in the name of the Lord, and two she-bears came out of the woods and tore up 42 of the boys." This is quite nasty, right? Prophets can do miracles, particularly the pre-classical prophet. Is the bald head a sign, a shaven head a sign of prophecy? It could be. It might also be that Elisha was simply bald.

In terms of pre-classical prophets and their formal means, kings hired prophets. Indeed, they hired bands of prophets, so the office of court prophet became quite popular. That's Nathan's job, for example. But eventually the court prophet would separate from the band and give the king oracles that the king did not want to hear. Epitomizing this is a court prophet from the court of King Ahab, Jezebel's husband. His name is Micaiah ben Imlah. At one point King Ahab complains about him so much, he says, "I hate him, for he never prophesies good concerning me but only evil." If the prophet says bad things are going to happen to the king, that's probably a legitimate prophet.

Thus we come to Elijah. Elijah, epitomizing the pre-classical prophet, is cast in the role of Moses. For example, Moses has a theophany, a revelation of God on Mt. Sinai; Elijah has a revelation of God on Mt. Horab, the "E" source's name for Sinai. Elijah performs a sacrifice on Mt. Carmel; the entire altar is consumed with fire. The people see this miracle, and they bow down and worship God. Moses does exactly the same thing in Leviticus. He offers a sacrifice and thereby consecrates his altar. The fire consumes the offering, and the people bow down. In the Hebrew you can see the words being repeated. Like Moses, Elijah has no tomb. Moses, as you know, is buried in secret. For Elijah a chariot comes down from heaven, a fiery chariot, and takes him back up, and that produces the legends that Elijah will at some point come back. In our discussion of canon very early in the series, we saw how the Christian canon puts the prophet Malachi at the end, predicting the coming of Elijah.

In terms of Elijah himself, what does he do? What is his role? His task is not easy. He goes up primarily against the king of the north, King Ahab, and his wife Jezebel. Jezebel you probably think of as someone who's like a prostitute or at least a woman whose morals are suspect. Actually, Jezebel does have her problems: she lies, she steals, she cheats, she engages in libel, she apostasizes, she murders, but she's actually quite faithful to her husband, Ahab. I mean, the one thing she doesn't do is engage in some sort of sexual crime. The reason she gets this reputation is because, right before her death, we find in Second Kings, Chapter 9, "she painted her eyes and adorned her hair, and she stood looking down from the window." This is a woman who knows enough to put on makeup right before she dies. I give her credit for that.

Elijah is not only dealing with Ahab's political crimes, but he's also dealing with Jezebel's sponsorship of her own gods. Jezebel is from Sidon; she worships one of the Baals. So Elijah has to explain to the people, Baal-worship is evil, it's apostatizing, you should only worship the one God. But for the people to whom Elijah is giving these oracles, this did not make much sense. They could not much more conceive of agriculture without Baal than they could conceive of agriculture without rain because they are living in a Canaanite environment and Baal is the nature god. So Elijah has to explain why Baal is simply a false god.

He is thereby depicted as contrasting the powers of YHWH and Baal. In his contest with the priests of Baal on Mt. Carmel, he has the priest on Mt. Carmel set up one sacrifice, he sets up another, and he says to the priest on Mt. Carmel, "Have your god Baal send fire down and consume the sacrifice." Then you can picture him just kind of sitting there, tapping his foot, flipping his fingers, and waiting, and he begins about noontime to taunt the priests of Baal. He says, "Where is your God? Is he on a journey? Is he meditating? Has he gone aside?" "Gone aside" in Hebrew means, "Has he gone to the bathroom?" "Perhaps he's asleep and you have to wake him up."

This is taunting the Baal-worshipers, and ultimately what we see with Elijah is that his God finally sends down fire from heaven and consumes that sacrifice. Throughout the rest of Elijah's career, he will not only combat Baal-worship, he will also establish the model by which future prophets, both pre-classical and classical, find their voice and establish the means by which they can convince the covenant community that their voice is the one that needs to be heeded.

Lecture Eighteen

The Prophets and the Fall of the North (1 Kings 16—2 Kings 17, Amos, Hosea)

Scope:

Amos and Hosea, the first two classical prophets whose words are preserved in the canon, proffer critiques expressed in poetic form against the government of Israel, the priesthood, and the rich. Despite their warnings concerning both personal behavior and political machinations, the Kingdom of Israel falls to Assyria in 722 B.C.E. Following brief comments about the roles of Elijah and Elisha and an introduction to the "minor prophets," this lecture describes the rhetoric used by Amos and Hosea, as well as the setting to which they delivered their oracles. We conclude by examining the fulfillment of their warnings: the fall of the North, as attested in both biblical and extra-canonical sources.

Outline

I. Elijah contrasts the powers of YHWH and Baal.

A. The Canaanite nature god cannot provide food, but in the midst of famine, YHWH's prophet is miraculously fed, and he can miraculously feed others, as he does for the widow of Zarephath.

B. On Mt. Horeb, Elijah witnesses wind, earthquake, then fire, but YHWH comes in the silence: He is neither in, nor controlled by, nature (1 Kings 19:1–18).

C. Yearly, Mot (death) overcomes Baal, but Anath revives him with appropriate rituals. Elijah raises a dead boy, while the "dying/rising god" cannot resurrect himself.

II. In addition to calling rulers to account, pre-classical prophets also sanction political events.

A. Elijah's successor, Elisha, arranges the coup that deposes Ahab and places Jehu on the throne.

B. The prophetess Huldah legitimates the Book of Deuteronomy.

C. Prophetic signs can solidify political symbols.

1. By the separation of Solomon's kingdom, with Solomon's son Rehoboam continuing the Davidic line in Judea in the South and Jereboam I ruling in Israel, the North (1 Kings 11:26ff.) receives prophetic warrant.
2. The prophet Ahijah states that Solomon had to be punished: "Because he has forsaken me, and worshiped Ashtoreth the goddess of the Sidonians, Chemosh the god of Moab… and has not walked in my ways, doing what is right in my sight… as David his father did" (1 Kgs.12:33).
3. The prophet sanctions the split by symbolizing it: "Ahijah laid hold of the new garment that was on him, and tore it into twelve pieces."

III. The prophetic corpus.

A. The twelve "minor prophets" are collected together after the major latter prophets (Isaiah, Jeremiah, and Ezekiel).

B. This collection is also called "The Book of the Twelve."

C. The minor prophets are: Hosea, Joel, Amos, Obadiah, Jonah, Micah, Nahum, Habakkuk, Zephaniah, Haggai, Zechariah, and Malachi.

D. The order is roughly chronological, from earliest to latest.

E. The Book of the Twelve equals the length of each major prophetic scroll.

IV. Prophetic rhetoric: arresting expressions and evocations of Israel's history. These devices continue the covenant practice of self-criticism.

A. Amos opens with a series of pronouncements against Israel's neighbors: Judah, Edom, Moab, Ammon, and so on.

1. The nations listed first are condemned for their treatment of outsiders (usually Israel and Judah).
2. Israel and Judah are then condemned for internal social oppression.

3. Israel's crime is more heinous in that the people reject God's blessings.
4. Amos 2:10–11 invokes the liberation from Egypt and the early days of Canaan.

B. Free association and puns:

Thus the Lord God showed me
Behold, a basket of summer fruit.
And he said, "Amos, what do you see?"
And I said, "A basket of summer fruit [*Kayitz*]."
Then the Lord said to me
The end (*Kaytz*) has come upon my people Israel (Amos 8:1–2).

C. Reversal of expectations: Amos adopts the rhetorical forms of cultic proclamation but announces the opposite of what was expected: "Woe to you who desire the day of the Lord! Why would you have the day of the Lord? It is darkness and not light." (5:18ff.).

D. Devices associated with the wisdom tradition (Proverbs, Ecclesiastes, Job):
1. Rhetorical questions and images from nature: "Do two walk together unless they have made an appointment? Does a lion roar in the forest when he has no prey?" (Amos 3:3–4).
2. Comparisons: "Thus says the Lord: 'As the shepherd rescues from the mouth of the lion two legs, or a piece of an ear, so shall the people of Israel who dwell in Samaria be rescued, with the corner of a couch and part of a bed'" (Amos 3:11–12).

E. Striking characterizations excoriated the upper class: "Hear this word, you cows of Bashan…who oppress the poor, who crush the needy, who say to their husbands: 'Bring that we may drink…'" (Amos 4:1ff.).

V. The focus of the pronouncements.

A. Of particular concern to the prophets was religious complacency, people who observe the rituals while ignoring the poor in their midst.
1. "Come to Bethel and transgress;

Bring your sacrifices every morning;
Your tithes every three days…
For so you love to do, O people of Israel" (Amos 4:4)

2. "I hate, I despise your feasts
And I take no delight in your solemn assemblies…
Take away from me the noise of your songs;
To the melody of your harps I will not listen.
But let justice roll down like waters,
And righteousness like an ever-flowing stream" (Amos 5:21–24).
3. Hos. 6:6 makes the point starkly: "I desire mercy, not sacrifice."

VI. Amos.

A. Amos, although from Judah, proclaimed his message in the cultic shrines of Israel during the reign of Jereboam II (787–747), a time of economic prosperity.

B. He identifies himself (1:1) as "among the shepherds of Tekoa."

1. With only two exceptions, the *Tanakh* uses *ro'eh* for shepherd; Amos uses *noqed.*
2. Comparative philology and Ugaritic cognates indicate that the *noqed* is a shepherd who cares for temple flocks destined for sacrifice.

C. Amos divorces himself from such connections: "I am no prophet, nor one of the sons of the prophets… [i.e., a member of a prophetic guild], but I am a herder and a dresser of sycamore trees" (7:14). The line may suggest that Amos is a seasonal or migrant worker.

VII. Hosea.

A. Hosea's initial activity coincides with the last year of Jereboam II (747 B.C.E.) and the Syro-Ephraimite war (Hos. 5:8–14, cf. 2 Kings 15:27–30).

1. In 734–732, Syria and Ephraim/Israel united against Assyria, but Assyria prevailed, and Israel was subjugated by the Assyrian king Tiglath-Pilesar III.
2. Hos. 12:12f. describes "Jacob" as "Fleeing to the land of Aram; there Israel did service for a wife, and for a wife he herded sheep." Jacob's desire is transformed into an unproductive Syrian alliance.

B. Hosea adapts traditions of Israel's past. Hos. 2:1ff. offers an allegory of Israel's covenantal history.

1. Reformation appears to be beyond both the ability and the will of priesthood, court, and people; only destruction will make renewal possible.
2. The allegory evokes the Baal cult: "In that day, says the Lord, you will call me 'my husband' and no longer will you call me 'my Baal'" (2:16–17).

VIII. The fall of the North.

A. Hos. 5:14 accurately observes, "I will carry off and none shall return." In 725–724, Israel violated its treaty with Assyria and turned to Egypt for protection. Sargon II of Assyria then began a siege that culminated in 722 when Samaria fell and Sargon deported about five percent of the population (see 2 Kings 17).

1. The Assyrian conquest is confirmed by external documentation.
2. An inscription from Sargon II concerning the conquering of Samaria includes the statement: "I led away as booty 27,290 inhabitants of it."
3. Sargon II's inscription goes on: "with the tribes of Tamud, Ibadidi, Marsimanu, and Halapa, the Arabs who live far away, in the desert… I deported their survivors and settled them in Samaria."

B. They "feared the Lord, but also served their own gods, after the manner of the nations from among whom they had been carried away… So they do to this day" (2 Kgs. 17:29–41).

Supplementary Reading:

Major commentaries in the series listed in the bibliography.

Questions to Consider:

1. Have either political or religious rhetoric changed much over the past two-and-a-half millennia?
2. What elements need to be in place for a culture to survive geographical displacement?
3. In the shared system of governance among kings, priests, and prophets, how is balance maintained?

Lecture Eighteen—Transcript
The Prophets and the Fall of the North
(1 Kings 16–2 Kings, Amos, Hosea)

In our discussion of the prophet Elijah and, indeed, of pre-classical prophets in general, we've noticed that often the Deuteronomic historian, the editor of First and Second Samuel and First and Second Kings, will sometimes use earlier materials such as the Moses tradition in order to develop models by which he can convey what these pre-classical prophets are doing. We've noticed that Elijah experiences a theophany on Mt. Horab much as Moses experiences a theophany on Mt. Sinai. But the theophanies themselves are different. Moses receives a law; Elijah, in fact, receives much of a prophetic commission. The theophany that Elijah experiences is, in fact, an anti-Baal polemic because Baal is a nature god manifested through rain, manifested through storms and in thunder.

On Mt. Horab, Elijah experiences an enormous storm, winds coming to rend the mountains and shatter the rocks before him, but then, we're told, "but the Lord was not in the wind." Then after the wind there is an earthquake, but the Lord is not in the earthquake, and after the earthquake there is a fire, but the Lord is not in the fire. The Lord is not in any of these manifestations associated with Baal. Following all these natural signs comes a stillness, such as you would find after a storm, and it's in that stillness that God speaks to Elijah. There is the difference between the God of Israel and Baal.

What does the God of Israel do? The God of Israel says to Elijah, "Hey, go back and preach my religion, my cult. Tell Ahab he's doing the wrong thing. Tell Jezebel she is engaging in apostasy. Let my people hear what they need to hear." So Elijah, commissioned in this anti-Baal theophany, goes back to engage in political concerns because those pre-classical prophets are heavily involved in what the government does. Following the theophany, Elijah actually does return, and what does he do? He is told by God,"Return on your way to the wilderness of Damascus, and when you arrive you shall anoint Hazael over Aram—Damascus, Syria—and you shall also anoint Jehu, son of Nimshi, over Israel [and that's in place of Ahab, who's now on the throne]."

So what God is suggesting is that Elijah produce a military coup. "You shall also," God tells Elijah, "anoint Elisha as a prophet in your place." How bloody does all this become? God continues, "Whoever escapes from the sword of Hazael, Jehu shall kill, and whoever escapes from the sword of Jehu, Elisha shall kill." So not only are pre-classical prophets engaged in giving political advice, they are themselves functionaries within creating the coup.

Elijah's successor, Elisha, actually does arrange this coup. Ahab is deposed. Jehu is placed on the throne. That's what pre-classical prophets do. Indeed, the division of Solomon's kingdom itself into Israel in the north and Judah in the south is arranged, if not facilitated, by a pre-classical prophet named Ahijah. Speaking for God, he announces that Solomon must be punished, as Ahijah puts it, in God's words, "because he has forsaken me and worshipped Ashtoreth, the goddess of the Sidonians and Chemosh, the god of Moab, and he has not walked in my ways doing what is right in my sight as his father, David, did." Ahijah actually sanctions this split by taking a new garment and ripping it into 12 pieces, symbolizing those 12 separate tribes prior to David's and then Solomon's unification of the kingdom. The country will be split apart.

The Deuteronomic historian confirms Ahijah's view by explaining to us that Solomon's heir, Rehoboam, is an unfit ruler. We've already seen that Solomon's kingdom is over-extended. The people are heavily taxed, and they want relief from those economic burdens that the throne is imposing upon them. So a group of envoys primarily from the north goes to Rehoboam, and they say, "We need some relief." Rehoboam has two groups of advisors: one group, an older group that served his father, the wise King Solomon, and a younger group, men with whom he was raised in the palace. We might think about the "J" source's description of those sons of God who abused their position. I think they might be referring to Rehoboam's advisors.

The older advisors say to Rehoboam, "Listen to the people, be nice to them, and they will love you." Rehoboam listens to his younger advisors, who actually tell him to tighten the ropes on them. Rehoboam listens to those younger men, and he says, "Well, my little finger is thicker than my father's loins. I'm more vigorous than he. I'm going to be stricter than he. I will put increasing burdens on you. Don't ask me for mercy. Don't ask me for favors. I am simply not going to give them." And the kingdom's split.

Indeed, Ahijah engages in aiding this split by facilitating the coup staged by Jereboam, and he's the one who will rule in the north. Jereboam is apparently one of the foremen on Solomon's building projects, so he's actually known in the capital, and he has some support from the Egyptian Pharaoh—his name is Shishak. The kingdom's split. Rehoboam, part of the Davidic line, stays in the south, ruling from Jerusalem. Jereboam takes the ten northern tribes with him and establishes his capital in the former Shechem, now called Samaria. What we will have throughout the rest of the Deuteronomic history, up to the end of Second Kings, is two parallel tracks of history: one from the southern kingdom, one from the northern kingdom. It's quite likely that the Deuteronomic historian is actually using court records to bolster his own particular take on what's happening with the government.

As the kingdom's split—and we have the northern kingdom not under Davidic rule but under kings who arise by coup and who are deposed by coup—we begin to find the origins of classical or writing prophecy. The earliest prophets we have include Amos and Hosea, and these are two prophets who prophesy up in the northern kingdom against the shrines in the north, places like Dan—you'll remember the shrine of Dan from the end of the Book of Judges, where Micah's Levite was dragged by the Danites up to that shrine at Dan—as well as places like Beth-El, and you will remember Beth-El from Jacob's dream of those ladders. Those shrines still continue, and that's where we locate Amos, our first classical prophet, and then Hosea.

In order to set the scene for Amos and Hosea, we'll begin with a brief—very brief—overview of the corpus called the "Minor Prophets." There were two groups of prophetic texts, one the major prophets—Isaiah, Jeremiah, and Ezekiel—and then the minor prophets, 12 of them. Why are they separated? It just depends upon the length of the scroll. Isaiah, Jeremiah, and Ezekiel are very, very long; they take up a scroll a piece. If you look at the 12 minor prophets, they will fit nicely onto one papyrus scroll. There are 12 of them. That's handy—it's easy to remember. There are 12 tribes. The Book of the Twelve will include Hosea, Joel, Amos, Obadiah, Jonah, Micah—You notice I have to check with my notes here because I can't remember them, either—Nahum, Habakkuk, Zephaniah, Haggai, Zechariah, and Malachi. Obviously we won't do them all; we'll hit the highlights.

I want to start with Amos and Hosea because their rhetoric is so exquisite—it's almost palpable; you can feel it—and because, when one looks at them in the context of their historical setting, one can see their involvement with the political climate internationally as well as the moral climate internally to the northern kingdom. Let's look, then, at their rhetorical strategies. Why do people actually bother to write down their materials in the first place? Which, if we think about it, is really quite extraordinary. The canonizers of this text wrote down the words of people criticizing the very establishment that the canonizers themselves represented. This is a covenant community that is very, very much interested in self-critique, and those words of the prophets will continue to echo through the generations. They are indeed still being read in churches and synagogues.

We'll begin with the prophet Amos, who opens with a series of pronouncements against outsiders. He says, "For three transgressions, O Edom, and for four, because you oppress the nations, I will not give you reprieve." "For three transgressions and for four, Moab"; "for three transgressions and for four, Syria." Now picture Amos doing this out loud. I suspect the people in the north would be with him all the way because he's complaining about the traditional enemies: Edom, Moab, Syria. The people are entirely with him. So it may well have come as a shock when Amos then explains to them, "Thus says the Lord, for three transgressions of Israel and for four, I will not give reprieve. I will not revoke punishment." Why? Because "they sell the righteous for silver. They sell the needy for a pair of sandals." It's that concrete imagery that will really grab. "They trample the heads of the poor into the dust of the earth, and they push the afflicted out of the way." That's the power of his rhetoric, and he's got you right there.

Amos does not use some of those key cultic terms we've seen before such as *berit* (covenant) or even *Torah*. Nevertheless, he does anchor his pronouncements in the covenant community's history. For example—this is Amos, Chapter 3, verse 1— "Hear this word that the Lord has spoken against you, O people of Israel, against the family which I brought out of Egypt." So just as we find in the law codes that Egyptian experience, freedom from slavery, becomes the model by which morality is ensured, it also becomes the paradigm, the template by which the prophets express their own concerns about the covenant community's responsibilities, although, as Amos points out, the community was rescued by God. The community doesn't heed that rescue and thereby, in effect, enslaves other people. They repeat history, but here they are in the role of Pharaoh rather than in the role of the oppressed.

How else does Amos get his views across? He actually uses a technique we know from divining, to go back to that earlier version of technical prophecy. Part of divining is to look out and see something and in that thing that you see get a message, as if today you would go outside and you would see a bird sitting where you had not seen a bird before and you take it as a positive omen—or a negative omen if it's on your windshield. Amos can do exactly the same thing.

Here is an example—and the reason this is so compelling is not only because he uses perfectly normal objects, but he enhances his view of something that's perfectly normal with puns. The problem here is we miss the puns in English translation: "Thus the Lord God showed me and behold a basket of summer fruit [something that anybody could find], and he said, 'Amos, what do you see?' and I said, 'I see a basket of summer fruit.'" The Hebrew for "summer fruit" is *kayitz*. And "the Lord said to me, the end [*kaytz*] shall come upon my people Israel." From *kayitz*, summer fruits, to *kaytz,* the people would have heard the harshness even of those expressions, those hard "K" sounds, and they would remember every time they picked up a basket of summer fruits.

Amos also plays upon the people's expectations only to reverse them. All cultures have rhetorical expectations. If somebody begins "The Star-Spangled Banner," we pretty much know how it's going to end, right? If somebody begins a cultic liturgy, a creed, for example, or a familiar prayer in church or synagogue, we know how it's going to end. The people in ancient Israel knew the same. For example, in cultic settings they would talk about the Day of the Lord, something to expect when God's righteousness would become fully manifest, and they would say, "The Day of the Lord, the Day of the Lord." Amos picks up on it, "The Day of the Lord, the Day of the Lord," but then he goes on to say, "It is darkness and not light," totally changing their expectations of what they might have expected.

He also invokes material that sounds very much like the curses we find at the end of Deuteronomy. We might think back here to those suzerainty-vassal treaties that end with a series of blessings if you do what the suzerain wants and end with a series of curses if you disobey the suzerain's commands. "I withheld the rain from you. I smite you with blight and mildew. I sent among you a pestilence after the manner of Egypt." It sounds like the end of Deuteronomy; it's actually Amos, Chapter 4. I think the people would have recognized this particular litany of curses as stemming directly from those suzerainty-vassal treaties. They would have recognized the covenant connections even in the words.

In addition to cultic language and treaty language, Amos also invokes rhetoric from schools of wisdom. We'll experience wisdom later. Well, we've already experienced wisdom, but we'll experience wisdom literature later when we get to books such as Proverbs and Job. The wisdom school itself had a particular form of rhetoric. They would, for example, ask rhetorical questions. For example, "Do two walk together unless they've got an appointment? Does a lion roar in the forest when he has no prey? Does a young lion cry out from its den if it has caught nothing?" My students frequently add, "If a tree falls in the forest and no one is there, can you hear the sound?" Amos does not say that.

But these rhetorical questions go on. "Is a trumpet blown in the city and the people are not afraid?" That's getting a little bit closer. "Does disaster befall a city unless the Lord has done it?" So we go from simple wisdom literature, conventional questions, to the idea of national disaster. Amos is able to take this wisdom literature and use it for his own use. Indeed, sometimes those rhetorical questions will actually be answered by the prophet. "Does a young lion cry out from its den unless it has a prey?" A few verses later Amos will give this incredibly striking image, "Thus says the Lord, as the shepherd rescues from the mouth of the lion two legs or the piece of an ear, so shall the people of Israel who dwell in Samaria [the northern capital] be rescued with a corner of a couch and part of a bed." This is so palpable you can envision it—you can even see it.

Wisdom literature will also develop, by stepping-stone construction, a pattern, one building upon the next building upon the next. Amos will do exactly the same thing. As he speaks of the Day of the Lord and explains, "It is darkness and not light," he goes on, "It is as if someone fled from a lion and was met by a bear"—you can't win in this type of wisdom literature—"or went into a house and rested his hand against the wall and was bit by a scorpion." For Israel's crimes it seems as if there is no redemption.

Enacting this particular metaphorical force, Amos will engage a rhetorical trope that we find with other prophets subsequently, categorizing the people of Israel—and for the southern prophets, the people of Judah—as unfaithful, adulterous wives, as women who are unconcerned with morality. In fact, many biblical scholars these days look at the prophets as engaging in misogynistic, anti-woman rhetoric, but this is, in fact, part of their culture; it's patriarchal culture.

This is Amos excoriating the upper class: "Hear this, you cows of Bashan, who oppress the poor, who crush the needy, who say to their husbands, 'Bring, that we may have a drink.'" "The time has surely come upon you," Amos says, "when they shall take you away with hooks, even the last of you with fishhooks." From ladies mincing as they go, saying, "Bring me a drink," to fishhooks stuck into flesh—this is why Amos's words still carry across the centuries.

Amos had a particular concern with reviving the cult. He was infuriated when members of the upper class would go to the cult and offer sacrifices at those shrines and then continue to oppress the poor. I think contemporary religious leaders and clergy have exactly the same problem. Folks who go to church on Sunday oppress the poor on Monday. Individuals who go to the synagogue on Shabbos on Saturday morning the next week engage in standard business practices. This is endemic to any sort of religion.

Amos brings this idea directly into the people. He says, speaking for God, "Come to Bethel and transgress. Bring your sacrifices every morning, your tithes every three days. For so you love to do, O people of Israel." You can hear the dripping sarcasm here. His most well-known oracles reinforce this point. Speaking for God, Amos says, "I hate, I despise your feasts. I take no delight in your solemn assemblies. Take away from me the noise of your songs. To the melody of your harps I will not listen." Then he goes on in a couplet that has been cited by liberation theologians and American politicians and civil rights workers: "Let justice roll down like waters and righteousness like an ever-flowing stream." That's what he wants.

The prophet Hosea will say the same thing in a much simpler way, "I desire mercy, not sacrifice." Now, when the prophets here complain against the cult, they are not actually saying, in fact, get rid of the cult. This type of hyperbole is a standard form of ancient rhetoric, both Near Eastern in general and Hebrew rhetoric in particular. What the prophets will do is say, "I want this instead of that," but what they are really doing is saying, "This is more important than that."

These diverse rhetorical techniques as well as their marvelously effective employment— and I hope you've been able to hear this—raise questions about Amos's own identity. I mean, who is this guy that he would have come up with such amazingly diverse and powerful sayings from the wisdom tradition, from the cult—"baskets of summer fruit"—that even a peasant could see? We know Amos is actually from Judah, the southern kingdom, and he goes up north to issue his oracles. This is as if somebody, say, from Dallas or Atlanta would go to Boston or Bangor to give particular views. It's amazing that people in the north would have even listened to him. His setting is during the reign of Jereboam II. You'll remember Jereboam I as the man who split away from Solomon's heir.

The time is 787 through 747. It's actually a time in the north of enormous economic prosperity. The north, or at least the upper class, is doing extremely well, but in a good many economies, when the elite is doing extremely well, they may be doing so because the poor are contributing everything. So what we've got is a substantially bifurcated economy. Typically, classical prophets tell us something about their background. Hosea gives us more details than, in fact, we may actually want about his marital life, his children. Amos actually tells us very little. Although it is conventional for prophets to identify themselves by means of their family background, to explain who their father is, no father is listed for Amos. That's actually a break in the convention, and it has caused people to wonder if Amos's father was so unimportant his name did not bear mentioning. Did he even know who his father was?

In a case like this we might pose that Amos is not from the upper classes but actually may be a peasant or from the shepherd group who recognizes injustice and somehow feels compelled to protest against it. Amos identifies himself right at the beginning of his book as "among the shepherds of Tekoa." The word he uses for shepherd, *noqed*, is not actually the standard word that we find for shepherds elsewhere, for example, "David is the good shepherd." A *noqed* is a shepherd who cares for temple flocks destined for sacrifice. Because of that, some scholars have suggested that Amos actually was involved with a cult, that he may have originally been a priest and then separated from it when he noticed those abuses. It's possible.

Others have suggested that Amos was part of a band of prophets, like those guilds we saw in discussion of the pre-classical prophets. Whether he was or he wasn't, he wants to make clear to people who listen to him that he is not associated with the priesthood now and he is not associated at all with prophets. This is what he says: "I am not a prophet nor one of the sons of the prophets. I am a herder and dresser of sycamore trees." Sycamore trees grow sycamore figs; they are the food of the poor people. In case you were wondering, to dress them actually means to puncture them, which is how they become fertile and how they grow.

Amos, in terms of his oracles, never explicitly states that the people will repent. It's not clear whether he expects them to or not. There is a happy ending in Amos, Chapter 9, verses 11-15, a promise that, "In that day I will raise up the booth of David that has fallen. I will restore the house of the fortunes of my people Israel. I will plant them upon their land, and they shall never again be plucked up." But many scholars think this is from a later hand. The prophecies of Amos and Hosea spoken in the north were eventually edited or readapted by scribes down in the south so that, when the northern kingdom fell to Assyria in 722, some of the refugees clearly brought with them the literary traditions of the north, the prophet Amos and the prophet Hosea. By the very reference here to the booth of David, that brings us back to that royal grant covenant with the south. This sounds very much like a southern editor rather than Amos himself.

The north is destroyed in 722. Amos's prophecies about the Day of the Lord being darkness and not light seem to have come true. This particular fall is actually witnessed by the prophet Hosea, whose initial activity coincides with the last years of the reign of Jereboam II, around 747 B.C.E., and, on the international horizon for Hosea, what is called the Syro-Ephraimite war. Amos knows about the empire of Assyria on the horizon, but for Amos the major problems are internal to the cult, to economic oppression internally.

Hosea becomes much more involved in external concerns, and here we find a classical prophet in the mold of those pre-classical prophets like Elijah and Elisha giving the king and the people advice about treaties, politics, and international alliances. For example, in 734–732 B.C.E., the kingdoms of Syria and Israel—Israel called here Ephraim, think about that Elohist (E) source— Syria and Ephraim unite against Assyria. So we have Assyria and Syria—please do not confuse them. Assyria is the major empire in the Middle East, and the Assyrian war machine is making its way, country through country, town through town, attacking and bringing additional peoples into its empire. Syria and Israel are afraid that they are going to be next, and they are right.

It turns out that Assyria was able to prevail against those combined forces, and under the leadership of the Assyrian emperor, Tiglath-Pilesar III—we just don't have names like that these days— Tiglath-Pilesar III subjugates the northern kingdom so that the kingdom of Israel becomes an Assyrian vassal. Hosea actually describes this in Chapter 12, describing Jacob as fleeing to the land of Aram—that's Syria. "There Israel did service for a wife, and for a wife he herded sheep." This is Hosea's complaint against the alliance between Israel and Syria, here using the ancient traditions of Jacob going to Laban to find a wife, Rachel and Leah.

But here this is not a good sign; the ancient tradition becomes a negative example. Hosea says, "Look, your ancestor Jacob went into service and you've done exactly the same thing. Jacob should never have worked for Laban. He was tricked, and you've been tricked, too." Hosea's concerns are archly political. He advises that Jereboam II stay out of that alliance with Syria because, in his view, God will provide everything that's needed. Here again you can find that suzerainty-vassal model, which says, "God alone should be your ruler. Don't have any other alliances with any other nations." We can even hear here that anti-monarchical source in First Samuel, "Don't be like the other nations," because it means treaties and bringing foreign gods into your temple and your shrines.

Hosea is counseling isolationism. But that's not what he got. It may actually have been the case that Hosea's counsel would not have worked. Assyria, given its strength—and we know about Assyrian strength from numerous extracanonical materials; the Assyrians kept great records, and we have parts of their archives as well as *stelae*, inscriptions on stone pillars explaining how they conquered various places, including the north of Israel—Assyria would have conquered

Israel anyway. It simply came a little bit sooner, probably because of that Syro-Ephraimite alliance.

In 725 and 724, the Assyrian emperor, Shalmaneser V, sent members of Israel's upper class into exile. In the ancient world, conquering empires would take the elite of a community, the elite of a kingdom—the king, the royal court, the priests, and often the artisans—and ship them somewhere else. They are in the business of population movement. Then they would ship other people in. The idea was here that, if you removed the leaders from your land and stuck them somewhere else, they would not be able sufficiently to regroup and get back home. Even if they did get back home, other people would be there. It's an absolutely brilliant strategy. If your empire lasts long enough and that first generation of exiles dies out, your empire will probably remain. Hosea, Chapter 5, verse 14, notices this initial exile. "I, even I, will rend and go astray. I will carry off and none shall return." Hosea apparently continued to prophesy until the actual fall of the northern kingdom, the conquering of the capital, Samaria, in 722.

At the time that Israel is captured there is no hope. Hosea gives us a sense that perhaps there might be. He describes his initial relationship with his wife as commanded by God, God telling him, "Hosea, go take a wife of harlotry"—He does. He marries a woman named Gomer—"and have children in harlotry." That's his view of Israel making foreign alliances. But ultimately God says, "My relationship with Israel, now committing adultery with these foreign nations, will eventually be reconciled." Hosea puts it this way, "I will allure her and bring her into the wilderness again and speak tenderly to her, and there she shall answer as in the days of her youth, as in the time when she came out of Egypt." He goes on, evoking images from the Baal cult, "In that day, says the Lord, you will call me 'my husband,' [*adoni*] and no longer will you call me 'my Baal, my Lord.'"

But that's not what happens. In 722 the kingdom is destroyed. The 10 tribes of the north are exiled. The remaining literature and some refugees from the north flee to the south and create new legends and give the south additional material by which it will establish its own identity. And that's what we'll see in the next lecture.

Lecture Nineteen

The Southern Kingdom (Isaiah, Deuteronomy, 2 Kings 18–23)

Scope:

The Northern Kingdom fell, but both its memory and its reconfiguration continued to affect the identity of Judah. This lecture picks up with the foundation of the new northern Kingdom. It then turns to the Southern Kingdom's response to Sennacherib's threat. This establishes the context in which Isaiah issued his oracles and Hezekiah, prompted by those oracles, promoted religious reform. We then turn to the second southern reform, sponsored by King Josiah and promoted by the implementation of the Book of Deuteronomy.

Outline

I. The resettled peoples in the North intermarried with remaining Israelites.

- **A.** They came to be called "Samaritans" from Israel's capital, Samaria, and they will become the enemies of the people in the South. The "ten tribes" are lost to history but preserved in legends.
- **B.** The people of the South yearn for the reconstitution of all the tribes, and from this, certain legends develop.
  1. They are the Native Americans.
  2. They are the British (from *Berit* [covenant] and *ish* [man]—a false etymology).
  3. They were relocated to China, India, or Afghanistan.
  4. They will be reintegrated into the covenant community in the Messianic age.

II. The loss of the North after 722; preservation in the South after 587.

- **A.** Israel, compared to Judah, has a less visible theological system.
  1. With the emphasis on only the Mosaic covenant, Israel perhaps believed that with expulsion, the suzerain was no longer protecting the vassal.
  2. The people may have lacked a strong clergy.
  3. They lacked a viable "canon."

B. Distinctions between the exile of the Israelites and the exile of the Judeans by Nebuchadnezzar.

1. Assyria fractured ethnic groups in exile; the Babylonians established exiled groups in self-governing neighborhoods.
2. Assyria was not conquered until the Babylonian campaigns of 612, over a century after Samaria fell; Babylonian captivity lasted forty-eight years.

III. The school of Isaiah.

A. Scholars argue that the biblical book entitled "Isaiah" is a composite representing at least three prophetic voices addressing different historical settings.

B. First Isaiah, chapters 1–24, 28–39.

1. The "first Isaiah" flourished during the second half of the eighth century.
2. The first Isaiah had at least two children, each with a symbolic name (cf. Hosea's children): She'ar-Jashub (7:3), "a remnant will return," and Maher-Shalal-Hash-Baz (8:1–4), "The Spoil speeds, the prey hastens."
3. His "call" (Isa. 6) occurs "in the year King Uzziah died" (742), after a reign of forty years.
4. His prophetic "school" (cf. 8:16–17) continued into the post-exilic period.

IV. First Isaiah's oracles.

A. Along with the various rhetorical forms and images associated with Amos and Hosea (woe oracles, the adulterous wife, personification of the rich as indolent women), Isaiah develops the parable (cf. 2 Sam. 12:1–12).

B. Most famous of these is the "parable of the vineyard" (5:1–7), in which God is the planter and Judah the vineyard that fails.

C. For Isaiah, the golden age is not the wilderness period (as it was for Hosea), but Davidic Jerusalem, and it is Jerusalem he seeks to save.

1. Isaiah, seeking Judean political neutrality, counsels against involvement in the Syro-Ephraimite War (7:1–16; see 2 Kings 20) through the oracle of Immanuel:
   a. "Behold a young woman has conceived and shall bear a son, and shall call his name Immanuel. This

child shall eat curds and honey when he knows how to refuse the evil and choose the good."

b. References to a "virgin" birth derive from the Septuagint, which renders the Hebrew "young woman" as *parthenos*.

2. Isaiah 9 and 11 describe an ideal king; the imagery develops into messianic desiderata.
3. Judean royal theology also contributes to messianic speculation.

D. Like Amos and, especially, Hosea, it is not clear whether Isaiah expects the people to repent.

1. "Go and say to this people: 'Hear and hear, but do not understand; see and see, but do not perceive…' until the cities lie waste, without inhabitants" (6:9–13).
2. Rather than prophesying total destruction, Isaiah promulgates a "remnant theology," as his son's name, She'ar-Jashub (and see 10:20–23), suggests.

V. King Hezekiah (ca. 704), likely prompted by Isaiah, instituted a series of religious and political reforms (2 Kings 18).

A. Among these reforms was the symbolic end to vassalage by stopping sacrifices to the Assyrian emperor.

B. Domestically, cultic reforms included the razing of "high places" and "sacred poles" and the removal from the Temple of Nehushtan the bronze serpent that Moses had made for apotropaic cures (18:4).

C. Public policy reforms included the Jerusalem water conduit (Hezekiah's tunnel, the Siloam tunnel, a 1,700-foot excavation through solid rock).

VI. The reforms ended with King Hezekiah's death.

A. His successor, Manasseh, returned Judah to vassal status (2 Kings 21).

B. Manasseh also reintroduced apostasy: rebuilding the high places and erecting sacred poles, constructing altars to Baal, and so on.

VII. Josiah, Manasseh's grandson, attempted a second reform based on the laws of Deuteronomy (2 Kings 22–23).

A. Deuteronomy is ostensibly Moses's last will and testament, only discovered during Josiah's Temple renovations (22:8–10).

1. The prophetess Huldah, when visited by a consortium of priests, (indirectly) proclaims the book to be authentic (22:14–20).

2. Deuteronomy abolishes previously legitimate altars (Deut. 12:1–31; 12:5–6).

3. It disenfranchises the Levites, who had presided over the local shrines.

4. It centralizes the cult in Jerusalem (the Samaritan Pentateuch locates the centralization in Samaria, on Mt. Gerizim).

B. Of particular concern are monarchical interests: the divine legitimation of the king. He is exhorted (17:18) to "write for himself in a book a copy of this law." The LXX translates "copy" as *Deuteronomion*, "Second law."

C. Deuteronomy's notable contributions to biblical law include:

1. Promoting the education of children by inculcation, cf. 6:7: "You shall teach them [the Laws] diligently to your children, and you shall talk of them when you sit in your house, and when you walk by the way, and when you lie down, and when you rise up. And you shall bind them for a sign upon your hand, and they shall be for frontlets between your eyes; and you shall write them upon the doorposts of your house, and upon your gates."

2. The sign and frontlets are *Tefillin* or phylacteries, two small square leather boxes containing scriptural passages worn on the forehead and left arm.

3. The doorpost/gate reference is to the *Mezuzah* (Hebrew for "doorpost"), a case containing Deut. 6:4–9 (the "Shema"); 11:13–21, and El Shaddai.

VIII. The hopes created by the Deuteronomic reform were dashed when Josiah, having reneged on his participation in the Syrian-Egyptian alliance, is then killed by Pharaoh Neco at Megiddo. The failure of the reform and the rise of Babylon set the stage for the prophecies of Jeremiah and for the Babylonian exile, the topics of the next lecture.

Supplementary Reading:

Commentaries in series listed in the bibliography.

Michael D. Coogan, (ed.), *The Oxford History of the Biblical World* (New York: Oxford University Press, 1998).

Questions to Consider:

1. What are the benefits, and the dangers, of interpreting prophetic oracles outside their original historical situations?
2. How does the international scene affect Judean policies, both political and religious?
3. How and to what extent does Deuteronomy respond to the prophetic calls for social justice?

Lecture Nineteen—Transcript
The Southern Kingdom
(Isaiah, Deuteronomy, 2 Kings 18-23)

When the northern kingdom falls to Assyria in 722, all that remains of the covenant community is the southern kingdom. There is still a Davidic king on the throne in Jerusalem, there is still a sense of this eternal covenant, and, although the northern kingdom is gone, its influences remain on the south, indeed, on biblical literature and even on contemporary legendary development.

In terms of history, the combination of the people moved in by the Assyrians and the indigenous population remaining in the land comprise a new group of people who become known as Samaritans. The irony is, as history goes on, the Samaritans in the north become the enemies of the people in the south. Even when you get up into New Testament times, you will find materials such as the parable of the Good Samaritan, and that itself suggests the ongoing enmity between these two population groups.

In terms of legendary development, people in the south continued to yearn for the reconstitution of those 12 tribes, and eventually past the biblical period we have developing legends both of the ingathering of the exiles and the messianic age and also these stories of 10 lost tribes who today frequently show up in pages of things like *The National Enquirer*. There are, in fact, legends of the 10 lost tribes. Some of them are quite early, some of them more recent. My favorite happens to be that the 10 lost tribes somehow found their way to the Western Hemisphere and are now Native Americans. That model actually comes about from some Cherokee inscriptions found in Tennessee, my home, which, if read backwards, look sort of like Paleo-Hebrew. I don't think that's actually the case. Others have suggested that the Israelites exiled by Assyria moved to Afghanistan. That's actually possible because Assyria did have territorial holdings in that area. Others have suggested northern India, China, and there is one Jewish legend that suggests that God moved them to some mystical place beyond some mystical river waiting for the Messiah to come and at that point reconstitute the tribes.

Although the northern tribes are lost to history, indeed, their very existence and the literature that they produced had ongoing value for people in the south. Refugees from the north would bring their material down, and the northern literature, their history, and their etiology wound up bolstering the self-identity of the southern kingdom. This becomes extremely important when the south itself faces Assyrian onslaught, and finally in the sixth century when the south is facing the new empire on the block, the Babylonians.

If we look at reasons why the north fell, and I think the south itself would have considered that, we might be able to get some sense on why the south was able to preserve its ethnic identity when it, too, was taken into exile. For example, the south had the strong concern for the royal grant, the Davidic covenant. In the south the Davidic king is taken into exile, but when Babylonian exile ends, a Davidic king is still present. It helps to have a particular figurehead or politician around whom the community can rally. Because the northern government was based on a series of military coups, there was no national leader and no natural leader, indeed, for the people in the north in exile to follow.

The people in the north may have lacked a strong clergy. The people in the south, particularly when they went into Babylonian exile, not only were able to bring temple functionaries, but they were able to gather clerical support in exile. This is the beginning of the "P" code, which we've already seen in our discussion of source criticism in the documentary hypothesis. It may also have been that the people in the north lacked a canon, a literature that could bind people like the American Constitution or the Declaration of Independence binds us today. People in the south decided it was imperative that they compile their history. The Deuteronomic historian is beginning. The priestly writers are beginning. The "J" material, even the "E" material brought down from the north, provide a repository for the exiles from the southern kingdom, the exilic community in Babylon, to establish their self-identity.

Indeed, the conditions of the exile itself differed. The Assyrians split up communities, but the Babylonians, when they put a community in exile, allowed that community to remain together, as if it were in some sort of golden ghetto. With communities remaining together, they can retain their identity much easier. Moreover, the Assyrian exile lasted much longer than the Babylonian exile. Assyrian exile lasted well over 100 years. There was nobody left from that initial generation to go home and rebuild. The Babylonian exile lasted under 50 years so that, indeed, there were people in Babylon who may well have retained vague memories of living in Jerusalem and at least passed on those memories to their children. The time is close enough to keep that hope of return alive.

The southern kingdom also knew what it was like to face threat. Thus we come to how people in the south with prophets like Isaiah and, as we'll see later, Jeremiah, and with law codes like the Book of Deuteronomy, were able to preserve their identity—religious, political, ethnic—despite incursions first by Assyria, indeed, sieges by Assyria, and later, when the Assyrian empire is conquered by Babylon, still retain their ethos, their self-identity, who they are as a covenant community.

So let's begin now by looking at exactly what the southern kingdom did, because they, too, knew about Assyria. They knew about the fall of the north, and Sennacherib, the Assyrian emperor, also had his sights on the southern kingdom. Things were not easy for them back then. We'll begin with the first prophet, the first major prophet from the southern kingdom. This is the prophet Isaiah, the first of the major prophets as opposed to the minor prophets we discussed in the last lecture. The prophet Isaiah has a corpus in the canon that goes for 66 chapters. It's enormous. Biblical scholars, as is their wont, came to the conclusion that Isaiah did not write all of this material. In the same way that biblical scholars questioned whether Moses wrote the Pentateuch and came to the conclusion that the Pentateuch is actually comprised of a series of different sources ultimately compiled by a single editor, so, too, with the prophet Isaiah.

Today biblical scholars are wont to divide up Isaiah's prophecy into at least three different time periods with three different styles of writing and three different authors. The first Isaiah, who is my major concern in discussing the early southern kingdom, is represented primarily by Chapters 1 through 24. Then we skip a couple of chapters, and then 28 through 39. This prophet flourished during the second half of the eighth century, in other words, the 700s. This particular prophet had at least two children, both with symbolic names, and we've already seen the function of names. One was named She'ar-Jashub, "a remnant will return." That already gives us a sense on Isaiah's view of what will happen. Yes, part of the south will, in fact, fall; the Davidic royal grant will not fully hold. But God's promises cannot simply be revoked *in toto*. Part of the kingdom, a remnant, will return. Isaiah knew that.

Isaiah also had another child whose name in Hebrew was the somewhat awkward, Maher-Shalal-Hash-Baz, similarly awkward in English: "the spoil speeds, the prey hastens," or, as the new English Bible reads, "speedy, spoiling, prompt, plundering." This is a difficult name to give to a child, but it also suggests what Isaiah saw upon the horizon. The Assyrian empire would come; there would be some collapse of the southern kingdom. By having children with these two names, Isaiah was able to demonstrate, whenever these children showed up in public, yes, capture would occur. Yes, disaster will strike part of the kingdom, but, nevertheless, "a remnant will return."

We get a sense of Isaiah from his call-narrative, that generic conventional form that explains how God calls upon, commissions, a particular prophet. Isaiah's is a magnificent view of the heavenly throne, and, indeed, from Isaiah 6, that call-narrative, other prophets will build. Ezekiel has a similar call-narrative, and we'll see this throne vision again when we get to the prophet Daniel. Here is how it starts. Isaiah tells us that he receives his call in the year that King Uzziah died. This is actually 743 B.C.E., and it is an important time because Uzziah had been on the throne for about 40 years. So here we have a major time of transition. What now will happen to the political situation? We also know that Assyria is on the horizon. They are already at the borders of the north, and they are moving inexorably toward Israel and then Judah.

What else does Isaiah tell us? He tells us in his throne vision that God is looking for somebody to help. God is sitting on a throne, a magnificent throne, his train trailing in the temple. That is still his house. Jerusalem needs to be preserved. He says, "Who will help?" and Isaiah says, in effect, "Not me," because, as is typical, prophets do not want their commission. It's a dangerous job. Isaiah says, "I am not worthy. I have sinful lips," but God arranges for a seraph, one of the seraphim—these heavenly beings—to touch his lips with a coal from the altar (that's from that temple altar where the sacrifice is offered), and Isaiah's lips are thereby purified. God can then say, "Who will go?" and Isaiah says, "*Hineni*, here I am. Send me." That's Isaiah's commission.

And what does he tell us? He tells us that the people, in fact, need to repent—standard prophetic rhetoric—but the way he conveys it is to manipulate those prophetic forms in a new and arresting way by pulling on the earlier tradition and developing it. For example, we already have the formulation of the parable, the short story which is meant to convey a particular meaning. We've had one example of this in the Book of Judges where Abimelech, the false judge's brother, Jotham, tells a parable to the people of Israel explaining how all the trees looked for a leader and eventually they settled on the bramble bush—the false judge.

We've also had a parable told to King David by the prophet Nathan, the parable of the ewe lamb, which explains how a very rich man, when a traveler came to visit him, instead of taking a lamb from his own flock, went to a poor man who had only one little ewe lamb whom he fed by hand, whom he took at his table and fed and treated even like a daughter. The rich man slaughtered the poor man's ewe lamb, and Nathan says to David, "And what should be done with such a terrible thing?" David says, "Well, obviously the rich man should be killed," and Nathan looks at him and says, "You are that man because you took Bathsheba and slaughtered Uriah."

So the parable form is already well-known. Isaiah gives us a magnificent example, which becomes a standard trope: Israel as the vineyard. One of the reasons this parable works is because Isaiah forces the covenant community in the south to provide its own response to the parable, just as Nathan forces David's hand.

God plants a vineyard, takes care of it, puts up a watchtower, and makes sure everything is perfect, but the vineyard does not yield for God. It produces wild things, weeds. What now is the vineyard owner God to do? Isaiah ends this parable by saying, "And now, inhabitants of Jerusalem, people of Judah, judge between me and my vineyard. What more was there for me to do for my vineyard?" God through Isaiah gives his own answer, "I will remove its hedge, and it shall be devoured. I will break down its walls, and it shall be trampled upon." Through the parable, Isaiah is able to predict what will happen to the covenant community. Indeed, it's immediately after this parable that Isaiah gives us his call, telling us that Isaiah will be the voice of God to explain the covenant community's fate. It's a staggering and fantastic sense of organization.

Isaiah, like most prophets, is involved not only with morality and repentance, Isaiah is also heavily, heavily invested in political concerns. Like Hosea, he advises political neutrality, and he counsels King Ahaz, from whom, by the way, we actually have archaeological seals remaining—it's attestation of this king—not to get involved in the Syro-Ephraimite alliance. When the kings of Israel and Syria noticed that the Assyrian empire was on the horizon, they formed an alliance. We saw this with Hosea. Isaiah says, "Don't get involved. It will not help." He also tells Ahaz, "Don't get involved with Assyria, either," because Ahaz is very worried. If he doesn't sign on to the Israelite alliance, they might attack him (and, indeed, they did). Should he go to Assyria for protection? Should he engage in that alliance? What should he do?

He eventually goes to Assyria against Isaiah's wishes and makes an alliance, at which point Israel under Ahaz becomes a vassal state. In order to explain why this is not a good thing, why Ahaz should never have even considered Assyrian connections, let alone connections with Israel and Syria, Isaiah tells an oracle set in the king's throne room. This is Chapter 7, right after that call. This oracle remains, surprisingly enough, one of the foundation statements of early Christianity and contemporary Christianity. This is Isaiah talking to Ahaz. He said, "Look, the Lord himself will give you a sign regarding these various alliances. Behold, this young woman has conceived and she'll bear a son, and she'll call his name Immanuel [which means "God with us"], and this child shall eat curds and honey. And when he knows how to refuse the evil and choose the good, the land before whose kings you are in dread will fall. There is no reason therefore for you to engage in political alliance." This child is likely the future king Hezekiah who takes the throne in 715.

What happens here is that, when the Hebrew of Isaiah is translated into Greek, "that young woman," the Hebrew *alma,* is translated as *parthenos*, which means "virgin," and this then becomes, for the evangelist Matthew in the New Testament, a sign of the birth of the Messiah. Matthew actually quotes the Greek version of Isaiah, Chapter 7, verse 14: "Behold, a virgin will conceive and bear a son, and you will call his name Immanuel." But Isaiah writing in the 700s is not going to predict something that's going to happen 700 years later. He's giving a very specific oracle to a king at a very, very specific time.

Isaiah's predictions about an ideal government—and he had great hopes for Hezekiah—will ultimately find their way into messianic predictions. But that's not actually what happened to the kingdom of Israel. Isaiah, I think, did not expect Judah to survive even though

Judah had that royal grant, because after he is commissioned he tells us that God told him to prophesy but with the result being that the people would not hear and the people would not understand: "Go and say to this people, hear and hear but do not understand, see and see but do not perceive until the cities lie waste without inhabitants." So the call convention is inverted. Most prophets are called to bring the people to repentance; Isaiah is called here to seal their doom. Rather than prophesying total destruction, Isaiah, as you know, has this view of remnant theology: "a remnant shall return." He speaks of a shoot from the stump of Jessie—that's David's father—returning. The royal grant is there but in a transformed way.

Isaiah becomes very influential during the reign of King Hezekiah and, indeed, prompts Hezekiah to engage in a series of reforms both international and internal. Since there was a transition in the Assyrian government at the time, it makes good sense for Hezekiah to do that. Internationally, he attempts to throw off Assyrian vassalage. Of course Assyria doesn't like this and begins a siege of the kingdom of Judah. Internally, he begins a reform of the temple. We can see this in Second Kings, Chapter 18. He goes into the temple and removes, for example, a bronze serpent that tradition says dates all the way back to the time of Moses but had become an idol for the people.

Regarding public policy, he constructs a water conduit. We actually have archaeological remains of this water conduit, including the inscription. It's a six-line inscription written at the time when the two teams of diggers actually met. One thinks of the transcontinental railroad. This became exceptionally important during the Assyrian siege of Jerusalem because it allowed Jerusalem to have free-flowing water inside. He razes some of the high places, those external shrines, pulls down sacred poles, and tries to wipe out Baalism, which is still strong in the area. Unfortunately what happened is that his successor, King Manasseh, returned the kingdom of Judah to vassal status. He had little choice in the matter. But he also returned the kingdom of Judah to various forms of pagan encroachment. He rebuilt the high places. He erected those special poles. He also apparently sacrificed one of his children. That old view of human sacrifice, that Canaanite view, comes back around. Isaiah offers oracles of hope, oracles of renewal, but ultimately the southern kingdom would fall.

Before it fell, however, there was yet one more reform, and that's a reform that occurs under King Josiah. Now, whether you think Josiah was prompted by simply a coincidental political happenstance or whether Josiah is an exceptionally manipulative, politically astute king, I leave up to you. Here is the story. King Josiah, needing to reform the country once again, engages in renovations of the temple building, and in the process he happens to discover a scroll. The scroll winds up being, in fact, the Book of Deuteronomy. Those scholars who think this is actually a true account suggest that the Book of Deuteronomy had been composed in the north, brought down by refugees to the south, and at that time secreted in the temple, ultimately to be found 100 years later or so by Josiah.

What does Josiah do? He implements the concerns of Deuteronomy. He first makes sure that the text is legitimate. He consults a local prophetess—her name is Huldah—and then he decides, "Yes, I will put this new law into place." What does Deuteronomy allow him to do? It allows him to centralize the government. For example, he pulls down, destroys, all of those external shrines. We might think of shrines like the one at Shiloh where Samuel and Eli were functionaries, or, in the northern kingdom, Dan and Bethel.

What this does is it disenfranchises the Levites who were out serving at all those shrines, but, for Josiah's benefit, it centralizes the cult in Jerusalem. This is extremely helpful if you happen to be the leader in Jerusalem because now the temple becomes the only place where you can offer sacrifices, and that means increasing monies coming in as well as the need for pilgrimage to Jerusalem, and thereby Josiah will have a much more economic base.

The text itself regarding the centralization of the cult is actually quite vague. The Samaritans, those people up in the north, have their own version of the Book of Deuteronomy. Whereas Deuteronomy suggests to the people in the south the cult should be centralized in Jerusalem, the Samaritan Pentateuch suggests that that cult should be centralized in Samaria on Mt. Gerizim. One has to be a little careful about what this original text says.

It also asserts that kingship is okay—here against some of that anti-monarchical material we had in First Samuel—but what the king is exhorted to do is avoid all those sins that Solomon had committed. The king is not to multiply wives. The king is not to overextend the economy. The king is not to engage in excessive trade in horses, which is, in fact, what Solomon did, and we have the legend of Solomon's stables. And the king is exhorted, in Deuteronomy, Chapter 17, "to write for himself in a book a copy of this law." The Septuagint translates "copy"—more colloquially, "repetition"—as *Deuteronomion*, a "second law," but it really means "a copy." That's where the name "Deuteronomy" comes from. The king, so says this book, "shall keep this law with him, and he shall read in it all the days of his life, that he may learn to fear the Lord his God by keeping all the words of this law and these statutes and doing them."

Deuteronomy, as we've seen, has some very notable materials in terms of how to deal with the poor and the oppressed, how to celebrate Sabbath, and why to celebrate Sabbath. A good much of Deuteronomy also finds its way into both Christian and Jewish liturgical formulation. Deuteronomy, for example, is exceptionally interested in inculcating knowledge to children. This is, as we'll see later, a connection with wisdom literature. This is Deuteronomy 6:7: "You shall teach them [meaning the laws] diligently to your children, and you shall talk of them when you sit in your house and when you walk by the way and when you lie down and when you rise up." Deuteronomy goes on to say, "You shall bind them for a sign upon your hand and they shall be for frontlets between your eyes." In contemporary—indeed, in ancient—Jewish practice, we have examples of *tefillin*, phylacteries from the Dead Sea areas, ancient, before-Jesus materials. Phylacteries are straps with little boxes connected to them that religious Jews today still put on their head for frontlets between their eyes and wrap seven times around their arm and over their hand for the sign upon their arm. These are, in effect, praying tools.

The text goes on, "You shall bind them for a sign upon your hand, and you shall write them upon the doorposts of your house and upon your gates." Well, the word for "doorpost" or "gate" is *mezuzah*, and this explains why Jewish families even today have little scrolls and little holders attached to the doors of their house. It's simply commanded in Deuteronomy, and it is followed up today.

Deuteronomy also has that very famous line, "Hear, O Israel, the Lord is our God, the Lord is one," or "the Lord alone." Deuteronomy, therefore, provides us an example of how an ancient text winds up providing the means for the covenant community to identify itself even in Babylon—can you picture?—with these signs, these praying tools, these positioning of laws on your gates and on your houses. You become self-identified. It is an example as well of how the covenant community can prevail across the centuries.

The hopes created by Isaiah with his view of the remnant returning, and, indeed, created by the Deuteronomic reform, are dashed. Political circumstances become increasingly difficult. Assyria is on the rise. Josiah the king decides that he will make an alliance with Egypt for protection but then ultimately pulls out of the alliance. Egypt then takes reins against Josiah. The pharaoh whose name is Pharaoh Neco—finally we have a pharaoh with a name—goes to battle against King Josiah. They meet at the Megiddo Pass, which is, by the way, in Greek, "Harmageddo"—Armageddon. It's a place where disasters happen. They meet at the Megiddo Pass; King Josiah is killed. The reform is dashed. Josiah's heir brings back the community into apostasy.

That leads us to the time of Jeremiah, and what will Jeremiah build on? Jeremiah, to a great extent, will build on the prophet Isaiah, and what we will wind up seeing is a sense of a remnant perhaps returning but also a continuing hopelessness. Where are we then with the literature of the southern kingdom? We have all of that material from the north brought down south. We have the "E" writer telling us patriarchal stories. We have the prophecies of Amos and Hosea edited by people in the south. We have the prophecies of that first Isaiah, the remnant returning. The second Isaiah, by the way, prophesies during the time of the Babylonian exile. There is yet a third Isaiah, the last 10 chapters of the book, the prophecies from the time of the return from exile. They are all simply put together in one particular school.

We have other people who are prophesying at this time, such as Habakkuk and Micah. I think the best way of summing up what's happening in the south is to give you a statement from Second Kings regarding the abuses of King Manasseh, because this is where the Deuteronomic history will end and how the Deuteronomic historian explains why the southern kingdom fell. Here is how it goes: "Judah had done abominable things." So this is the word of the Lord, the God of Israel: "I am bringing such evil upon Jerusalem and Judah, I shall wipe out Jerusalem as one would wipe a dish, wiping it and turning it upside down. They shall become a spoil and a prey." You can hear Isaiah's child in the background, "the spoil speeds, the prey hastens." "They shall become a spoil and a prey to their enemies." But, as Isaiah would put it, "a remnant will return."

Lecture Twenty

Babylonian Exile
(2 Kings 24–25, Jeremiah, Isaiah 40–55, Ezekiel)

Scope:

The royal court and upper classes of Judea, taken into exile in Babylon, preserved and enhanced their identity as a people—through prophetic support, the development of a theology of catastrophe, and the consolidation of their historical and legal traditions. This lecture begins on the eve of the exile, with the collapse of King Josiah's reforms and the prophetic warnings of Jeremiah. It then introduces the prophecies, narratives, and laws by which the Judean exiles promoted and maintained communal identity: the Second (or Deutero-) Isaiah (Isa. 40–55), and Ezekiel.

Outline

I. The siege of Judah.

- **A.** "In the 14th year of King Hezekiah, Sennacherib King of Assyria came up against the fortified cities of Judah and took them" (2 Kings 18:13).
  1. Recognizing the disaster of the Kingdom of Israel, the South had to respond.
  2. To prevent catastrophe, King Hezekiah pays enormous tribute, including stripping the gold from the Temple, but the siege prevails.
- **B.** The end of the siege.
  1. Herodotus (*Hist*. II.131) attests that the Assyrians suffered a defeat on the borders of Egypt because their equipment was ruined by some ravenous field mice, a notice some scholars connect with the Judean situation.
  2. Sennacherib's own version implies that after a successful attack on Jerusalem, Hezekiah agreed to increased tribute, which he would send directly to Nineveh.
  3. The Deuteronomic historian attributes the lifting of the siege to divine intervention: "And that night the angel of the Lord went forth and slew 185,000 men in the camp of the Assyrians" (2 Kings 19:34; cf. Isa. 36–39).

4. Judean theologians concluded that the royal grant protected Jerusalem (Isa. 10:24ff.).

II. The failure of the Josianic reform and the end of national self-determination.

A. Babylon defeats the Egyptian-Assyrian coalition at the Battle of Carchemish in 605 (see Jer. 46:2; 2 Kings 24).

1. Judah is now under Babylonian control.
2. Jehoiakim, King of Judah, rebels after a three-year submission but dies (in 598) before Babylon retaliates.
3. Jehoiakim's son, Jehoiachin (Jeconiah), surrenders to Nebuchadnezzar (Nebuchadrezzar) in 597 (see Jer. 21:2; 2 Kings 24; this surrender is attested in Babylonian records).
4. Probably between 3,000 and 10,000 people are then deported.

B. End of the Judean monarchy.

1. Mattaniah (probably another son of Josiah) is made king and renamed Zedekiah to symbolize his vassal status (1 Chr. 3).
2. Zedekiah seeks an alliance with Egypt (Jer. 17; 1 Kings 25; Ezek. 17).
3. In retaliation, Nebuchadnezzar destroys Jerusalem, forces a second deportation, takes the Temple valuables to Babylon, and executes Zedekiah.
4. Gedaliah, a friend to Jeremiah (Jer. 39–40), is appointed governor but assassinated by a member of the royal family.

III. Jeremiah.

A. Given this dismal situation, Jeremiah reflects an intense spiritual struggle.

B. His oracles are juxtaposed with events in his life such that his personal tragedies mirror the nation's doom.

1. His "temple sermon" provokes a judicial hearing.
2. His prophesying put his life in danger: Manasseh probably executed prophets (2 Kgs. 21:1b), and King Jehoiakim certainly did (2 Kgs. 26:20–33; Jer. 2:20).

C. His solution to Judah's failings is a "new covenant" (31:31ff.), in which YHWH "Will put my law within them, and I will write it upon their hearts…"

IV. After Gedaliah's murder, Jeremiah and his scribe, Baruch, are taken by Judean refugees to Egypt.

A. The Book of Lamentations, although traditionally attributed to him, manifests his sorrow but not his themes or style.

B. From Jeremiah's exile develops the legend that the ark, last seen when Solomon placed it in the Holy of Holies (1 Kings 8), was brought to Egypt.

C. Second Maccabees 2:4ff. suggests that Jeremiah hid the ark on Mt. Nebo and proclaimed, "The place shall be unknown until God gathers his people together again and shows his mercy."

V. Ezekiel proclaimed both invective and hope to the Babylonian exiles ca. 593–563.

A. Probably part of the first deportation of 597, Ezekiel found an exilic community confident that rescue was imminent and the Temple, inviolable.

1. These Judeans linked their position with that of Abraham: "The word of the Lord came to me, 'Son of man, the inhabitants of the waste places…keep saying, 'Abraham was only one man, yet he got possession of the land; but we are many; the land is surely given to us to possess'" (33:24).
2. Ezekiel insists that this view is incorrect; the people are not yet deserving of redemption.

B. His message is less one of consolation than of justification.

1. The people's apostasy caused YHWH to bring about the exile.
2. Redemption will follow repentance (36:24): "I will take you from the nations, and gather you from all the countries, and bring you into your own land."
3. But this will occur only "after many days…in the later years" (38:8–16).

C. Personal empowerment.

1. Earlier prophets and the Deuteronomic history spoke of sin as a corporate problem, and its results could be inherited (e.g., the sins of Manasseh precipitate the exile).

2. Ezekiel stresses individual responsibility: "The son shall not suffer for the iniquity of the father, nor shall the father suffer for the iniquity of the son; the righteousness of the righteous shall be upon himself, and the wickedness of the wicked shall be on himself" (18:20).

D. Symbolism.

1. Ezekiel's prophecy is enhanced by highly symbolic terminology (wheels within wheels [the "chariot vision"]; the valley of the dry bones).
2. He also engages in symbolic actions (Ezekiel is commanded not to mourn the death of his wife, to remain in particular positions for extremely long periods of time).
3. Perhaps the intensity, if not complete oddity, of his pronouncements and visions is best seen in the context of exilic trauma.
4. His visions foreshadow changes in prophetic language as prophets find increasing resistance to their proclamations: after exile, what more could be threatened?

VI. The Second Isaiah offers a message of consolation.

A. YHWH, not Marduk, controls history.

1. Because exile was predicted, prophecy of restoration is also credible: "A voice cries, 'In the wilderness prepare the way of the Lord; make straight in the desert a highway for our God'" (40:3).
2. The return of the exiles will be a new Exodus (Isa. 43).
3. Babylonian gods will go into captivity as Babylon is destroyed (Isa. 46–48).

B. YHWH's universal sovereignty and suffering servant.

1. Isa. 44:5 anticipates universal recognition of God and the covenant community: "This one will say, 'I am the Lord's'; another will call himself by the name of Jacob."
2. The "suffering servant" motif extends the *diaspora* promise: "I will give you as a light to the nations, that my salvation will reach to the end of the earth…" (49:1–6; cf. 42:1–4; 51:4ff.).
3. Isaiah's image of Abraham reverses that in Ezekiel. Isa. 51:2–3 reads: "Look to Abraham your father and to

Sarah who bore you; for when he was but one I called him, and I blessed him and made him many."

C. King Cyrus of Persia.

  1. YHWH appoints Cyrus of Persia ("God's anointed," Heb: *Messiah*) to defeat Babylon (Isa. 44:24–45:13).

  2. In 539 B.C.E., the Babylonian king Nabonidus flees, and the Persian army takes Babylon peacefully.

  3. Cyrus will, in 538, sponsor an edict to permit those in exile to return home.

  4. This practice is confirmed by the Cyrus Cylinder, dated to 528 B.C.E.

Supplementary Reading:

Commentaries in series listed in the bibliography.

Michael D. Coogan, (ed.), *The Oxford History of the Biblical World* (New York: Oxford University Press, 1998).

Questions to Consider:

1. Are references to other nations in a universal monotheism indicative of inclusion, co-optation, colonialism, or all three?

2. How does one distinguish between a theology of hope and a theology of self-deception?

3. How does "religion" (defined as you will) in a *diaspora* or in exile differ from religion in the homeland?

Lecture Twenty—Transcript
Babylonian Exile
(2 Kings 24-25, Jeremiah, Isaiah 40-55, Ezekiel)

I often think that we should take pity on those poor prophets who had to speak to the covenant community in the southern kingdom of Judah. Their kings and their people were convinced that there was no way the country would ever fall. They had the promises to David, the Davidic royal grant. They knew that God would protect Jerusalem because Jerusalem, David's city, was God's own city. It was where God's temple was located. It was where the train of God's cloak stayed, as we saw in Isaiah's call vision. Indeed, people in the south even had history on their side.

Pity poor Jeremiah, for example, who had to deal not only with all these conventions of royal grants and theology but also with history such as the following: According to the Deuteronomic historian, in the fourteenth year of King Hezekiah, Sennacherib of Assyria came up against the fortified cities of Judah and actually took them. One would think at this point people in Jerusalem would begin to panic. Recognizing that disaster was on the horizon, King Hezekiah actually did take some action. He paid a bribe to the Assyrians. This typically works in the Near East, and it seemed to work a little bit at that time; Sennacherib actually withdrew. But then Hezekiah revolts against Assyria, and this is what happens. The Assyrian campaign actually comes back, and it's ready to take Jerusalem.

Now, given the highly stylized nature of the Deuteronomic history, it's not exactly clear what happened. But this is what we find out in Second Kings, Chapter 18 and 19. There was a siege. The people were convinced they were going to die. Then suddenly, at the last moment, "That night the angel of the Lord went forth and slew 185,000 men in the camp of the Assyrians, and when the morning dawned, there they were all dead." Contemporary political analysts have a difficult time ascribing military victory to angelic intervention.

There have been some other suggestions as to what did happen to this actual historical siege of Jerusalem. Herodotus is often cited here, his book of *Histories*. I don't think this actually had any bearing whatsoever, but since biblical studies textbooks tend to cite it, I'll share it with you. According to Herodotus, the Assyrians had suffered a defeat on the borders of Egypt about this time, because their equipment was ruined by some ravenous field mice that had a taste for the leather. Therefore, the Assyrians needed to withdraw their troops on the borders of Judah in order to bolster their campaigns in other areas. It's a lovely story, but I don't think it helps us with the biblical tradition. Sennacherib in his archives provides us his own version. He implies here that the attack on Jerusalem was actually successful, at which point Hezekiah agreed to increase tribute yet again, which he promised that he would send directly to Ninevah, the Assyrian capital.

It's not exactly clear what happened, but we know what the effects are. The people in Judah are convinced nothing will ever happen to their kingdom, and this is the context in which we look at a prophet like Jeremiah on the eve of the attack against Judah by Babylon, trying to convince the kings, trying to convince the people, that, in fact, God might not protect Jerusalem, might not protect Judah. So let's look at Jeremiah and the fall of the northern kingdom to see how he expressed his views, what the political circumstances were, and how, in fact, the people once taken into exile did manage to preserve their identity through the priestly writers, through the second Isaiah, through the prophet Ezekiel.

In order to understand Jeremiah we need to understand his setting in life. You will recall that's the technical term, *Sitz in Leben*. He begins at about the time of Josiah's reform, which we discussed in the last lecture, when the Book of Deuteronomy was discovered during temple renovations. His call likely came in 627 B.C.E.—this is the thirteenth year of the reign of Josiah. Already political events on the horizon do not bode well, but at least Jeremiah at the beginning of his life could take some heart that the reforms would work. Alas, Josiah, as you know, is defeated by the Egyptians, by Pharaoh Neco at a battle set at the Megiddo Pass. The reforms are for nothing. The kingdom sinks back into apostasy. Jeremiah simply cannot fathom how this is happening. Moreover, Jeremiah had in his mind the Deuteronomic ideal that people who behave appropriately will be rewarded by God and people who sin will be punished by God. But then he notices that King Josiah, one of the good kings, dies in battle, and the reforms end. Where is God here?

Meanwhile, on the international horizon, an Egyptian-Assyrian coalition is designed to prevent Babylon from succeeding in its drive to conquer the entire Mesopotamian area, but that Egyptian-Assyrian coalition comes up against Babylon at the battle of Carchemish in 605, and they lose. Judah, which had previously been in vassalage to Assyria, becomes a vassal state of the Babylonian empire, and this is the context—official context—for Jeremiah's preaching. Things were not going well, and Jeremiah knew it. He knew that the government of Judah was unstable, and, as he watched the Babylonian empire deal with puppet kings, the situation went from bad to worse.

Under Babylonian control, Jehoiakim, King of Judah, rules for three years of submission, and then stupidly he rebels. He dies, in fact, before Babylon is able to take any stand against this rebellion. Jehoiakim's son, Jehoiachin, also named Jeconiah—there were two different names given for him—then surrenders to the Babylonian ruler. This is King Nebuchadnezzar, also pronounced "Nebuchadrezzar," and we have both spellings from antiquity. Jehoiakim's son, Jeconiah, surrenders in 597, and at this stage Babylon engages in what other ancient Near Eastern empires do. They begin to deport upper-class members and royal members and priestly members of the capital city. Babylon deports between 3,000 and 10,000 people from Jerusalem, including the king. They are taken into exile, where they remain in Babylon. We're going to leave them there for just a little bit.

Meanwhile, back in Judah, Mattaniah, who is probably related to Josiah, perhaps one of his sons or grandsons, assumes the throne under Babylonian protection. Babylonians rename him Zedekiah simply to symbolize his vassal status. But Zedekiah, established by Babylon, in yet another remarkably politically stupid move, seeks an alliance with Egypt and rebels against Babylon. In retaliation, in the year 587, King Nebuchadnezzar re-enters Judah, re-enters Jerusalem, and, at this point, burns down the temple constructed by Solomon, burns down God's house, the setting of Isaiah's call vision. He burns down the place that everybody in Judah and Jerusalem consider to be inviolate. He destroys the city, forces a second deportation, takes the valuables left from the temple's destruction into Babylon, and executes Zedekiah.

Gedaliah, who is actually a friend of Jeremiah—and we see him referred to in Jeremiah, Chapters 39 and 40—is appointed governor, but he's soon assassinated by a member of the Davidic royal family, one of the few who are left in Jerusalem. Given this incredibly dismal situation, one can understand why the Book of Lamentations is often attributed to Jeremiah. He did not write it, but, as you can hear even in the name Lamentations, this is a text that somehow bears his stamp.

That Jeremiah took all of these international events seriously is confirmed by his own call-narrative, and thus we go back to that convention of the prophetic commission. We learn in Chapter 1 that he is from the town of Anathoth, which is a little over two miles northeast of Jerusalem. He's from an area that would be affected by any sort of political policy because events in Jerusalem—the news, indeed, the attacks—would certainly trickle out to the suburbs. He's also intimately familiar with events regarding the cult. It's often suggested that Jeremiah is a descendant of one Abiathar who served as high priest under King David, but Abiathar was subsequently deposed by Solomon in favor of another priest whose name is Zadok. Abiathar was actually banished to Anathoth, Jeremiah's village, because he was involved in a coup, a failed coup, against King Solomon. He attempted to put Solomon's brother, Adonijah, on the throne. If Jeremiah is connected to this priestly family, one can understand Jeremiah's intense concern about the temple cult as well as the royal family. There are specific connections to Jerusalem here.

The call narrative also tells us that Jeremiah's father, Hilkiah, was a priest and therefore Jeremiah must have known about those old priestly traditions, no doubt, including the idea of the Davidic royal grant, because the priests and their scribes would have passed on that tradition from Second Samuel 7. Given this Judahite theology, given the historical events, given the fact that the temple was there in Jerusalem and it looked like it would stay there forever, how is Jeremiah ever going to communicate to the people that something might, in fact, go wrong? He tries to tell the people that the kingdom will fall. He lets them know, in fact, that at some point God will come back and help them but at this point the best they can do is hold on to their traditions. This despair comes out in his sense of what will happen to the people because he believes the covenant has actually fallen.

He predicts, therefore, an ideal future covenant, no longer one established in written literature but one established by the heart. This is Jeremiah's view of the new covenant, which we've actually already mentioned in our discussion of where the term "New Testament" comes from. As he states in Chapter 31—YHWH, speaking through Jeremiah—"I will put my law within them, and I will write it upon their hearts. No longer shall each person teach a neighbor and a relative, saying 'know the Lord.'" We might hear in the background, hear Deuteronomy: "Teach this diligently to your children when you walk by the way, when you sit down, and when you rise up." Jeremiah knows that the Deuteronomic reform did not work. Teaching, public presentation, no longer works. The covenant will be written on the heart: "No longer shall each person teach a neighbor and a relative, saying 'know the Lord,' for they shall all know me from the least of them to the greatest."

Jeremiah engages in a series of his own lamentations describing his heartbreak at the deportations and the fall of Jerusalem. His scribe, whose name is Baruch—from whom, by the way, we actually have a seal left; it's now in a private collection, so it's difficult for archaeologists to get a really, really close look on it, but it does, perhaps, perhaps, seem to be Baruch's actual seal—Jeremiah and his faithful Baruch continue to issue oracles. They are condemned by the kings. They are condemned by the priests. Apparently no one in Judah or Jerusalem likes them. That's part of the job of the prophet. No one likes them; they give bad news. But everybody needs a prophet.

What finally happens? In 582 Gedaliah is murdered. As you know, this prompts the third exile. People in Jerusalem who were still left needed to get away to avoid the Babylonian ongoing destruction. A group of them actually take Jeremiah and Baruch with them to Egypt, which is here remaining a place of safety. We've seen throughout this military history that Egypt goes from being in alliance with the people to being their enemy. At this point Egypt is against Babylon. It's part of that old view, the enemy of my enemy is my friend.

Egypt, at least at this point, is on Judah's side. Jeremiah goes to Egypt, where apparently Baruch actually compiled some of Jeremiah's oracles, and here is where the Book of Jeremiah comes from. It's also Jeremiah's being brought to Egypt that begins part of the legend of the lost ark. I mention this because of the movie, *Raiders of the Lost Ark.* So there becomes, even in contemporary American thought, this idea that the ark is important. The ark had been in the temple in Jerusalem. The temple in Jerusalem is burnt down by Nebuchadnezzar. Where is the ark? From Jeremiah's exile develops the legend that the holy ark was last seen, by the way, when Solomon put it in the Holy of Holies. Nobody has mentioned it since (First Kings, Chapter 8). That Jeremiah and his companions brought it down to Egypt is possible.

First Kings 14 mentions a raid against Jerusalem by the Pharaoh Shishak, and we saw him as part of Jereboam's support when the united kingdom separated. According to First Kings 14:26, "In the fifth year of Rehoboam, Shishak king of Egypt came up against Jerusalem. He took away the treasures of the house of the Lord [that's the temple] and the treasures of the house of the king." Then the Deuteronomic historian adds, "He took away everything." Could Pharaoh Shishak have brought the ark with him to Egypt at that time?

From the Old Testament Apocrypha, the deuterocanonical collection, we have a text called Second Maccabees. Second Maccabees, Chapter 2, suggests that Jeremiah hid the ark on Mt. Nebo and proclaimed, "This place shall be unknown until God gathers his people together and shows his mercy." For Jews in the Second Temple Period under Hellenistic rule, the ark remained a mystery, and they wanted it back. I think what Second Maccabees is doing here is connecting the ark, say, with Moses and with Elijah, hidden but ultimately to return in a new form when God's true rule breaks in.

The most likely scenario is that it was either burned down by Nebuchadnezzar, or, if Nebuchadnezzar did despoil the temple prior to the full destruction of Jerusalem, that Nebuchadnezzar brought it with him to Babylon. We will see reference in the Book of Daniel to some of those temple treasures, but I think Daniel was not actually recording history. I think that material is more legend than fact.

Jeremiah, Chapter 3, suggests that the ark remains in the communal memory of the people even if it's not there. It's not in physical space, but it's around. Jeremiah suggests, "When you have multiplied and increased in the land in those days, says the Lord, they shall no longer say, 'the ark of the covenant of the Lord,'" as if somehow that's a refrain that Jeremiah here has repeated, like a litany, "the ark of the covenant of the Lord." Jeremiah goes on, "It shall not come to mind or be remembered or missed, and nor shall another one be made." In Jeremiah's view—and this is associated with this idea of the new covenant—you don't need an ark because Jerusalem itself will be the Lord's throne. The nations will gather in Jerusalem. The exiles from the northern kingdom, the 10 lost tribes, will return, and the people, as Jeremiah puts it, "will no longer stubbornly follow their own will." These are glorious predictions of a future to come that we obviously haven't had yet.

Jeremiah's text, by the way, is just as mysterious as his fate. We're not exactly sure what happened to him after he went to Egypt. Part of our problem is that we have two quite different versions of the Book of Jeremiah. We have the Hebrew, or Masoretic, text, which is actually quite long, and we have the Greek, or Septuagintal, text, which is much more compact. Complicating this even more, the Dead Sea Scrolls have both traditions represented among their remains. There are two editions, therefore, of the Book of Jeremiah. Could it be that Jeremiah's scribe Baruch prepared one in diaspora, in Egypt, perhaps the longer one, and a shorter one retained by people in Judah? Could it be that Baruch prepared two different versions for two different liturgical settings or two different groups of readers? We simply do not know.

As the refugees in Egypt bring Jeremiah and Baruch with them in order to have a prophetic voice to keep their community intact, so the Judahites deported to Babylon have their own prophets, and that prophetic voice helps in allowing people from the southern kingdom to retain their identity, whereas people in the north were unable to do so. The notable prophets who exist in exile are first Ezekiel and then second Isaiah.

So let's look first at Ezekiel. Ezekiel proclaimed both a message of hope, an incredible, in fact, possibly pornographic, invective to the people in exile from about 593 to about 563. Ezekiel may have been part of that forced deportation in 597, and when he arrived in Babylon he found a people still confident. The initial people taken into exile thought, "Oh, this is not going to last very long. This is just a minor blip in history. Of course the covenant with David will be preserved. Of course God has loyalty to Judah and Jerusalem. We're here to be punished, yes, we probably deserve it, but it's not going to last all that long." Ezekiel finds a people with an enormous amount of hope, and it's his job to say, "Hunker down people, we're going to be here for a quite a while. Your punishment is not at an end yet."

These Judeans link their position with Abraham. This is Ezekiel citing them: "The word of the Lord came to me, son of man" [which is how God refers to Ezekiel. Here it simply means, "you human being."]. "Son of man, the inhabitants of the waste places [that's Babylon] keep saying, 'Abraham was only one man, yet he got possession of the land, and we are many. The land is surely given to us to possess.'" In other words, we're going to get it back. Ezekiel insists this is incorrect; the people are not deserving of redemption yet. His message, then, is one less of consolation than it is of justification, that God is still in control. Nothing has gone wrong. The people deserve their fate. It is their apostasy that forced YHWH to put them into exile. Redemption will follow, but it requires repentance. This is Ezekiel 36: "I will take you from the nations and gather you from all the countries [and we might think of those exiles in Egypt] and bring you into your own land," but, as Chapter 38 goes on, "after many days in the later years."

Ezekiel, in order to convince the people that they need to repent, changes one of the views promulgated by Deuteronomy. Deuteronomy, and indeed much of the earlier religious thought of the community, suggested that sin was a corporate problem. Deuteronomy speaks in the plural, "If you sin you will be punished." What Ezekiel wants to do is emphasize the idea of individual personal responsibility. He cites the proverb, "The parents have eaten sour grapes, and the children's teeth are set on edge." We suffer for what our parents do—that's Ezekiel 18. But, according to Ezekiel, "The son shall not suffer for the iniquity of the father, nor the father suffer for the iniquity of the son. The righteousness of the righteous shall be upon himself, and the wickedness of the wicked shall be upon himself." Every individual creates his or her own fate. If something goes wrong for one of us, it's because we deserved it and not because there is some sense of inherited guilt.

Obviously this is still going to cause a problem when it comes to questions of the theodicy because, if an individual is still behaving and the individual suffers—and of course we think of Job here—Ezekiel's system doesn't work. But at least here the people unburdened or without the justification of corporate guilt have to take on more personal responsibility.

To this point, Ezekiel's message fits very, very well within the biblical prophetic tradition, but there are parts of his oracles that are strange, peculiar, aberrant, bizarre. Ezekiel's prophecy, for example, is enhanced by exceptionally rich symbolic imagery. He begins his call vision with a description of a divine chariot of wheels within wheels of four living creatures, each with four faces and four wings. This is the beginning of what's known in Judaism as *merkabah*, "mysticism." This is the vision of God's chariot, God's throne. People are still trying to figure out what exactly Ezekiel saw. He also has the very well-known vision of the valley of the dry bones in Chapter 37. "Suddenly there was a noise," Ezekiel says, "a rattling, and the bones came together, bone to its bone, and I looked. There were sinews on them, and then flesh had come upon them, and then skin had covered them." This is incredibly graphic. It's his view of how the covenant community, like a corpse, will ultimately regain sinew, regain flesh, and literally pull itself back together. It's as if he is struggling to find the language to express what he's seeing, and, even when it comes to his description of God, language somehow fails him. He describes God in his call vision, Chapter 1, as "the appearance of the likeness of the glory of God." He simply can't get close linguistically.

He also engages in highly symbolic action. Jeremiah had done the same thing. For example, Jeremiah, in order to describe the yoke of the Babylonian exile, the Babylonian kingdom, actually put a regular yoke around his own shoulders, which a local priest broke off of him because local priests didn't like Jeremiah. Ezekiel is, for example, commanded not to mourn the death of his wife (Chapter 24). He remains lying on his left side for 390 days and then on his right for another 40 days to symbolize time in exile. He is commanded to eat food cooked over human dung, and connected with these bizarre actions are his invectives against Judah and also Israel. They are highly stylized, but they are also highly sexual, even misogynistic. Some people have called them pornographic.

He describes the kingdom of Israel and the kingdom of Judah as women, as adulterous women. We've already seen that with Hosea. But he also describes how God will rape them in the streets and display them naked before the people after whom they have gone in search of love affairs. The allegory in Chapter 23 of the sisters, Aholah, meaning "her tent"—that's Samaria—and Aholibah, meaning "my tent is in her"—that's Jerusalem—is so difficult that I will not read it to you. Chapter 23, if you can bear it. Perhaps the intensity if not the complete oddity of these visions represent for Ezekiel the trauma of exile. The people hadn't expected it; they still can't come to terms with it. It may be that the only way Ezekiel can grab their attention is through such shocking pronouncements. As prophecy goes on, as we move from Amos and Hosea through the first Isaiah to the time of the Babylonian exile, people will become used to prophetic rhetoric. If you get used to rhetoric it's much easier to ignore it. Through shock Ezekiel is at least able to gain the attention of the people.

His visions and his rhetoric foreshadow visions and rhetoric yet to come, that of apocalyptic literature, which really comes to the fore after the exile is done in the Second Temple Period, beginning, in fact, with some proto-apocalyptic material in the third Isaiah. This actually brings us to the second Isaiah, Ezekiel's younger contemporary during the Babylonian exile. By the time Isaiah is prophesying, the people have come to believe Ezekiel's message, "The end of exile has not come" and the message is now not one of perseverance per se but one of consolation, that God really does love this people, that God will retain the covenant, and that God will redeem these people. Because the exile was predicted, the second Isaiah said, "therefore restoration is also likely."

As the second Isaiah puts it in Chapter 40, "A voice cries in the wilderness, 'Prepare the way of the Lord. Make straight in the desert a highway for our God.'" In other words, build that highway out there because we're going back home. This is the statement, by the way, at the beginning of the Gospel tradition where John the Baptist is called "a voice in the wilderness," and you can see here punctuation problems. For the second Isaiah, it's "Go out into the wilderness and build a highway." For the Gospel of Mark, it's "a voice in the wilderness crying." This is simply Christian adaptation of prophecy, perfectly normal for first-century Jewish or Christian writers.

Evoking past tradition, the second Isaiah presents the return of the exiles, as in return of the exiles in Babylon, as, in fact, a new Exodus, the coming out of Egypt again, and he demonstrates here and elsewhere how Israel's own history serves as the model here for Israel's redemption. We might think back to those prophets of the north for whom Israel's own history served as a sign of their ultimate demise. History is usable material. You can use it to console; you can use it to complain. Finally, Isaiah also asserts that the Babylonian gods will go into captivity as Babylon is destroyed—that's Chapters 46 through 48. This is an alternative version of that peripatetic journey of the ark. Just as the ark went into exile—into Philistine territory—and came back, so ultimately the Babylonian gods will go into exile, but they will not return.

Isaiah's words of comfort would have also received support on the international front because, by the year 550, Persia is the empire on the rise, and King Cyrus of Persia looks like he's fated to take over. He had consolidated his empire, and he is encroaching on Babylon. Isaiah, Chapter 44, verse 5, anticipates the universal recognition of God, perhaps facilitated by the Persian conquering of everyone. This is Isaiah 44: "One nation will say, 'I am the Lord's as another will call himself by the name of Jacob." The Gentile nations will all stream to YHWH. They stay Gentiles. They don't become Jews, they are not circumcised, and they don't keep the dietary laws in this view, but they begin to worship the one true God. This motif extends into the *diaspora* promise that we saw already back with Abraham, who was guaranteed, "You will be a blessing to the nations."

This is Isaiah: "I will give you as a light to the nations that my salvation will reach to the ends of the earth." This is symbolized by Isaiah's vision of the suffering servant: beaten now, despised now, but ultimately showing God's own glory. For Isaiah, the suffering servant is primarily the nation of Judah, the Jews, the kingdom of Israel, which eventually will carry God's message throughout the empire. This message of consolation and vindication so different from Ezekiel even uses some of Ezekiel's own imagery because the second Isaiah, too, will go back to Abraham but here using Abraham as the model for God's blessing.

Second Isaiah's words are themselves vindicated by King Cyrus of Persia. Isaiah proclaims that Cyrus of Persia has been appointed the Lord's anointed. The Hebrew is *mashiah*, "Messiah." The Greek translation would be "Christ." He is appointed Lord's anointed to defeat Babylon, and that's exactly what happens. In 539 B.C.E., the Babylonian King Nabonidus flees his capital, and Persia comes in quite peacefully and takes over. In 538 King Cyrus of Persia promulgates an edict permitting the Jews in exile in Babylon to return home. We have something, an archaeological remain called the Cyrus Cylinder, in which this practice of returning the exiles back home is actually recorded.

The Jews go back home, and they have with them the literature of the exile. They bring as well the priestly material, the "P" code, and, through the priestly material and then third Isaiah and all of these traditions combined, when they return home they still have their own identity, but the problem is that what they find when they go back is not quite what they had anticipated.

Lecture Twenty-One

Restoration and Theocracy (Isaiah 56–55, Ezra–Nehemiah, Haggai, Zechariah, Malachi, Ruth, Jonah)

Scope:

This lecture addresses the situation encountered by those who returned from Babylon: the policies of Persian rule; disappointment in Jerusalem's condition; the failed messianic potential of the Davidic heir, Zerubbabel; and power struggles between Aaronides and Levites, priest and prophets, and those who returned from exile and those who remained in the land. The lecture then turns to two phenomena developed under these conditions: the breakdown of classical prophecy and the increasing concern with assimilation in general, intermarriage in particular.

Outline

I. The early Persian period.

- **A.** The Cyrus Cylinder (cf. Isa. 44:28; 45:1; 47ff; Ezra 1:2–4; 2 Chron. 36:23: Ezra 6:3–5) states: "I returned to [these] sacred cities on the other side of the Tigris, the sanctuaries of which have been ruins for a long time, the images which [used] to live therein, and established for them permanent sanctuaries. I gathered all their inhabitants and returned their habitations."
  1. Under Persian rule, the Judeans are encouraged to rebuild their Temple with funds provided from the royal treasury.
  2. Cyrus allows the return of Temple vessels plundered by Babylon (2 Kings 24:13).
  3. Persia's tactics were politically expedient: toleration of a subject nation's cultural practices and limited autonomous governance. Both fostered stability and provided a bulwark against the growing Greek threat.
  4. The Jewish military colony at Elephantine notes that Cambyses (529–522) did not damage their temple despite destroying "all the temples of the gods of the Egyptians."

B. Darius I (522–486) divides the empire into twenty satrapies; Judah belongs to Avar Nahal, "beyond the river."

1. Persia offered satrapies substantial autonomy, developed an efficient means of communication, and facilitated the flourishing of commerce.
2. The satraps (first the Davidide Zerubbabel, then the courtier Nehemiah) were chosen with regard to local concerns.

II. For many, the Jerusalem anticipated by the Second Isaiah was a severe disappointment.

A. "Zion has become a wilderness, Jerusalem a desolation; O holy and beautiful house where our fathers praised you have been burned by fire, and all our pleasant places have become ruins" (Isa. 64:10–12).

B. Second Isaiah's universalism ("light to the nations") transforms into siege mentality: "I have trodden the wine press alone…I trod them with my anger and trampled them in my wrath" (Isa. 63:3).

C. Haggai deplores the languishing of the cult and the poor condition of the Temple: "Who is left among you who saw this house in its former glory? How do you see it now? Is it not in your sight as nothing?" (2:3)

1. The Temple's rebuilding did not, contrary to expectations, usher in an age of prosperity.
2. Hag. 1:6ff. and Zech. 6:8–9 reveal a people who are starving, freezing, and poor.
3. Many questioned the value of serving YHWH. As Malachi opens, "'I have loved you,' says the Lord; but you say, 'How have you loved us?'"

III. Contributing to the disappointment was the failed restoration government.

A. Haggai exhorts the priest (Joshua) and the governor (Zerubbabel) to take courage and work.

1. Ezra and Zechariah attest to their collaboration.
2. Zerubbabel disappears from history and leaves no heir. Persian authorities may have removed or even executed him.
3. The Davidic line is lost here.

B. Levites and Aaronides.
   1. Levites sought to regain power wrested from them under Deuteronomic reform.
   2. Aaronides still worked to consolidate the power accorded them by the P source/the Babylonian Judean establishment.

C. The struggle for power was ultimately won by the Aaronide priests.
   1. The legitimacy of the priesthood was established in the symbolic rites of investiture (comparable to a royal coronation) involving Joshua (Zech. 3:1–9).
   2. Priestly rule is epitomized in the authority accorded Ezra by his own community and by the Persian government.
   3. For Malachi, the task of religious and moral instruction passes from the prophets, whose authority rested on revelation, to those entrusted with a hereditary commission, the priests.

IV. The breakdown of classical prophecy.

A. By the Persian period, classical prophecy was on the verge of collapse (Ps. 74:9; Lam. 2:9; Zech. 13:2–5): "I will remove from the land the prophets… And if anyone again appears as a prophet, his father and mother who bore him will say to him, 'You shall not live, for you speak lies in the name of the Lord…'"
   1. The movement's demise followed the exile: What more could prophets threaten, after exile, the destruction of the Temple, Persian rule, and famine?
   2. Prophetic promises, such as those of the Second Isaiah, failed.
   3. Sin prospered, and righteousness was ineffectual (Mal. 3:14; Eccl. 9:13–15).
   4. Malachi was unable to take for granted even the most basic element of Israelite theology: God's love for the community.

B. A contributing factor was the demise of the monarchy.
   1. Government was in the hands of priests and their Persian sponsors. Whom was the prophet to condemn? The priests were themselves associated with divine sanction, and the Persians did not care.

2. The post-exilic period needed unity, which prophetic argument threatened to undermine; without the countering force of the throne, prophetic critique would create political imbalance.

V. Genealogy and ethnic identity become increasingly important as Judea recognizes itself to be part of an empire.

A. Ezra legislates that Judean men divorce their foreign wives; genealogy becomes increasingly important (cf. 1, 2 Chron.).

B. Likely written to combat this ethnocentrism are the novellas of Ruth and Jonah.

1. The novellas offer positive views of gentiles but implicitly warn against assimilation.

2. Ruth, continually identified as "Ruth the Moabite," seduces Boaz on the threshing floor, a scene reminiscent of Genesis 19. Ruth the Moabite becomes David's great-grandmother.

3. Jonah—attempting to escape the divine command to preach to Nineveh—is first tossed overboard, then swallowed by a great fish, and ultimately left to the burning sun while the Assyrians repent.

Supplementary Reading:

Commentaries in series listed in the bibliography.

Michael D. Coogan, (ed.), *The Oxford History of the Biblical World* (New York: Oxford University Press, 1998).

Kenneth M. Craig, *The Poetics of Jonah: Art in the Service of Ideology*, 2nd ed. (Macon, GA: Mercer University Press, 1999).

Questions to Consider:

1. How are moral values promulgated in circumstances of despair?
2. What adaptations do cultures make when they become part of an external empire?
3. What prompted the post-exilic stress on genealogy and the concern for assimilation?
4. How might Ruth be compared to Abraham? What are the implications of her Moabite ancestry?
5. Is Jonah a comedy or a tragedy?

Lecture Twenty-One—Transcript
Restoration and Theocracy
(Isaiah 56-55, Ezra–Nehemiah, Haggai, Zechariah, Malachi, Ruth, Jonah)

When King Cyrus of Persia promulgated his edict in 538 B.C.E., permitting the Jews in exile in Babylon to return home, great excitement no doubt occurred. The people in Babylon had been bolstered in part by their memories of what they had left behind. The next generation had heard stories from their parents about the glories of the temple, the glories of Judea, and, indeed, they had been bolstered as well by the prophecies of second Isaiah, saying, "Go build a highway in the wilderness. Head home. God's glory is about to break through. You will be a blessing to all nations." With enormous hope people left, they followed Cyrus of Persia, and they returned home.

Unfortunately, things were not as they had hoped they would be. The destruction that Nebuchadnezzar had brought when he destroyed Jerusalem had not been repaired. The city was in ruins. The infrastructure was completely destroyed. Moreover, the people who had not been taken into exile resented the return of those from Babylon. So we have the community at odds with each other, a land in destruction, and very little hope. That's where we begin with the discussion of the immediate post-exilic period. How is this community going to put itself back together? Where is the leadership to come from? Is the Davidic king going to last? What will the priests do? What will happen to the people who were left? Who will take over?

In order to get a handle on what's going on during this period, we have to look at a variety of different types of literature. We have, for example, from the prophetic corpus the third Isaiah. The first Isaiah we've already met preaching during the reign of King Hezekiah; the second Isaiah providing hope and consolation to people during exile; and the third Isaiah reflecting upon the shattered dreams of the people who had returned. We also have information from the prophets Haggai, Zechariah, and Malachi, who are exhorting the people first to rebuild the temple and then, subsequently—particularly with Malachi—exhorting the priests to function properly. The cult needed to be revived, and people needed to renew their trust in it. That becomes the job ultimately of the prophetic school to bolster the priesthood.

We also have historical material from Ezra and Nehemiah, Persian envoys entrusted by the government with developing the economy, the stable political system, and, indeed, solidifying the priesthood of the exilic community. Finally we have a couple of short stories or novellas, if you will.

Part of the problem of the post-exilic period was the new sense of self-definition for the people. This is the time when they are changing from being an ethnic group, Judeans, to being a combination of both an ethnos and a religion. We're now finding a time when people no longer simply affiliate with the group, as would a stranger or a resident alien. This is a time when people can actually convert to Judaism. So we have here questions about how the Judean population becoming Jews will relate to Gentiles. The two books in question are Ruth and Jonah.

Let's start out with a basic history of the early Persian period. An artifact from the sixth century B.C.E. from Persia, the Cyrus Cylinder, which we mentioned in the last lecture, provides information on Persian policies. This is what the cylinder states: "I returned to these sacred cities on the other side of the Tigris [which includes the area of Judea], the sanctuaries of which have been in ruins for a long time [and one has to deal with strained syntax here], the images which used to live therein, and established them permanent sanctuaries. I gathered all their inhabitants and returned their habitation." In other words, not only for Jews but also for several of the other population groups that the Babylonians had taken into exile, Cyrus said, "Go back home." This was exceptionally astute on the part of the Persian empire. By encouraging exiles to return home, and indeed rebuild their temple, Cyrus was able to develop a new infrastructure, and the people leading that new government had their loyalties to Cyrus of Persia. Thereby he had allies in all these new kingdoms that he had, in effect, inherited from the Babylonian empire.

Persia's tactics were sufficiently politically expedient that we have evidence of them from other places throughout the ancient Near East. You might recall the community at Elephantine in Egypt, the Jewish military colony that had the god Yahu and Mrs. Yahu. Among their documents we have some information on Persian policies in the late sixth century, talking about the King Cambyses, a successor of Cyrus of Persia, who began his rule about 529. The Elephantine papyri note that when the Persians came in they did not damage the Jewish temple down there, although the Persians destroyed all the temples of the gods of the Egyptians. The idea was to keep here the loyalty of the Jewish military colony and avoid having the Egyptians, bolstered by their own priests, engage in some sort of revolution against Persia.

In Judah's case Cyrus had a secondary goal here. The new empire on the horizon is Greece, and it often helps to have someone on the shores of the Mediterranean protecting your initial investments. That's what the Jews, to some extent, were able to do for the Persian empire. So here we are, under the rule of Persia beginning with Cyrus and continuing on with people like Darius I, who ruled from about 522 for about 30 or 40 years after. The empire winds up getting divided into various satrapies; Persia now has Judea firmly in its hand. The Persians offered their various satrapies a fair amount of autonomy. They didn't need to have complete control over everything as long as they knew that the government was not likely to revolt. The Persian empire sponsored, and the Jews were able to take advantage of, new efficient means of communication which facilitated commerce. They also had, at least the Jews also had, their own king.

Returning from Babylon we find a king, or at least a ruler, whose name is Zerubbabel, and you can hear simply in his name that Babylonian echo. This is a community and a kingship that has to some extent assimilated with Babylon. The priests and the prophets of the immediately returning exilic community had enormous hope for Zerubbabel. Although they didn't have the government they used to have, although this was no longer the glories of Judea, there was enough there that at least part of the population, particularly those who had returned from exile, could get a sense that perhaps the community might be able to rebuild and at some point reestablish the glories that they had originally had.

We'll leave Zerubbabel for a minute and talk briefly about the disappointed hopes of some of the others, because, while the upper classes were able, for the most part, to exult in the relative freedom they had with Persia, some of the exiles didn't have that much authority, and a good many of the people who had been left in the land had even less. Third Isaiah attests to the disappointment of the return and indeed gives us a hopeful vision that, when redemption comes, it will not be brought about through Persian rule. It will not be brought about so much by human endeavor. It will be brought about by divine fiat, by the heavenly hosts entering into history, God straightening up the mess that Nebuchadnezzar had originally caused. This is Isaiah 64 describing what he thought of Judea when he returned: "Zion has become a wilderness, Jerusalem a desolation. Our holy and beautiful house where our fathers praised you has been burned with fire, and all our pleasant places have become ruin." I suspect that's what a good many people who returned from exile thought.

Second Isaiah's universalism, this vision of being a light to the nations, has become less a universal mandate. Now it's more of a siege mentality. There is isolationism coming in with the third Isaiah. As part of his despair, speaking God's word, third Isaiah says, "I have trodden the winepress alone. I trod them with my anger and trampled them with my wrath." There's no hopeful means of communicating with Gentiles from this particular viewpoint. For this situation, the divine promise of redemption remains, but it's not anything that people can do themselves. Isaiah explains, again speaking for God, "I am about to create new heavens and a new earth. The former things shall not be remembered or come to mind, but be glad and rejoice forever in what I am creating. For I am about to create Jerusalem as a joy and its people as a delight." And it remains wishful thinking.

Haggai, too, another prophet who would return from Babylon, finds conditions in post-exilic Judea absolutely deplorable. He laments the languishing of the cult, the very poor condition of the temple. There had been some early renovations about 538 when the first group of exiles returned, but not much had been done. Haggai's disappointment is exacerbated because the Persian government had promised help in rebuilding the temple, but the exilic population who had returned did not take advantage of that help. Cyrus had promised the funds. Who was using it?

By the time of 520, close to 20 years after Cyrus had promulgated his edict of return, the temple was still in ruins, and this is when Haggai begins to write. As he puts it to the people who had come back with him, "Who was left among you who saw this house in its former glory? How do you see it now—is it not in your eyes as nothing?" Which, in fact, it was. So under Haggai's urging and subsequently under the prophet Zechariah's urging, and under the combined efforts of the governor Zerubbabel, that Davidic descendant, as well as a high priest whose name is Joshua, the temple renovations began, and the basic structure was finally completed about the year 515. The same general information that we get from Haggai and Zechariah is confirmed in the Book of Ezra, Chapter 5.

But the temple's rebuilding did not, contrary to Haggai's hopes and Zechariah's hopes, lead to a glorious view of redemption. I suspect some of these people who were involved in the renovation would have thought, "Once we get this temple built God will retake his seat in the throne of the temple. Everything will be right in heaven and on earth." But that's wishful thinking, and it's not quite what happened.

Zechariah, whose oracles, at least in Chapters 1 through 8, were promulgated between, say, 520 and 518, continues to reveal a people despondent. This is his vision of what will be, but not yet of what was: "Thus says the Lord of hosts, 'Old men and old women shall again sit in the streets of Jerusalem, each with a staff in hand because of their great age. And the streets of the city shall be filled with boys and girls playing in those streets.'" That's the vision of the peaceful community, like a heaven on earth, where people are settled underneath their own vines and fig trees. It's actually the prophet Micah, but this is the ideal, and they simply didn't have it in the post-exilic period.

Indeed, the more the prophets made promises, the less the people could trust them. There was not much left that the prophets could say. Could they threaten exile unless the temple was built? As my daughter would have said, "Been there; done that." What else could they possibly do? By the time we get to the prophet Malachi, who comes at some point after Haggai and Zechariah, but his oracles are, in fact, difficult to date—probably some time in the first half of the fifth century—the people had begun to question even the most basic elements of Judean theology. They wondered why they should continue to serve God. This is the way Malachi opens, "I have loved you, says the Lord, but you say, 'How have you loved us?'" which, given their situation, is not an illegitimate question. Where is the glory? Where is the redemption we had been promised?

God laments in Malachi, "A son honors his father and servants their master. If, then, I am a father, where is the honor due me? If I am a master, where is the respect due me?" From Malachi's perspective, God was not being honored either as a parent or as a master. The people were lacking in hope and therefore lacking in any sort of religious response that Malachi considered legitimate. Indeed, not even the priests were doing what they were supposed to do, and Malachi's invective goes particularly against the priesthood rather than the people. We can hear echoes even here of Amos's complaints about the cult hundreds of years before.

The priests are particularly important here because, in the absence of a Davidic king, with the collapse to some extent of the royal grant theology, it's the priests who were supposed to pick up the pieces. If the priests don't do their job, the community is not going to last. If the temple is rebuilt but there are no caring officiants, it's nothing. So Malachi winds up saying, "Oh, that someone among you would just shut the doors so that you would not kindle fire on my altar in vain." For Malachi, the priests are just going through the motions—what's the point?

Contributing to the disappointment was the ultimate failure of the restoration government because the government, no matter what it could do, still remained under Persian control. This was no independent Davidic monarchy. Haggai spoke directly to the people who had some sort of ability to engage in restructuring the temple and restructuring the government. He addresses Zerubbabel, the Davidic descendant and Persian-appointed governor, and Joshua the high priest in strong exhortation. This is Haggai: "'Take now courage, Zerubbabel,' says the Lord. 'Take courage, Joshua the high priest. Take courage, indeed, all you people of the land and work, for I am with you,' says the Lord of Hosts. 'According to the promise that I made with you when you came out of Egypt, my spirit abides among you. Do not fear.'"

There is exhortation, and at the beginning there is high hope that perhaps this government will indeed succeed. Zechariah, for example, has a vision of the high priest Joshua standing before the angel of the Lord. We might think of Isaiah's call vision here, where priests and prophets are brought to the heavenly throne room. Here is Joshua, the high priest, standing before the angel and the accuser. This is like a prosecuting attorney. The Hebrew was *ha-satan;* hence we get "satan." We'll return to him when we get to the Book of Job. Here he is simply an accuser. He stands on the high priest's right hand to accuse him, and God the Lord says to *ha-satan*, the accuser, "The Lord rebuke you, *ha-satan*. Is not this man a brand plucked from the fire [something to be redeemed and restored]?"

Zechariah goes on, "Joshua was dressed with filthy clothes as he stood before the angel." Priests are supposed to wear white garments. There is a sense of investiture in how they dress and how they present themselves. "The angel said to those who were standing before him, 'Take off his filthy clothes,' and to the high priest the angel said, 'I will clothe you with festive apparel'" (Zechariah 3).

Zechariah also prophesies about Zerubbabel, "This is the word of the Lord to Zerubbabel: 'Not by might nor by power but by my spirit,' says the Lord of hosts. What are you, great mountain? Before Zerubbabel you shall become a plain." Now, if Zerubbabel is good enough to turn a mountain into a plain, that's high hope. We didn't even get a molehill out of him. Even Ezra attests the collaboration: "Then Zerubbabel and Joshua set out to rebuild the temple, the house of God in Jerusalem, and with them were priests helping." That's Ezra 5.

But Zerubbabel disappears from history. After references in Haggai and Zechariah and Ezra, we do not know what happened to him. I have my suspicions that the Persian government, recognizing the hope that some of the priests and prophets had put in him, simply decided he was too much of a liability and perhaps got him out of the way. Perhaps he simply faded off, not having accomplished very much and without descendants to continue the Davidic line. After Zerubbabel there is no firm Davidic line that historians can trace down. At this point the Davidic heirs pass into legend. Although the New Testament attributes to Jesus descent from King David, the genealogies we have in the Gospels of Luke and Matthew do not agree even past the time of King David. So the Davidic line is, at least as far as we can tell, lost. Hope for that royal grant, that promise, passes into messianic speculation. It's no longer there for politics.

Not only is the government in disarray, so is the priesthood. We've already seen struggles between the Levites and the government when King Josiah closed down all the high places and centralized the cult. Deuteronomy thereby limited the power of the Levites. But some of this limitation also had to form a means of coalescing. When the temple is destroyed by Nebuchadnezzar, not only is the government taken into exile but so are many of the priests, and it's during the time of the exile that the Aaronide priests, the priests who traced their descent from Moses' brother Aaron, begin to take over the cultic symbols and develop the laws. This is the time during the exile, and immediately after that the "P" code is written—the priests responsible for Genesis, Chapter 1—we've already seen that.

What these Aaronides needed to do in order to establish their authority—because there were other rival groups of priests, for example, the Zadokite priests whom Ezekiel sponsored—the Aaronides, in the process of editing the Pentateuch, actually rewrote their own history. When in doubt, as it were, send Moses back up the mountain and get a new law. We can actually trace this out through a bit of source criticism. They needed to figure out a way to establish their own authority. Here is how they did it. They noticed that, in "J" and in "E," Aaron, Moses' brother, is appointed to be high priest but the major thing he does is construct the golden calf. His reputation is not that good. Even in Deuteronomy all he does basically is construct the golden calf and then die.

What do the Aaronides do? They come back in, and they create at least three scenes whereby God invests the Aaronide priests, Aaron and his sons, with authority. In Exodus 29 the "P" code writers come in and provide us the ordination ceremony of Aaron and his sons. In Exodus 40, Aaron and his sons get the blessing of a perpetual priesthood throughout their generations. It is as if the Davidic royal grant established for the monarchy is now given to the priests and the priests would function as God's cultic representatives in perpetuity. Finally, in Leviticus 8, continuing into Leviticus 9, we have Aaron's coronation—and it really is a coronation—and then he offers a sacrifice and delivers a priestly blessing.

"P" also revamps polity, the idea that people would go to the temple and offer sacrifices, into a much more regularized system. Now people have to go and offer sacrifices. The only place they can do it, as we know from Josiah, is in Jerusalem, and who's going to function? The priests, the Aaronide descendants. So since the cult now becomes much more formalized, one needs a formal clergy through inheritance, through descent, in order to facilitate the cult. This was absolutely brilliant on the Aaronides' part.

Sometimes my students fuss about this and call it evil or Machiavellian, but it may have been that, through this Aaronide gesture, that's the only way the covenant community would have survived. The monarchy was no longer functional. The prophets had nothing left to tell the people. They had threatened and promised all they possibly could. It would be the priests who would be able to keep the people together by providing them a written record. We have Ezra's reading of the Pentateuch to the people and providing them laws and providing them a cult and holding onto those religious traditions. It's the priests who wind up saving the covenant community, ironically enough, and their influence remains so strong that the culture becomes a theocracy, and the priesthood comes to dominate Judean civilization all the way down to the second century, when we begin to find another monarchy coming in.

Priestly rule, I suspect, would be epitomized by the prophet Ezra. He is both priest and prophet, and his legitimacy is established not only by the other priests who will defer to him but also by the Persian government itself. The Persians seemed to like priestly rule. It was safer than having kingly rule. Ezra himself apparently returned from Babylon during the second or even a third wave of returnees under King Artaxerxes in the middle of the fifth century, so we're now down several decades from the time of Haggai and Zechariah. And, as you know, he brought with him an early version of the Pentateuch, as we've described before, the Book of the Law of Moses, which he read to the congregation, and that's described in Nehemiah, Chapter 8.

For Malachi the priests needed to do their job. They weren't really doing it. The idea of the prophetic voice was in shambles. We come now during the post-exilic period to what might be considered the end of prophecy, and, as we'll see in a lecture or two, prophecy will eventually die out, and we find in place of prophecy both wisdom literature and apocalyptic visions. We can see the end of prophecy already in Zechariah—this is Chapter 13—"I will remove from the land the prophets, and if anyone again appears as a prophet, his father and mother who bore him will say to him, 'You shall not live, for you speak lies in the name of the Lord.'" You can't trust a prophet these days, in the post-exilic period.

Why did prophets die out? In part because there wasn't anything left to threaten and, I suspect, in part because of the demise of the monarchy. As we saw in our discussion earlier of the origins of prophecy, the prophet begins work when the office of judge splits, and then we have the prophet serving as the conscience of the monarchy. But if you no longer have a monarchy, in fact, you no longer need a prophet. At this point in the post-exilic period the important thing is not to provide invective against the ruling class. You need somebody who is going to support the ruling class because they are sufficiently fragile. Prophets no longer had a specific audience. They could rail against the priests as Malachi did, but the population doesn't get much out of it except despising the priests, which is not what you want if you want to build a society.

Haggai and Malachi could not do very much. When Ezra takes over as both priest and prophet, we find fewer prophetic oracles, the type of poetry that we saw with Isaiah or Amos or Hosea. What we find now is the priest-prophet combination legislating morality, indeed, legislating whom one could marry and how. One of the distresses that Ezra found when he returned is that people who were left in the land, as well as some of the earlier returnees, had married local women and not all Judean—now Jewish—women. They had married women from Samaria, perhaps Persian women, or others who had come into the territory. Ezra discovers that the children of these women were no longer even speaking the language of the Jews. They didn't know Jewish tradition. They didn't know anything about the Exodus or Sinai. They were, in fact, from Ezra's perspective, pagans, and Ezra takes the drastic move of insisting that the Jews divorce their foreign wives, push away those foreign wives and those foreign children.

We begin to see in the post-exilic period not only in Ezra but continuing on through the Chronicler—First and Second Chronicles—a concern for genealogy, a concern for passing on the lineage, the tradition, both in terms of inculcation—that's Deuteronomy, teaching your children—but now also in terms of ethnic identity. It becomes biological. This is the negative view of the Gentiles, but it's not the only view that we have in this particular period. We also have the books of Jonah and Ruth, difficult to date, but I agree with those scholars who want to put these books in the post-exilic period functioning as counterarguments to this idea of putting away your foreign wives. The epitome of the counterargument is the Book of Ruth. It's an absolutely fascinating story.

Here is the basic storyline, and you can hear in it, both the idea that Gentile women can be even better to, say, an Israelite mother than seven sons, but also still a little bit of an ambivalence. Yes, the Gentile women might actually be fine, but they still make us a little bit nervous. The story of the Book of Ruth starts out with a woman named Naomi, her husband, and her two sons leaving Israel, leaving the town of Bethlehem, because there is a famine. Bethlehem is not only the city of David, but the word "Bethlehem" itself actually means "House of Bread." So here we have "House of Bread" and famine—something is obviously wrong. They settle in the land of Moab, and Moab, as you know, is one of the perpetual enemies of Israel. We've already talked about the Moabites as descended from the incestuous relationship between Lott and his daughters.

They settle in Moab, the sons marry local women, and finally all the men in the family die. Naomi, the mother-in-law, decides she wants to return to Bethlehem—the famine is over—so she announces this to her daughters-in-law. Her daughters-in-law say, "We want to go with you." One daughter-in-law is named Orpah; the other is named Ruth. Naomi says, "There is no point. I'm not going to give you any more sons to marry. I have no hope in my own life. I'm a bitter old woman. Go back to your mother's house." In fact, she says, "Find a new husband. Establish your own life."

After much tears, Orpah finally kisses Naomi and turns, but Ruth cleaves to Naomi. In fact, the word used here is *davaq*. It's the same word that we find in Genesis 2 when Adam says, "A man shall leave his father and mother and cleave to his wife." That's as close as Ruth gets to Naomi. So, as Adam says, "We will become one flesh," that's Ruth's view, and she says to her mother-in-law—these are famous lines—"Whither thou goest, I will go, and your home will be my home, and your God will be my God." Naomi, who has nothing left to say, basically allows Ruth to come after her.

When they arrive in Bethlehem the women find lodging, and Ruth goes to glean in the fields of an older relative. It turns out the older relative, whose name is Boaz, is available, and after a few brief comments passed back and forth between Boaz and Ruth, Boaz actually likes Ruth. He's heard how she is taking care of her mother-in-law. Ruth says to Boaz at one point, "May I continue to find favor in your eyes, my lord, for you have comforted me and spoken kindly," etc. Naomi gets the idea, "Well, Boaz is a relative; perhaps he might redeem us," the idea being, in the sense of lever-relationships, that a woman who is widowed without a child would marry ideally a brother-in-law but sometimes a near kinsman and that near kinsman, a brother-in-law, would have a child with the widow, and that child would inherit the dead husband's property and name.

Naomi actually says to Ruth when she gets this idea in her head, "Take a bath, put on your best clothes, put on some perfume, go down to the threshing floor late at night, and wait until the man Boaz's heart is heavy with wine. Mark where he lies down. Go lie down next to him. Uncover his feet [which, as you know, is a euphemism for genitals], and he'll tell you what to do." I would call this a seduction scene. You've got to give Naomi some credit here. And Ruth agrees.

She goes down to the threshing floor at midnight, Boaz wakes up, notices his feet are uncovered, looks at Ruth, and says, "Who are you?" which is a good question. Ruth responds to him, "Spread your cloak over me, my lord, because you are next of kin." They have a brief conversation. Boaz gets Ruth out of the way before anybody notices her. As he said, "Let it not be said that a woman has come to the threshing floor." Through this relationship, Boaz, in the very next chapter—and it's only a four-chapter book—announces to the closer relative that he, Boaz, will redeem Ruth, will marry Ruth, and ultimately Boaz and Ruth become married. Ruth gives birth to a son, and through that line we eventually get King David.

What is this book saying? That a Gentile woman—indeed, descended from the Moabites—becomes great-grandmother of the greatest hero in Israel. Why, therefore, put away your foreign wives? If this Moabite woman can do so much for her mother-in-law, how much more could some of these foreign wives during Ezra and Nehemiah's time do?

Similarly with the Book of Jonah we also have a little bit of a problem. Jonah, as you know, is the one successful prophet. He preaches to the Ninevites, and they, in fact, convert. Jonah is actually identified as a prophet in the Deuteronomic history. He lived prior to the time of the fall of Nineveh. If Jonah hadn't prophesied and they hadn't converted, Nineveh would have been destroyed, and, if we add up the dates, the northern kingdom would never have been destroyed either. There is an ambivalence here. The Gentiles can be good. They can repent. But they also may wipe you out, so we need to be a little bit more careful than we might have thought originally.

Lecture Twenty-Two

Wisdom Literature
(Song of Songs, Proverbs, Ecclesiastes, Job)

Scope:

From the "Sumerian Job" (fourth millennium) and the "Babylonian theodicy" to Cynic *chreia*, authors have attempted to make sense of the world and their place in it. The biblical contributions to this "wisdom literature" range from the optimistic Song of Songs to the practical Proverbs to the pessimistic Ecclesiastes. The most famous, and most controversial, example of biblical wisdom is the Book of Job: combining prose and poetry, resignation and resistance, and complicated by a problematic textual tradition, the book requires the "patience of Job" for understanding. Following a brief introduction to wisdom literature, this lecture addresses the Book of Job through its characterizations of Job and God, and the text-critical problems that contribute to the book's complexity.

Outline

I. The international implications of empire, while manifested in the xenophobia of Ezra and Nehemiah and the irresistible universalism of YHWH according to Ruth and Jonah, take on a third form: "wisdom," a tradition well established in the Near East.

II. Biblical wisdom is partially epitomized by the books ascribed to Solomon: Song of Songs (Song of Solomon, Canticles), Proverbs, and Ecclesiastes.

- **A.** Song of Songs (Song of Solomon, Canticles) is actually less a text of "wisdom" teaching than a celebration of the joys of love, emotional as well as physical.
  1. Its literary parallels are less Proverbs and Ecclesiastes than Egyptian love poetry.
  2. The song's overt sensuality complements the earthiness of Genesis and Judges, as does its powerful woman's voice.
  3. Under Hellenistic influence, the song became regarded as a spiritual allegory of the love between Israel and God or the Church and the Christ.

4. Some interpreters propose that parts may be parody (e.g., "Your hair is like a flock of goats streaming down Mt. Gilead" [4:1]).
5. Current multicultural readings call attention to the fact that the Hebrew can bear either of two translations of "I am black and/but beautiful."

B. Proverbs, a cross-cultural form for promoting proper attitudes and behaviors, receives divine sanction by Lady Wisdom herself (1–9).

1. The proverbs encourage (male) readers to cleave to Lady Wisdom and avoid the paths of Strange (foreign, adulterous) Woman (Dame Folly).
2. Wisdom as a character is increasingly developed in the Old Testament Apocrypha/Deuterocanonical writings (e.g., Wisdom of Solomon).
3. She finds herself contributing to the *Shekinah*, the feminine manifestation of the divine, in Judaism, and the *Logos*, the pre-existent form of the incarnate Christ, depicted in the Prologue of the Gospel of John.

C. Ecclesiastes (Qoheleth, "leader of the assembly") negotiates life in a world of ennui.

1. Tradition suggests that the Song of Songs is the product of Solomon's youth; Proverbs, of his adult prime; and Ecclesiastes, of his age.
2. The text combines a pessimistic view of life ("Vanity of vanities…all is vanity" [12:8]; "there is nothing new under the sun" [1:9]) with utilitarian advice following from it (eat, drink, and be merry [cf. 9:7]; rejoice in your youth [cf. 11:9]).
3. Everything has its season (3:1–8); risk taking is advisable ("Cast your bread upon the waters" [11:1]); fear God (12:13, perhaps from the hand of a later editor).

III. Job and the question of theodicy.

A. Robert Gordis states, "There is not, nor can there be, universal agreement on such major issues as the structure, the unity, and the basic meaning of the book, or even on such relatively minor questions as its style, date, and origin."

1. Perhaps the book offers less a solution to the problem of suffering than an opportunity for readers to engage the question.
2. Various appropriations include Goethe's *Faust*; MacLeish's *JB*; H. G. Wells's *The Undying Fire*; and Heinlein's *Job, A Comedy*.

B. Job's character.

1. The traditional interpretation, premised on the prose frame, views Job as an ideal figure who continually engages in pious action; accepts the loss of his property and the death of his children with faithful resignation; refuses to follow his wife's advice, "Curse God and die"; repents of any possible doubt; and submits before divine majesty.
2. A variant view makes Job an existentialist "everyman" demanding meaning from a chaotic world. Appropriately, this Job is not Jewish or Israelite (he descends from Esau). This is the Job of G.K. Chesterton: "The *Iliad* is great because all life is a battle; the *Odyssey* is great because all life is a journey; the Book of Job is great because all life is a riddle."
3. Some see the book as a satire depicting a hypocritical protagonist who confirms the Satan's accusations (pious when rewarded; argumentative when his life is destroyed; pious again when the opportunity of restoration is presented) and a tyrannical, unstable God who demands worship as a form of extortion.
4. Perhaps Job is a realist who is sure only of his righteousness but recognizes that the world lacks justice. This is the Job who tells God: "I know you can do all things…" but, so knowing, pities humanity: "I mourn in dust and ashes" (42:2–3).
5. There may be mutually exclusive Jobs: one from the prologue and one from the poem, with the epilogue fitting both.

C. The prosaic Job remains faithful.

1. "Then Job arose, and rent his robe, and shaved his head, and fell on the ground, and worshiped. And he said, 'Naked came I from my mother's womb, and naked I shall return. The Lord gave, and the Lord has taken

away; blessed be the name of the Lord.' In all this, Job did not sin, or charge God with wrong" (1:20).

2. The poetic Job bewails his fate, curses the Deity (e.g., 16:11), curses his birth, and longs for his death (from the opening line).

D. How are we to understand God, who permits Job's suffering, then condemns Job's friends for defending traditional theology in insisting on a correlation between faith and fate?

1. Eliphaz appeals to mystical visions (4, 15) and describes suffering as a form of discipline and a mark of divine love (5).
2. Eliphaz also echoes the Deuteronomic view that "the sins of the fathers are visited upon the sons" (22) and bolsters it with appeal to the corporate community's mutual responsibility.
3. Bildad, invoking traditional wisdom (8), and Zophar, appealing to esoteric wisdom (11), recapitulate Eliphaz's arguments.
4. Elihu adds that suffering serves to deter sin (33, 36), such as pride.
5. Does God favor Job because he speaks from experience rather than theory?
6. Or is the Deity simply arbitrary?

E. Complicating interpretation are the whirlwind speeches (38:1–40:5; 40:6–41:34).

1. Does the whirlwind indicate that God is unknowable, yet operating purposefully? "Where were you when I laid the foundations of the earth, tell me, if you have understanding. Who determined its measurements, surely you know" (38:4).
2. Might the point be less what is said but the theophany itself, that the divine is not indifferent (42:5: "I have heard of you by the hearing of the ear, but now my eye sees you")?
3. Or is it all just sound and fury?

F. Text critical and translation issues.

1. Job 13:15 yields three mutually exclusive translations:

KJV: "Though he slay me, yet I will trust him."
RSV: "Behold he will slay me, I have no hope."

Anchor Bible: "He may slay me, I'll not quaver."

2. Job 19:25 traditionally reads, "For I know that my redeemer lives…," but the translation is uncertain.

Supplementary Reading:

Marcia Falk, *Love Lyrics from the Bible, The Song of Songs: A New Translation and Interpretation* (San Francisco: HarperCollins, 1990).

Roland E. Murphy, *The Tree of Life: An Exploration of Biblical Wisdom Literature* (New York: Doubleday, 1990).

Questions to Consider:

1. Why would ancient Israel canonize pessimistic wisdom, such as Ecclesiastes and Job?
2. Is the God of Job the God of the *Akedah*? Of Jephthah? Of Saul?
3. How does the scribe, responsible for wisdom, relate to king, priest, and prophet?

Lecture Twenty-Two—Transcript
Wisdom Literature
(Song of Songs, Proverbs, Ecclesiastes, Job)

We've seen in the post-exilic period a certain ambivalence regarding the Gentile nations. On the one hand we have Ezra and Nehemiah insisting that Jewish men divorce their foreign wives, and on the other we have books like Ruth and Jonah suggesting that Gentiles might actually repent and contribute enormously to the ongoing life of the covenant community. The ambivalence shows up in particular in the prophetic tradition and then in the priestly tradition.

But when we look at the wisdom tradition to which we are turning in this lecture, we find an amazing influence by and indeed respect for the international community, the international wisdom community. We've already seen this earlier in discussions of Solomon's court, where people from the nations would come to experience the wisdom that he himself promulgated and the wisdom of the other people he brought into his court. That's why the Queen of Sheba came to visit him.

Wisdom literature itself is an international phenomenon. We have, from the fourth millennium B.C.E., from the kingdom of Sumer, a theodicy, a document that describes why bad things happen to good people, why the wicked prosper, why the innocent suffer. The question is as old as humankind, I suspect. From Babylon itself there is a text called the "Babylonian Theodicy." This question is not unique to Israel, and, indeed, when we go over to Greece we find Cynics making aphorisms, questions, and couplets trying to describe why the world is the way it is. Why does sometimes nature aid us and why does sometimes nature kill us?

Various genres can raise the question and, indeed, provide some answers to this issue of theodicy. Scientific treatises might tell us why nature functions the way it does. New discoveries in neurology or psychiatry might explain why some people are good and some people are sociopathic. Poetry can explain or at least explore some of these questions that we simply cannot answer fully by rational means, and it's a combination of poetry and the wisdom literature as genre within which the Bible, especially, raises some of these questions.

Biblical contributions to wisdom literature take a variety of forms. We have the relatively upbeat Book of Proverbs, which is primarily instruction to young men on how to get along in life: what to do, what not to do, whom to follow, whom not to follow. We also have the somewhat depressing book of Ecclesiastes, also called Qoheleth, for whom the world is just set. "There is nothing new under the sun," as he puts it, and he provides basic information like, "Eat, drink, and be merry, because that's just the way the world is." With it we also have the Book of Job, and on that we will concentrate in this lecture.

But first I want to give a little bit of a foretaste of some of this other wisdom literature that the Bible has. I also want to bring in one other text that I don't really have an opportunity to discuss. I'm stuck with only 24 lectures; I need at least 48 to cover this text. That's a text called the Song of Solomon. It's not really wisdom literature, it's love poetry, but it is attributed to King Solomon, and therefore I feel more or less legitimate that I can slide it into the wisdom school. So let's just stop for just a bit and take a look at this wonderful text.

It's a collection of poems, independent poems spoken first by a woman, then a man, back and forth and back and forth. They rejoice in the joys of each other's body. They rejoice in the idea of physical love, and, indeed, it's not even clear that they are married. Tradition suggests that the man is Solomon and the woman perhaps a member of his court. Later legend suggests the woman might actually be the Queen of Sheba. This text is, in fact, at home in the Bible. We often think of biblical literature as holy and, indeed, holier than the rest of us. It's to be up there on a pedestal somewhere, and we can revere it but we can't really wrestle with it. Song of Songs is there to be enjoyed. Its overt sensuality compliments the earthiness that we found in some of the stories in Genesis and certainly in Judges, if we think of Ehud and Deborah. Its powerful woman's voice recollects the Song of Hannah, the Song of Deborah, Ruth, and Miriam crossing the sea.

The Song is clearly erotic. We can see it right at the beginning: "Let him kiss me with the kisses of his mouth, for your love is better than wine." The poem gets increasingly passionate and indeed increasingly graphic. Lest there are people here under 18 listening to this tape, I will not read aloud for you Chapter 5, verses 4 to 5, but I encourage you on your own to take a look. Under Hellenistic influence, after 333, when Alexander the Great came through and

Jews suddenly found themselves part of the Greek empire, and later on as people began to speculate about this text, the idea that this was love poetry didn't settle quite so well. In the Jewish tradition, by the first century of the Common Era, certainly by the beginning of the second century, this text is looked at as an allegory of the love between God and Israel. In the church, similarly, it becomes an allegory of the love for Christ and the church. That doesn't keep it from being love poetry, but it makes it a little bit safer to be recited in churches and synagogues.

Indeed, today some scholars have gone over this poetry and thought that perhaps it's not just erotic love poetry. Some even consider it to be comedy. There is this wonderful line in Chapter 4 where the man is describing his ladylove. He says, "Your hair is like a flock of goats streaming down Mt. Gilead." The problem is, if you actually watch goats going down a mountain, they tend to go one by one by one. This woman's hair is not overly thick if this is, in fact, a line of parody rather than a line of compliment. Others, particularly feminist scholars, have seen this text as a man's fantasy because the woman is so in love that she actually risks censure by people in the community. She actually puts her own life at risk by being able to follow her man and hoping to do so.

Finally, the Song gives rise to controversy in translation. We've already seen some difficulties in translation regarding text criticism where the Greek and the Hebrew disagree, for example. Here the Hebrew was abundantly clear; the issue is how to translate it. It's part of the opening chapter which had until the past two or three decades frequently been read, "I am black but beautiful," with the idea being that this woman has been out in the sun, she's been darkened by the sun, and the standard of beauty in antiquity, at least for this poem, is that one be fair skinned. I think about *Gone with the Wind* with southern belles walking outside with umbrellas lest they get a single freckle.

Given concerns today for inclusive language and multiculturalism, it's becoming increasingly common in scholarship as well as in formal productions of the Bible to translate, "I am black and beautiful," as if those terms are not mutually exclusive. The Hebrew can bear either translation. How you translate this becomes up to you. But recognize that translation carries more than simply historical meaning. Translation very much can affect the reader, and one can notice the negative effects that that earlier translation had on a good many people who read this text.

Moving on to our actual example of wisdom literature, we start with Proverbs. We've already had some hints of the type of techniques wisdom literature has—for example, enumerations. We've heard this in the prophets: "For three transgressions and for four" or examples from the natural world: "Does a lion roar unless it has found a prey?" Indeed, rhetorical questions, and that's the type of form we find in Proverbs. But Proverbs actually goes on beyond this type of secular protocol and beyond simple exhortations to people on how to behave.

The unique biblical contribution to wisdom literature that Proverbs provides is a concern not only that "the fear of the Lord is the beginning of wisdom," in other words, if you don't have faith, wisdom is for naught—that's already in Chapter 1—but also a focus on a figure called Sophia in Greek, *Hochma* in Hebrew, or in English typically referred to as "Lady Wisdom." We have in Proverbs a father exhorting his son, "Get wisdom. Get insight," but this wisdom is personified as female. "Do not forsake her; she will keep you. Love her, and she will guard you. Prize her highly; she will exalt you. She will honor you if you embrace her." It's as if wisdom, hypostatically, is standing there right in front of him. "She will place on your head a fair garland." This is how to win the race—you go for wisdom. "And she will bestow on you a beautiful crown." This is how you become royal—you gain wisdom.

Proverbs thus encourages its male readers to cleave to Lady Wisdom. She's better than any possible real woman could be. She's totally faithful. She's the wife behind the successful man, as it were. She's the ideal lover, the ideal spouse, and, like the woman in the Song of Songs, she actually pursues her man—here not for physical delights but for metaphorical ones. This is Lady Wisdom's description: "Wisdom has built her house. She has hewn her seven pillars." So if you've heard about the seven pillars of wisdom, it comes from the Book of Proverbs. "She has slaughtered her animals. She has mixed her wine. She has also set out her table [because wisdom is a banquet at which anyone can feast]. She has sent out her servant girl. She calls from the highest places in town [public announcement]. You that are simple, turn in here. To those without sense, she says, 'Come eat my bread and drink the wine I have mixed.'" Her call is irresistible. If you want to succeed, if you want to love God, if you want to know what God wants from you, follow Lady Wisdom.

But be careful because Lady Wisdom has a counterpart who is often referred to as "the strange woman" or "the foreign woman" or sometimes simply "Dame Folly," often conveyed in this text as an adulterous wife, and her path leads not to life but to death. If you listen to the words of Dame Folly and follow her, you will go in the opposite direction from which Lady Wisdom would lead you. This is Dame Folly—she too calls out, says the Book of Wisdom: "You who are simple, turn in here. And to you without sense she says, 'Stolen water is sweet, and bread eaten in secret is pleasant.' But they do not know," says the author, "that the dead are there with Dame Folly and that her guests are in the depths of Sheol." They are in hell.

So here the young man in Judean civilization, Israelite civilization, has a choice. Do you follow Lady Wisdom, or do you follow her counterpart? This is what my children would refer to as a no-brainer. Of course you go with Lady Wisdom; but watch out, because graphically Proverbs will describe the negative results if you don't follow Wisdom but if you follow Dame Folly.

This idea of the hypostatic wisdom, wisdom personified as a woman, develops in the Old Testament Apocrypha, the deuterocanonical materials such as the wisdom of Jesus ben Sirach, also called Ecclesiasticus, and the wisdom of Solomon. The figure of wisdom becomes so developed that she becomes almost like a goddess. The tradition eventually develops in Judaism to the idea of the *Shekinah*, the feminine presence of God, and it actually underlies the description of the Logos. The term is a masculine term, but the Logos in early Christianity, the Logos who in the Gospel of John was with God at the beginning of time, has as characteristics the descriptions of Lady Wisdom from the earlier material. So wisdom speculation will continue on in both church and synagogue.

The next wisdom text we can look at is the Book of Ecclesiastes, also known as Qoheleth. If we think of Song of Songs as a text written by Solomon in his youth and Proverbs as a text written during middle age, Ecclesiastes is typically ascribed to Solomon at the end of his life when he's dealt with everything that can be. He's seen all that there is. He's been through his 300 wives and his 700 concubines, and he's done his international relations, and there is nothing left to amuse him. There is nothing left much at all. This is a text of ennui. I don't think Solomon wrote it, but I can understand the ascription.

This text contains an exceptionally pessimistic view of life—not that life is terrible but there is just not that much new to appreciate. "Vanity of vanities. All is vanity," a phrase you are probably familiar with, comes from Chapter 12 of Ecclesiastes. Another translation is, "Everything is futility. There is no point." Chapter 1, verse 9, does, in fact, suggest "There is nothing new under the sun." So, with a world like that, what does one do simply to get up the next morning? There are some hints here: "Eat, drink and be merry," which is a summary of Chapter 9, verse 7. "Rejoice in your youth." If you've got energy and you've got strength, enjoy it because indeed it's sort of downhill from there. I don't really think so, but that is what the text suggests. The text also suggests that, "Everything has a season," and one can either look at that in a pessimistic way—Oh, it's winter again—or one can look at it in a helpful way: To everything there is a season, a time to be born, a time to die; the world can function in an appropriate and, indeed, ordered way.

So unlike the Book of Job, as we'll see, where the world is chaotic and that causes obvious distress for Job, here in Ecclesiastes perhaps the problem is the world's too ordered. The nice thing about the biblical canon is we can read one text next to the other, so if one particular worldview becomes too much for us there is an alternative there. As I mentioned very early on in this series, this Bible does not always give us answers. It raises questions, and it provides us different resources once we can find those answers.

For people interested in economics, this particular text of Ecclesiastes provides us some business advice. You've probably heard the expression, "Cast your bread upon the waters." What that actually means is send out your grain overseas in hope of a profitable return. It's not simply giving breadcrumbs to ducks. It's a good economic view. Some commentators suggest that Ecclesiastes was edited by a more upbeat, more optimistic final redactor because there are various spots in this book that suggest that things are really okay in the end and God loves us, which is probably true. Whether that happy material is also from the original author who himself, or even herself, simply couldn't make up his mind/her mind as to how the world functions, or whether it comes from someone else, it allows us to read Ecclesiastes either as simply a document of pessimism or as a document of world knowledge coupled with both experience and a little bit of hope. One might say, "Been there; done that," but one might also say, "You know, the world progressed the way it should have progressed and, indeed, eat, drink, and be merry because it is a pretty good world after all." How you read this text is actually up to you, and that's basically the advice for Job. How you read it is up to you.

Biblical scholar Robert Gordis, who has written some excellent material on Job, said the following, "There is not nor can there be universal agreement on such major issues as the structure, the unity, and the basic meaning of the book or even on such relatively minor questions as its style, its date, and its origin." Job is simply out there as a mystery both in terms of origin and in terms of interpretation. Sometimes I think that this book less offers a solution to the problem of suffering, to the question of theodicy, than an opportunity for readers to engage the question.

If one thinks about the Bible as a text that is simply up there giving us God's word, then Job does not function well for us. Job, rather, gives us permission to question everything else that's in that text, to go back to the Book of Deuteronomy, which says, "The good prosper and the wicked suffer," and say, "Well, maybe not." I can raise questions to this. I can question my life in the world. I can question the justice of God. Indeed, numerous authors in various cultures and times have raised precisely these questions influenced by the Book of Job, from Goethe's *Faust*; which has a Joban background, to Archibald MacLeish's *JB*. H. G. Wells raised the question in *The Undying Fire;* Heinlein more recently wrote a book called *Job, A Comedy*. Plays, poems, operas, novels—people are still wrestling with Job, and I suspect they are never going to find an answer that will suit everyone.

Job's character poses us the first problem because the character, in fact, differs as we move from the prose or, in fact, prosaic opening to the poem in the middle and then to the prose conclusion, the prose epilogue. The traditional interpretation of Job is premised on the prose frame, and it views Job as an ideal figure who engages in pious action. He is religious, he's good, he loves God, and he accepts the loss first of his property and then the death of all of his children with a faithful resignation. His wife says to him, "Curse God and die."

The Hebrew, by the way, actually says, "Bless God," but that's simply a euphemism. We know what she is saying.

This is a Job who has no doubt, and he submits himself before divine majesty. He's the moral exemplar. A variant view of this makes Job an everyman, an everyman who desires meaning from life. It's this existential quest. This is a Job who is not specifically Jewish; he's anyone. Indeed, we find out at the beginning that Job is from the land of Uz, and Uz, as we know from Genesis, is one of the descendants of Esau. Job may well be an Edomite. He's not a Jew; he can be everyone. This is the Job of G. K. Chesterton, who said about the book, "The *Iliad* is great because all of life is a battle. The *Odyssey* is great because all of life is a journey. And the Book of Job is great because all of life is a riddle." He doesn't, however, provide us an answer to this.

In this sense Job might be a mirror of our own lives: We can't make sense of it, but we simply struggle through, muddle through, and do the best we can. I am attracted to, although I am not convinced by, the argument that Job is a satire depicting a hypocritical or at least practical protagonist who confirms the Satan's accusations at the beginning. This is a text, perhaps, that says, "Well, you know what? God is sort of arbitrary, but if you behave yourself for the most part, you will succeed, and if you are wicked at the end God will punish you." This is a Job who finally says, "Well, God's is the only game in town, and I'm going to play it." It's a Job who realizes that God's power is much more than anything he can bear. He is simply going to submit because that's all, in fact, he can do—cynical, satirical, and depressing.

Or perhaps Job is simply a realist. He is sure of his righteousness. He knows he hasn't done anything wrong, but he also recognizes that the world lacks justice. This is perhaps the Job who tells God at the end, "I know you can do all things" but then so knowing, in fact, winds up pitying humankind. This depends upon how you want to read the line, "I mourn in dust and ashes." Is Job repenting from what he does not know about God's greatness, or is Job mourning because he recognizes that humankind has to deal with a God who is not on call, with a God who permits evil to exist in the world, with a God who will sometimes respond positively and sometimes negatively? This is the God of Cain and Abel. We never know when God will act positively or when God will cause us to suffer. These may be several mutually exclusively Jobs: one from the prologue, one from the poetry, one from the epilogue. They are all a possibility.

Let's go back to the prosaic Job at the beginning. Job has just been bereft of everything, and, in total equanimity, totally sanguine, Job responds, "Naked came I from my mother's womb and naked I shall return. The Lord gave; the Lord has taken away. Blessed be the name of the Lord," and the narrator adds, "In all this Job did not sin or charge God with wrong." On the other hand, as soon as we get to the poem, Job curses his fate, argues against God, assaults God, curses his birth, and longs for his death, and that's in the opening couple of verses. The first line of the poetry reads as follows, after this: after Job's entire household/family has been killed, Job's body has been besieged with boils, and he's sitting on a dung heap. You can't get any lower than this. The poem says, "Why did I not die at birth, come forth from the womb and expire? Why were there knees to receive me or breasts for me to suck? Now I would simply lie down and be quiet. I would be asleep and then I would be at rest." This is a man who not only longs for death but wishes he had never been born in the first place. This is not, "Naked came I from my mother's womb." This is a guy who is suffering, and the emotion that he feels is palpable. For the Job of the poem, death would be a comfort, and it would remove him from the tortures that God places upon him.

Worse, contributing to Job's anguish are his three so-called friends. They are called friends at the beginning. By the time we get toward the end of the poem they are simply called men. They are ostensibly there to comfort and console him (that's Chapter 2), and what they wind up doing is giving him the old tried and true answers to the question of theodicy. They explain to him, "Well, you know, Job, how we're supposed to understand God." I'll give you those in a minute, but notice at the end that, after the friends, after three rounds of discussion, give Job the tried and true answers, God winds up condemning the friends and blessing Job. So I'm still worrying about what to do with God.

Eliphaz, the first friend, appeals to mystical visions and describes suffering as a form of discipline and a mark of divine love, so he says, for example, "Happy is the one whom God reproves. Therefore, do not despise the discipline of the Almighty." That's Chapter 5, Verse 17. Discipline is one thing. Having your entire family killed and being reduced to an itchy, scratchy boil-filled person sitting on a dung heap is a little bit more than simple discipline. Job's not going to buy that one. He's hardly in a position to be happy based on God's reproof.

Eliphaz also echoes the Deuteronomic view that punishment comes from evil, and so he condemns Job. If Job is suffering, therefore Job must have done something wrong. He says, "Is it for your piety that God reproves you and enters into judgment with you? Is not your wickedness great? There is no end to your inequities." You know, with friends like this. . . But Job knows he's been righteous, so he simply can't respond, "Oh yes, I've been wicked. I'm sorry." Eliphaz concludes that Job should repent. He says, "If you return to the Almighty, you will be restored. If you remove the unrighteousness from your tents." But from what could Job possibly repent? He hasn't—at least as far as he knows and we as readers know—done anything wrong.

Bildad, the second friend, evokes traditional wisdom. He says, and good old rhetorical questions here, "Does God pervert justice? Does the Almighty pervert the right?" The problem with rhetorical questions is that you don't always get the answer you might have thought, and although Job does not answer directly to these questions, one can imagine what he's thinking: "Yes, justice here has been perverted. Yes, the right has been perverted." Bildad also continues, "How then can a mortal be righteous before God? How can one born of women be pure?" It's not normally in the Bible the anthropological view that we are simply wallowing in sin. That's not the way the Old Testament, the *Tanakh*, looks at humankind.

But even if one looks at human beings as somehow flawed, and indeed we are—that's why we have things like the Torah to keep us on the right path and means of atonement in case we mess up—it is one thing to say, "Well, we're all not particularly righteous." It's something else for Job to look at his own situation. Indeed, if one looks at Bildad's question from Job's perspective, Job might just as well say to Bildad, "Well, how come you're not here on the dung heap with me? If everyone lacks righteousness, why am I suffering and why are you doing quite well?"

Zophar, the third friend, appeals to esoteric wisdom. "Can you find the deep things of God? Can you find out the limits of the Almighty? It is higher than the height of heaven. What can you do? It is deeper than the pit of Sheol. What can you know?" In other words, "Job, God has a rationale here. God's wisdom so surpasses anything that humans can know that there is a reason for your suffering. Hold tight—eventually you'll know what that reason is." But this does Job little good. It's fine to be told there is a rationale to the universe and God has infinite wisdom, but that's not going to help Job, given his present circumstances. I also wonder if this particular friend Zophar actually knows all those mysteries himself. It sounds good, but does he really grasp the mysteries of the universe?

There is a fourth friend, this young man, Elihu, who some people think was added on by a later editor. He, for the most part, repeats what the other friends have said, but he doesn't begin the same way. We're told that the three friends had come to Job to comfort and console. Not Elihu. He's identified as a young man who is very angry not only at Job but at the three friends. He is angry at Job because Job has justified himself rather than God. Job is saying, "God, I am in the right; you're in the wrong," and Elihu says, "No, no, no. We simply can't have that. That's not good religion." He's also angry at the friends "because they had found no answer though they had declared Job to be in the wrong." He wants those friends to provide an answer that's going to convince Job that God is right and that Job has somehow sinned and that Job has misjudged God.

Elihu recaps the arguments made by the friends: God is just, God chastises with pain and punishment, and Job's situation is clearly that he has sinned. Elihu goes on for several chapters doing this (the enthusiasm of youth). He also adds that suffering serves to deter sin such as pride. And that may well be part of Job's problem. He is a somewhat prideful man. But on the other hand, we haven't been told he did anything wrong yet. Ultimately all these views are rejected. The Lord says to Eliphaz the Temanite, "My wrath is kindled against you and against your two friends, for you have not spoken of me what is right as my servant Job has." But Job has been the one who has been kvetching and complaining all the way through. Eliphaz is told to offer a sacrifice and to have Job pray for him and his fellows, which Job is happy to do once he's off the dung heap.

Then I wonder, why does God finally favor Job? Because he speaks from experience, perhaps, rather than from theory? Or is God simply arbitrary? Or do we have to separate the poetry from the prose? Are they simply two different stories that don't sit well together?

Complicating all of this are God's speeches to Job from the whirlwind. We've seen theophanies before—Elijah hearing the stillness, that still small voice on Mt. Horab, and Moses getting the law on Mt. Sinai—but we have not seen theophanies like this. Job asks for an ordered court. He says, "Would he plead against me with his great power?" No, says Job, "He would put strength in me. There the righteous would dispute with him." In other words, Job is asking for an orderly response. He wants a court of justice. He gets a whirlwind. Does the whirlwind indicate God's unknowability? "Were you there when I laid the foundations of the earth?" asks God. "Tell me, if you have any understanding, who determined its measurement? Surely you know?" Or is there an order to existence we fail to recognize, just as beasts in nature can eat their young but there is an order and indeed a beauty there? Might the point be less what is said than the fact that God responds at all, that there is a response?

If we think we've got a handle on this text, Job 13, verse 15, gives us four different ways of viewing it. The King James Version says, "Though he slay me, yet I will trust him." The Revised Standard Version, "Behold, he will slay me; I have no hope." The Anchor Bible, "He may slay me; I'll not quaver." The Revised English Bible, "If he wishes to slay me, I have nothing to lose." From the poetry to the prose there are no easy answers.

The easiest figure that we can grasp in this text happens to be the Satan, the accuser, and in the next lecture we'll begin with the Satan, the accuser, to find out how he affects Israelite theology. Then we'll move on to tales of Jews in the Diaspora.

Lecture Twenty-Three

Life in the Diaspora (Genesis 30, 37–50; Esther; Daniel 1–6)

Scope:

The Babylonian exile gave rise to the *diaspora*, the "dispersion" of the Judeans now known as "Jews" to places outside their homeland. As the eastern diaspora became a major center of Jewish life, new questions of self-definition arose: To what extent should community members acculturate themselves to Persian or Greek thought and practice, and what traditions would preserve their identity? To address these issues, we explore how the "court tales" of Esther and Daniel 1–6, through a combination of the humorous and the macabre, provide answers. We conclude with comparisons to earlier court stories, those of Joseph and Moses. But we begin with a brief note on how the "accuser" of Job develops into the demonic "Satan" as the Jewish community continues to come into contact with other nations, and, as we shall see in our final lecture, as it advances the genre of apocalyptic.

Outline

I. The least controversial figure in Job is *ha-satan*, "the accuser."

- **A.** In Zechariah, as in Job, *the* Satan ("the accuser") is the heavenly prosecuting agent whose task is to weed out evil and hypocrisy.
- **B.** Isa. 14:12–15 contributes to the mythic development: "How you are fallen from heaven, O day star, son of Dawn…You who said in your heart, 'I will ascend to heaven above the stars of God…I will make myself like the most high…' But you are brought down to Sheol, to the depths of the pit."
  1. Ugaritic texts speak of Shahar, god of Dawn, and his son Helal, Morning Star. Isaiah identifies the Babylonian king with Canaanite gods.
  2. "Day star" or "light bringer" is, in Latin, Lucifer.

II. The "tales of the diaspora" present as heroes figures representing the wisdom tradition: Daniel and Mordecai. It is to the Books of Daniel and Esther, and to a discussion of Jewish life outside Israel, we next turn.

III. The Book of Esther.

A. Dating.

1. Esther may well have taken shape during the Persian period. However, even if King Ahasueros is to be associated with Xerxes I, there is no external record of his having a Jewish queen or prime minister.

2. Esther exists in Hebrew as well as two Greek versions. The LXX version (the Deuterocanonical text [Old Testament Apocrypha]) has six major additions that give the story an overt religious component: the mention of God over fifty times, an explicit distaste for intermarriage (cf. Ezra and Nehemiah), concern for dietary regulations, and so on. Compounding the difficulties of determining an "original" story is the absence of Esther from Qumran.

B. The "rival wife" type scene.

1. In a variant of the convention, the Book of Esther offers rival wives (Sarah and Hagar, Rachel and Leah, Hannah and Peninnah), but the rivalry is presented through behavioral differences rather than through personal conflict: Esther only appears, can only appear, after Vashti is dismissed.

2. Vashti refuses the king's order to appear at his banquet.

3. Vashti refuses to leave her own banquet to attend the king (her rationale—disgust at being an object of display for drunken men, involvement with her own party, mean-spiritedness—is never explained). Vashti's refusal prompts a law that "all women will give honor to their husbands, high and low alike" (1:20).

4. Vashti's refusal results in a law mandating her banishment, i.e., Ahasueros writes into law the confirmation of her refusal.

C. The dangers of life in the diaspora.

1. Ahasueros is less malevolent than inept: He holds a banquet for "all his officials and ministers, the army of Persia and Media and the nobles and governors of the provinces," the entire infrastructure of the empire, for six months. He is almost always drinking or drunk. He chooses a bride not for political alliance but on the basis of a "beauty" contest in which each candidate spends a year marinating in myrrh, followed by one night with the king.

2. From this contest, he decides to marry Esther, even though he knows nothing of her background. "Esther did not reveal her people or kindred, for Mordecai had charged her not to tell" (2:10). Yet Mordecai insists such silence will not, ultimately, help (Est. 4:13).
3. The danger to the Jews comes first from Haman, the prime minister, whose hatred of Mordecai, Esther's uncle or cousin, extends to all Jews, then from those people in the empire who are willing to carry out the genocidal decree. The enmity between Haman and Mordecai may even have been predicted: Mordecai is a Benjaminite, as was Saul (Est. 2:5; 1 Sam. 9:1; each is explicitly identified as the "son of Kish"). Haman is an Agagite (Est. 9:24), and Saul's sparing of Agag and his taking of booty contribute to his tragedy (1 Sam. 15).
4. Esther does save her people. She, unlike Vashti, comes unbidden to the king. Further, she invites her husband to a banquet in which she manages to place Haman in a compromising position. He is then hanged on the gallows he erected for Mordecai.
5. The book consequently suggests that diaspora communities need to be aware that they may suddenly find themselves no longer welcome in the land they have made their home (one recollects the Exodus), and that even if the authorities wish to protect them, the local population may not.

D. The dangers of the Book of Esther.

1. By king's command and Esther's instruction, "The Jews struck down all their enemies with the sword, slaughtering and destroying them, and did as they pleased to those who hated them. In the citadel city of Susa the Jews killed and destroyed five-hundred people" (9:5–6). "The other Jews who were in the king's provinces also gathered to defend their lives, and gained relief from their enemies, and killed seventy-five thousand of those who hated them; but they laid no hands on the plunder" (9:16).

2. Although the desire to strike back at enemies and to rid the world of anti-Semitism is understandable, is holy war commendable (booty was not taken)?
3. Better is the way that the Book of Esther insists one celebrate the holiday of Purim—the date picked by Haman for the slaughter of the Jews, then hailed as a time of redemption: with "feasting and gladness [and] sending gifts of food to one another and to the poor" (9:22) and with "peace and security" (9:30).

IV. Daniel 1–6.

A. The earliest reference to a Daniel (Dan'el) is that of a Ugaritic king who lived in the fourteenth century B.C.E.

B. Ezek. 14:14 associates "Danel" with Noah and Job: three (gentile?) individuals known for wisdom. According to Ezek. 28:3, "Danel" knows secrets.

C. Dan. 1:1 dates the story to the "third year of the reign of King Jehoiakim" or 606 B.C.E. (2 Chr. 36:5–7). Jehoiakim's son, Jehoiachin, ruled when Jerusalem was captured in 587. Nebuchadnezzar reigned from 605 to 552 B.C.E. but did not invade Judah until after 605. Such chronological problems are typical of folktales.

D. The accounts of Daniel and the other Jewish youths taken into captivity reflect a time in which the imperial rule is ignorant and dangerous, rather than malevolent, and in which diaspora Jews live in peace, if not with a complete sense of security (contrasting Dan. 7–12, as we see in the next lecture). Consequently, the tales are most often regarded as products of the Persian (538–333 B.C.E.) or early Hellenistic (333–168 B.C.E.) periods.

E. Dan. 2.4b–7.28 is written in Aramaic, the common language of the Near East from the Babylonian exile until the incursion of Hellenism; Dan. 1, 8–12 are in Hebrew, which had become a liturgical language in the Second Temple period.

F. Complicating the linguistic history are the Septuagint and Old Greek versions, which contain additions to the Daniel cycle: the Book of Susanna, the Prayer of Azariah and the Song of the Three, and Bel and the Dragon (all three appear in the Old Testament Apocrypha). Still more books in the corpus were found among documents discovered in 1948 at

Qumran, the so-called "Dead Sea Scrolls." One, the Prayer of Nabonidus (4QprNab), may be an earlier version of Daniel 4.

G. Daniel raises many questions of special concern to those Jews living under foreign rule: Should we eat non-kosher food? Should idols be worshipped? Should one cease to pray to God according to royal decree?

V. The Jew in the foreign court.

A. Joseph is sold by his brothers into Egyptian slavery; Moses is born in Egypt and compelled by God to return; Daniel is taken into Babylonian captivity; Esther is brought to court as part of a beauty pageant. The Jews find themselves in foreign courts not of their own volition, but on arriving, they make the best of their circumstances: Joseph gains charge of Egypt (Gen. 41:37–45); Moses bests Pharaoh; Esther becomes queen and Mordecai, the prime minister (Est. 8:1–2); Daniel is "made ruler" (2:48).

B. All four cases present matters of the utmost seriousness: Joseph saves Egypt and his family from famine; Moses saves his people from death and slavery; Daniel's own life is continually threatened; and Esther saves her people from genocide.

C. Variations in the role of God also inform these stories: Joseph receives divine aid in all that he does, and he makes explicit that his ability to interpret dreams comes from God (Gen. 40:8; 41:16). Moses receives divine aid but must be prompted. Daniel, like Joseph, succeeds in service to the ruler through his God-given ability to interpret dreams, as well as to tell the content of them before the interpretation (Dan. 2:19–23). The Book of Esther does not mention the Deity.

VI. Developments of the genre.

A. The additions to Esther feature highly symbolic dreams that give cosmic import to the story. As the Book of Daniel continues, the hero is no longer the interpreter of dreams but one in need of interpretation of his own visions.

B. The changes mark a shift from folktale to apocalyptic literature, the subject of the final lecture.

Supplementary Reading:

Danna Nolan Fewell, *Circle of Sovereignty: A Story of Stories in Daniel 1–6* (Sheffield: Almond Press, 1988).

Michael Fox, *Character and Ideology in the Book of Esther* (Columbia, SC: University of South Carolina Press, 1991).

W. Lee Humphries, *Joseph and His Family: A Literary Study* (Columbia, SC: University of South Carolina Press, 1988).

James L Kugel, *In Potiphar's House: The Interpretive Life of Biblical Texts* (San Francisco: HarperCollins, 1990).

Lawrence Wills, *The Jew in the Court of the Foreign King: Ancient Jewish Court Legends* (Minneapolis, MN: Fortress Press, 1990).

Questions to Consider:

1. Can one distinguish between a historical event presented in folktale style and a folktale that purports to describe a historical event?
2. What circumstances, if any, might warrant the violence described in the Book of Esther?
3. Why were Esther and Daniel the only Hebrew narratives expanded in the LXX?
4. What is the theology of Esther?

Lecture Twenty-Three—Transcript
Life in the Diaspora
(Genesis 30, 37-50; Esther; Daniel 1-6)

From Proverbs to Ecclesiastes to Job, we've already seen the international concerns of wisdom literature. Since the questions these texts raise, from how to live the good life, to what's the point of living at all, to where is the justice in the world, are international questions, they are certainly not unique to the covenant community. These international concerns also influence much else of the covenant community's literature, its interpretation, and even its setting. In terms of interpretation, we'll begin this talk with just a brief comment or two about the development of the legend of Satan. We've already seen the accuser in Zechariah. We've met him in Job. But it's from international connections moving even from Hebrew into Latin that Satan comes to be the figure we know and worry about today.

Then we'll move on to some of the "court tales," questions about Jews in courts of foreign kings, with a focus on Esther, and then a look at Daniel to talk about how Israel dealt with its role as part of a global world, part of the Persian empire, later part of the Greek empire. This is not a community that exists in a vacuum.

So we'll start here with Satan. In Zechariah and in Job, Satan is simply *ha,* "the," *satan*, "the accuser." If you remember the old Perry Mason movies, this is Hamilton Berger, the person who doesn't often win but always brings a case against somebody who is typically innocent. Here *ha-satan* in Zechariah will bring a case against the high priest Joshua. In Job, the case is against Job, the righteous. Developing the imagery of Satan requires flitting through various parts of the Bible. When we look at the prophet Isaiah, we find in Chapter 14 the following: "How you are fallen from heaven, O day star, son of dawn . . . You who said in your heart, 'I will ascend to heaven above the stars of God . . . I will make myself like the Most High . . .' But you are brought down to Sheol, to the depths of the pit."

Ugaritic texts speak of Shahar, the god of dawn, and his son, Helal, the morning star. What Isaiah is actually talking about are Babylonian kings and Canaanite gods. These are political statements talking about the fall of those nations who have oppressed the covenant community. When this text is translated into Latin, we begin to see the development of satanic speculation. If we take the term "day star," which can also be read as "light bringer," and we bring that into Latin, we get "Lucifer," and that's where we start finding the development of Satan materials.

By the early Hellenistic periods, second to third centuries of B.C.E., after the time of Alexander the Great, as Israel comes in contact with Greek thought and Greek gods, the idea of evil gods then starts to influence the covenant community's view of its own theology, and satanic concerns begin to develop. We don't find them in the Old Testament materials, but we do find them well played out in the New.

As we move to other examples of international literature, translation, and concern, we find ourselves addressing the question, what is life like in the Diaspora, where people might not speak our language, where they are no longer speaking Hebrew but perhaps Persian or Greek? Where Hebrews, Jews, come into contact with people who don't share their values, indeed, don't even understand their values? We're talking here about something called the Diaspora. The term actually comes from a Greek word meaning "dispersion."

From the time of the Babylonian exile we find pockets of Jews living outside the land of Israel, in Babylon, but not Babylon only—in the Persian kingdom, in the Egyptian kingdom, later on in Greece, moving off to Rome, and in North Africa. How are these people to survive amid the alien culture? This might be considered the reverse of the question Ruth poses. Ruth is the Gentile who comes into Jewish territory. When we meet figures like Esther and Daniel, here we have Jews who are existing in Gentile territory. How much of their ethnic identity do they preserve? To what extent can they acculturate or assimilate? These are the questions Jews had to raise as they themselves found themselves either in the Diaspora or as Israel became heavily influenced first by Persian culture and then certainly by Greek.

Larry Wills wrote a monograph several years ago entitled *The Jew in the Court of the Foreign King*. This may well be a convention because the idea of a Jew in a foreign court actually applies through various texts in the Bible: Joseph in Pharaoh's court, Moses raised in Pharaoh's court, and then these latter tales of the Diaspora, Esther and Daniel.

So we'll start with a look at the Book of Esther, which I think is a terrific book, and see what advice this text gives us. Now, I warn you about Esther, because its canonical status has always been controversial. The Hebrew version of Esther never mentions the name of God. The early Jews debated whether it should be included in the canon or not. Martin Luther from the Protestant Reformation despised this book. Other people have loved it. It has caused enormous hope. It's also caused quite a good deal of tragedy.

Here is the Book of Esther. It's set in the Persian court, first line: "In the days of Ahasuerus," the same Ahasuerus who ruled over 127 provinces from India to Kush or Ethiopia. If you even think of the term "Ahasuerus," which is difficult for me to say and, in fact, difficult for most, it sounds sort of silly, and I think in Hebrew it's supposed to because at least the beginning of this text is not merely comedy; it's, in fact, farce. We don't know who this Ahasuerus is. He is typically associated with the Persian King Xerxes I who ruled from 485 to 464 B.C.E., but when we look at the details in the Book of Esther and then look to Persian records, which are, in fact, quite good, we find no confirmation of anything in this book. There is no external record of Xerxes having a Jewish queen or a Jewish prime minister. There is no evidence of a grand vizier named Haman who wanted to sponsor genocide. The easiest way and probably the most appropriate way of approaching the Book of Esther is to approach it as a book of fiction, which, through its storytelling, provides information to the people who read it. You might think of this as a very, very big parable.

Esther may have been composed during the Persian period. It's certainly set in the Persian court. But it actually may be a product of the Greek age as well. The text is exceptionally stylized, but the style itself fits both the earlier material, such as the Joseph material, as well as later materials, such as, for example, Hellenistic romances. In terms of the text, again we have a problem because the Book of Esther exists in different versions. There is the Hebrew text, the Mazoretic text—this is the one that never mentions the name of God—but the Greek translation of Esther, the text that's found in the Septuagint, has a substantial number of major additions to it, and the Greek text actually Judeafies the book. The Greek version of Esther mentions God over 50 times. It displays, in the spirit of Ezra and Nehemiah, a distaste for intermarriage. The Hebrew Esther marries the Persian king; nobody raises a fuss. In the Greek, everybody—Esther, Mordecai—they all raise a fuss. Intermarriage is bad.

The Greek text has an enormous concern for dietary regulations, keeping kosher. You will recall those laws from Leviticus. The Hebrew never mentions it. The Greek has a good many dreams, which are highly symbolic. Much as Joseph interprets dreams and Daniel interprets dreams, that's part of this Jewish tradition. The Book of Esther leaves that material out. So whether the Greek is the original and the Hebrew is derivative, or whether the Hebrew was original and the Greek derivative, or whether actually a third text, called the Alpha Text, which is not in anybody's canon—either in the Old Testament Apocrypha, the Greek text, or the Hebrew canon—whether the Alpha Text is the first one or the third, we simply don't know. The textual tradition of the Book of Esther is, in a word, confused. Making it even more confused, there is no copy of the Book of Esther found among the Dead Sea Scrolls, so we don't even know what its canonical status was, let alone what early records of this text suggested, how it read.

In terms of the book itself, it's completely artificial. It pulls upon motifs that we've already seen, drawing upon literary conventions. If we didn't have the Book of Esther, we probably could have written it based on material we already had. It begins, for example, not only with a foreign court, which we can see from Daniel or even the Joseph saga, it begins with a type scene of two wives in competition. We've seen that with Sarah and Hagar, with Hannah and Peninnah, and with Rachel and Leah. Here we have it with Esther and the first queen, whose name is Vashti.

But circumstances here are not quite the same as they were before. In earlier examples of this convention, the two wives duke it out over who's going to have a child, whether there is a barren wife or a fertile wife, or who will have the love of the husband, but they exist together, the two wives, in enmity. In this particular case, the first wife Vashti is off the scene before Esther ever arrives. Indeed, Vashti's dismissal from the court is what causes Esther to be invited into the court in the first place.

When we think of this particular text and how the convention plays out, here we move into farce. Ahasuerus basically throws parties. He spends most of the book either drinking or drunk. The first chapter is set out with an enormous banquet that he's thrown for all of his principles, his advisors, his captains, and his governors. Midway through the banquet he orders his queen, Vashti, to appear before him and his lords. Vashti, meanwhile, is hosting a banquet of her own for some other ladies in a different part of the palace, and she sends word back, "I refuse to come." Why she refuses we're never told, and scholars have, in fact, speculated about this as they do frequently when we have a fictional character. Clearly there must be some sort of motive. Does she despise her husband? That's easy enough to do. Does she find disgust at being asked to be an object of display before a group of drunken men? Is she involved with her own duties and doesn't want to give up her job as hostess? Is it simply mean-spiritedness, or is it, as one Jewish *midrash* says in expansion on this story, that she was suffering from an outbreak of pimples at the time and was simply too embarrassed to show up? The king says to her, "Appear in your royal crown." Another *midrash* reads, "She was asked to appear only in her royal crown and out of modesty refused to come."

Whatever her rationale, she incites the king's fury. Of course, she's a wife—she should have obeyed him. So the king, who is, I will continue to remind you, not bright, proceeds to consult his sages. What do you do if your wife disobeys you? He consults his sages, who knew the laws, for this was the king's procedure toward all who were versed in law and custom. He's a by-the-books kind of guy. We might here contrast him with Israelite law, where the laws are sane, where they tell you what to do, but they certainly don't legislate what to do if your wife doesn't show up when you call her. The king's advisors are very much concerned with this, however.

They note, "This very day the noble ladies of Persia and Media who have heard of the queen's behavior will tell against the king's officials, and there will be no end of contempt and wrath." So they come up with a new law. They advise the king to promulgate a law throughout his extensive empire, "that all women will give honor to their husbands high and low alike." So the king therefore passes a law that every man be the master of his own house. This is somewhat difficult to legislate, and I think here we can see part of the farcical aspect of this. The king of the Persian empire is now involved in minute domestic disputations. Ahasuerus, also advised by his eunuchs, who help him out here, decides to banish Queen Vashti, which may well have been exactly what Vashti wanted. She refuses to come to the court. He says, "Fine, I'll make a law you can't come to the court."

Now the king has a problem. He needs a queen. How is he going to get a queen? Now, if I were a king in antiquity and I needed a queen, I would go to my nearest rival and marry that rival's daughter or sister because, in antiquity, indeed, as we've seen through the monarchy up through the Middle Ages to contemporary times, monarchs marry other monarchs. They are good for economic alliances. They are good for political alliances. They prevent war. Not this king. He, on the advice of his ministers and other advisors, decides he's going to hold a beauty contest and he's going to pick the winner. How does this contest work? He sends messengers out to the entire empire, "Find me all the virgins you can." This is Persia—there are a fair number of virgins—and they are all brought to the palace, where they are entrusted to the care of one of the king's eunuchs, and they spend the next year marinating in myrrh and precious oils. Then each one, subsequently, night after night, one by one, visits the king in the evening and then in the morning goes to a second harem.

When I read this story when I was a child, I used to think they played canasta. I don't think that's actually what they were doing. But then the king has to decide which of these women he will accept, and he winds up accepting Esther, good girl that she is, who goes into the king taking only what the king's eunuch advised her. She's a girl who knows how to take advice. That's how Esther gets to be queen. This is clearly farce.

Part of the fiction is also taken up with Esther's uncle or cousin—the textual tradition differs on this. His name is Mordecai, and he is a bit of a problem here. He is a Benjaminite, as was King Saul, by the way, and Mordecai is related to a man named Kish, and, as you will recall from our introduction of Saul, Saul's father's name is Kish. So there is a connection here with that earlier Deuteronomic history. Mordecai at one point refuses to bow down to the king's prime minister—his name is Haman or Hamen, and he is an Agagite. The problem here is that it was Saul's sparing of Agag that led to his dismissal by Samuel. You might recall that wonderful line about "Samuel hewed the body of Agag to pieces."

So what we have in the Book of Esther is a replay of that ancient enmity between the Hebrews and the Agagites, between Saul and his enemy, but here Mordecai, Saul's descendant, will make good what his ancestor lost. Mordecai has obtained Haman's enmity because he has not bowed down. Haman decides he wants to commit genocide against the Hebrew people because he finds out Mordecai is a Jew, and he decides all Jews have to go. Haman, however, and, in fact, no one else, knows that Esther is Jewish because, when Esther was taken into the Persian court, Mordecai had told her, "Do not reveal your people or your nation." So she is a Jew in secret there in the Persian court.

How are things going to play out? As soon as the edict promulgating the death of the Jews is made, and it's made by casting *purim*, which means "lots" or "dice," Haman gets the king's signet ring. He also gives the king a nice bribe of silver and says to the king, "I want to get rid of this people who have their own laws and don't obey you." Well, it's true they have their own laws, but, as we've seen with laws and covenants, Jews who exist in foreign countries, who live there, have to obey the laws of the state. The king never even asks, "Well, what people is this?" He simply says, "Fine, do as you will."

Mordecai goes into mourning. He rends his clothes. Esther hears about it through palace intrigue, and she sends word to her cousin, "What's wrong?" Mordecai tells her what's happened and says, "You need to plead with your husband to rescue us," and Esther says, "Well, wait. The Persians have a law"—because that's what they do in Persia—"The Persians have a law that says you cannot go to visit the king if you've not been invited, on pain of death. Unless the king extends to you his golden scepter, you die. He's going to kill me." Mordecai says to her, "Look, perhaps it is precisely for such a time as this that you were put into the harem." He doesn't evoke God here, but one can read in some sort of divine or at least providential impulse. Mordecai also goes on to say, "Do not think your role as queen will save you. You will die if you don't do something, and then help will come from some other place"—God, perhaps, or somewhere else? Mordecai doesn't say.

So Esther gets herself together. She dresses up nicely, and she goes to the royal court, and, thank heaven, Ahasuerus extends his golden scepter to her. He says, "What do you want, O queen? I will give you whatever you want, even up to half of my kingdom," which is a very stupid thing for a king to promise. We can see here the irony. Vashti is dismissed from the court for refusing to come; Esther comes unbidden. In fact, Esther winds up doing everything that Vashti doesn't and in doing so slightly transgresses the law—not too bad but just a little bit, takes it into her own hands.

What does she do? She invites the king to a banquet, here again the reverse of Vashti, who refuses to come, and she says, "Come to my banquet, and have your minister Haman come as well." This is not quite what the king was expecting, but he's quick on the uptake, and he's always happy to party, so he, in fact, goes with her, and they have a banquet. Then they have another banquet, and Esther is setting her plot. Finally, finally, at the last banquet, when they are drinking and the king is happy, and the king says, "What can I give to you, Esther, even if it's up to half of my kingdom?" Esther responds, "Well, listen, if we were simply sold as slaves this would be okay, but my people have been sold to death, I and my people. Find me some way of protection. Stop this law." Ahasuerus says, "Who would have done such a thing?" and Esther looks at Haman and says, "The wicked Haman." The scene is nicely set.

This being a farcical text and somewhat contrived, at this point Ahasuerus leaves the room, ostensibly because he's upset. This gives Haman time to throw himself on the dining couch where Queen Esther is lying to plead for his life, and, of course, at this opportune moment Ahasuerus walks back in, sees Haman having thrown himself on his wife, and says, "Will you ravish my wife as well?" He thinks there is a rape in progress. He decides at this point to kill Haman, and, at this point as well, Esther keeps her mouth shut. Haman actually gets condemned for doing something he didn't do, attacking Esther, rather than condemned for something he did do, sponsoring genocide. Haman is hanged on the gallows that he had actually erected for Mordecai.

But the dangers of this text continue because the law has been passed that the Jews are to be killed on a certain day. As we know, the laws of the Medes and the Persians say, once the law is made you cannot revoke it. What's going to happen? Esther has to arrange with her cousin Mordecai and the king that a new law be promulgated, giving the Jews in the Persian empire the opportunity to defend themselves, which is actually quite helpful. What then happens? "By the king's command and Esther's instruction, the Jews struck down all their enemies with the sword, slaughtering and destroying them, and did as they pleased to all who hated them. In the citadel of Susa [which is where the Persian kings had their summer palace], the Jews killed and destroyed 500 people" (Ch. 9).

But that's not all, and here we move from farce into what I would regard as tragedy. The other Jews who were living in the king's provinces also gathered to defend their lives and gain release from their enemies and killed 75,000 of those who hated them, but, the text goes on to say, "they laid no hand on the plunder." It is as if these Jews in the Persian empire are engaged in holy war, and, as we've see before with holy war, you can kill people—indeed, you're supposed to kill people—but you're not supposed to take any of the booty. When we think back to that original conflict between King Saul and the Agagites, what was the problem? Saul conquered his enemy but took some of the booty and allowed the king to remain alive. At this point, Mordecai and his fellow Jews wind up slaughtering everybody. There is no one left among the enemy, but the booty is not taken.

This desire to strike back at enemies and to rid the world of anti-Semitism is certainly understandable, and holy war is indeed part and parcel of the way the ancient world functioned. The problem is, this text, the Book of Esther—it is called the *Megillat* Esther, the scroll of Esther—is read every year in synagogues on the Jewish Festival of Purim. Contemporary synagogues are not, these days, always reading the last couple of chapters about the destruction. In 1994, having heard this text read in Israel, a settler who was actually from the United States and moved to Israel the next day went to the mosque at Hebron, opened up with machine-gun fire and massacred over 30 Muslim people at prayer. This is a text that can inspire both hope and incredible hatred.

Better is the way, I think, the Book of Esther insists one actually celebrate the holiday. The holiday is celebrated on the date that Haman picked for the genocide of the Jews, and it's now turned into a celebration of life rather than death. We're told in Chapter 9 that the Jews in the Persian empire celebrated this holiday "with feasting and gladness and sending of gifts of food to one another and to the poor and with peace and security." That's the way the holiday needs to celebrated. That's the way it's traditionally celebrated. But we need to be careful because this is a text of enormous violence, and the farce turns to tragedy. If we continue to look at Esther as a book of farce, perhaps we might not take that ending quite so seriously, and I actually like the idea of not reading it out loud liturgically.

That's Esther and Mordecai, and they certainly survive in the court of the foreign king. Esther remains queen. Mordecai is given Haman's old job, and suddenly we have a Jewish grand vizier in the Persian empire. Ahasuerus certainly could have used it—he is not too bright—but Mordecai is appreciated by all the people, including the king.

And so we leave the Persian Court and move to the Babylonian court, and this brings us to the stories of Daniel. As with the Book of Esther, dating the Book of Daniel is no simple matter. The earliest references to a figure named Daniel or Dan'el—it's a slightly different spelling in the Hebrew—are to a Ugaritic king. There is actually a figure named Dan'el who lived in the fourteenth century B.C.E., the 1300s. The prophet Ezekiel in Chapter 14 associates one Dan'el with Noah and Job, perhaps three Gentiles, from Ezekiel's perspective, who are known for wisdom. Ezekiel tells us even, in Chapter 28, this particular Dan'el knows secrets.

The Book of Daniel itself, Chapter 1, Verse 1, dates the story to the third year of the reign of King Jehoiakim, and we met him when we talked about the Babylonian destruction of the southern kingdom. This would be about 606 B.C.E. Jehoiakim's son, Jehoiachin or Jeconiah, ruled when Jerusalem was captured in 587, and Daniel is in Babylon after the destruction of the temple. Now, I did that very quickly, and you probably didn't catch the dates, but the point is here, the dates of Daniel do not match up with the dates of the Babylonian emperors or the Hebrew—the Judean—empires, or the destruction of the temple. The dating here seems to be contrived. It's fictional. Daniel, based on his own dating, is in Babylon prior to the time that the temple was destroyed, but the text itself says the temple is already destroyed.

If we look at this, then, as a book of fiction, a book of folktales, then we can get a handle on it. The accounts of Daniel and the other Jewish youths taken into captivity reflect a time when imperial rule is ignorant and dangerous, much like the Book of Esther, rather than malevolent. When we get to the apocalyptic sections of the Book of Daniel, imperial rule becomes malevolent. The question is how to survive in foreign countries where the kings simply do not understand you rather than, for the most part, want to kill you.

The tales of Daniel are most often regarded as products of the Persian period from 538 to 333 or the early Greek period—Alexander the Great comes through in 333—up to about the year 168. Daniel, Chapter 2, Verse 4b until Chapter 7, Verse 28, is written not in Hebrew but in Aramaic, which is actually the common language of the Near East in the time of the Babylonian empire up to the rise of the Greek empire. Daniel, Chapter 1, and the remaining Chapters 8 through 12, happen to be in Hebrew, which, by the Second Temple Period, by, say, about 200 B.C.E., was becoming much more a liturgical language than a spoken language. Aramaic was, as it were, becoming the lingua franca of the period.

Complicating the history of the Book of Daniel, as with the Book of Esther, the Greek text has a different version or, indeed, has additions. You may have heard of the story of Susanna, this lovely young lady who was in the process of taking a bath when some elders came and attempted to attack her. That's an addition to the Book of Daniel. Or the stories of Bel and the dragon or the prayer of Azariah and the song of the three young men. These are all part of the Danielic corpus. They are in the Greek text, and they are in the Old Testament Apocrypha, but they are not in the Hebrew. Indeed, Danielic traditions continue even to the Dead Sea Scrolls, where additional books attributed to Daniel are there.

In terms of the folktales, the major questions are those of assimilation. Daniel raises questions like, should we eat non-kosher food? Absolutely not, the response is. Should idols be worshipped? Absolutely not, the response is, even if the refusal to participate in idol worship causes you to be thrown into a fiery furnace, and that's what happens with Daniel's three friends. Should one cease to pray to God according to royal decree? This is not asking for overt idolatry; it's asking for simply a refraining. One might think of sins of commission versus sins of omission. Should one cease to pray to God according to royal decree? Absolutely not, even if one's fate by doing so is to be thrown into a lion's den—and there is Daniel in the lion's den.

Through all these dangers, there is also a great deal of humor in these folktales. Daniel's enemies in the royal court always receive their just reward. Daniel manifests his interpretative gifts, his ability to interpret dreams, not only the way Joseph does—Pharaoh tells him a dream and Joseph makes the interpretation—but in this case

Nebuchadnezzar and the other kings will say to Daniel not only "Interpret my dream for me" but also "Tell me what I dreamt and then interpret my dream," which is a much harder thing to do. Daniel, like Joseph, of course, always gives the credit to God.

And we find in Daniel, Chapter 5, that very famous handwriting on the wall. "MENE, MENE, TEKEL, PARSIN," it says, which basically says, "Evil empires will be divided up and will fall." I think other empires since might note this handwriting on the wall sometimes applies to them, and for the Book of Daniel, which knew about the fall of the Babylonian empire and probably about the fall of the Persian empire, the handwriting on the wall did come true.

As biblical chronology moves from the patriarchs to Persia, this motif of the Jew in the court of the foreign king develops from Joseph to Moses to Mordecai to Daniel, and one can see in this, in fact, literary conventions. They are all in foreign courts not by their own choice, for example. Joseph is sold; Moses is brought there—he didn't ask for it; Daniel is taken into captivity during the Babylonian onslaught; and Esther is brought to the court as part of a beauty pageant and her cousin follows her. But they all succeed. Joseph gains charge over all of Egypt. Moses bests Pharaoh. Esther becomes queen and Mordecai the prime minister. And Daniel, according to Chapter 2, Verse 48 of his book, is made ruler. One can see how these stories would be, at the very least, uplifting to people within a minority group.

All four cases present matters of the utmost seriousness. Joseph saves Egypt and therefore his family from famine. He is there to protect. Moses saves his own people from death and slavery. Daniel saves his own life and by extension the life of every Jew in the Diaspora, and Esther saves her people from genocide. There are also variations on the role of God in all these stories. Joseph receives divine aid all the time. Moses receives divine aid, but he's got to be prompted—God's got to push him through. Daniel, like Joseph, succeeds through the gift of interpretation of dreams. In a major break with the convention, Esther never evokes God. Neither does Mordecai.

As these stories are compared, these tales of Jews in the foreign court, many more insights can be gained both in terms of individual narratives and as a collection, and you might want to pursue that at your leisure. The other thing that we find with these tales is these are tales also of wisdom. Daniel is a figure of wisdom. Mordecai, with his royal advice, is a figure of wisdom. Wisdom is one form that Israelite literature takes in antiquity. But, as we see with continuation of the Book of Daniel, in addition to novels and folktales and wisdom, there is one more genre yet to go. So for our last lecture we'll look at the genre of apocalypticism.

Lecture Twenty-Four

Apocalyptic Literature (Isaiah 24–27, 56–66; Zechariah 9–14; Daniel 7–12)

Scope:

With the weakening of classical prophecy and an increasing sense of hopelessness concerning universal justice, prophets began to envision a divinely inaugurated new heaven and new earth. This reorientation, combined with wisdom literature's interest in construction of the universe and the means of living the good life, the Zoroastrian dualism of Persia, and Hellenism's well-developed visions of an afterlife, gave rise to apocalyptic writing. Apocalyptic voices accomplished through rhetoric what they lacked in reality: assurance that world and time were ordered rather than chaotic, that suffering would soon end, and that those who persevered would be rewarded in the "world to come" ("messianic age") with resurrection and eternal life. This lecture describes the literary devices and sociological origins of apocalyptic and addresses the Old Testament's only "full blown" apocalypse, Dan. 7–12.

Outline

I. The genre "apocalyptic" (Greek: "revelation," "uncovering") takes its name from the last book of the New Testament: the Book of Revelation or the Apocalypse of St. John.

- **A.** Books are classified as apocalypses based on several features, not all of which appear in every apocalypse.
- **B.** The genre is notoriously hard to define.
- **C.** Apocalyptic materials sometimes are combined with other forms: the Apocalypse of Daniel is tacked onto folk tales.

II. What does apocalyptic writing do?

- **A.** It raises universal questions concerning the*Urzeit* (the time of creation) and the *Endzeit* (the end of time).
- **B.** It often leaves its symbols unmediated and unexplained; its audience may be familiar with the codes.
- **C.** It is primarily a written, not an oral, genre.
- **D.** It frequently offers a pessimistic view of history. Still, its determinism means that God has established a plan that

includes redemption for those who now despair. Popular in apocalyptic literature is a sense of de-evolution. When things get bad enough, then God intervenes.

E. Dualistic thought divides both mundane and supernatural realms into warring camps of good and evil.

  1. The cosmic war pits the heavenly hosts, led by the archangel Michael, against the forces of evil, led by such fallen angels as Mastema, Belial, and Satan, or the devil.

  2. On earth, the Sons of Light battle the Sons of Darkness (the Qumran War Scroll).

III. Daniel is an interpreter of dreams; he later becomes the visionary who needs others to interpret his dreams.

A. In one vision, he sees the Son of Man awarded an everlasting dominion and needs an angelic explanation.

B. Sometimes, these visions are unexplained, left to the reader's speculation.

C. The motif of secrecy is part of the apocalyptic genre; it is like reading a mystery novel and not having all the pieces.

D. Apocalyptic frequently gives itself a false or pseudonymous author by backdating its time of authorship.

IV. Most scholars date Daniel's apocalyptic materials to the eve of the Maccabean revolt (second century B.C.E.).

A. After Alexander's death (323), his empire was divided among his generals. To Ptolemy in Egypt went the satrapy "Across the River" (Dan. 2:41).

B. In 198, at the Battle of Paneas, the descendants of Seleucis of Syria gain Judea.

C. In about 168, rebellion breaks under the Seleucid Antiochus IV Epiphanes.

D. The Temple is profaned ("abomination or desolation" or "desolating sacrilege," Dan. 8:1–14, 11:30; 1 Macc. 1:54; 2 Macc. 6:2), circumcision and Sabbath observance are forbidden, and Jerusalem becomes a Greek *polis*.

E. The Hasmonean family (Maccabees) rout the Syrians and their supporters and replace the assimilationist families as rulers.

F. Daniel's vision is, ultimately, one of redemption. His apocalypse is eschatological, and we still await its fulfillment.

V. We are at our own eschaton now that we've reached the end of the course. Given the enormous scope of the Old Testament/*Tanakh*, we are unable to cover many subjects:

A. The court histories of David.

B. The Elisha story.

C. The promise of the prophet Micah.

D. The poetry of the Psalms and Lamentations.

E. The artistry of Jonah.

F. The post-exilic enmity between Judea and Samaria.

G. The development of the worship system.

H. The change in community self-definition, from a tribe to a kingdom.

I. The canonical process, or how the texts were put together.

J. The Ancient Near Eastern parallels to these materials.

K. The tale of Joseph and Mrs. Potiphar.

L. The Philistines.

M. Archaeological remains, such as the Moabite inscriptions.

N. Tragedies, such as the rape of Jacob's daughter Dinah.

O. Developed stories on Abraham's childhood, on Moses's marriage.

P. Messianic speculation.

VI. There is much in this text still to explore. Now you should have a good sense of how rich the material really is.

Supplementary Reading:

John J. Collins, *The Apocalyptic Imagination: An Introduction to Jewish Apocalyptic Literature*, 2nd ed. (Grand Rapids, MI: William B. Eerdmans, 1998).

Jacob Neusner, William Scott Green, and Ernest S. Frerichs (eds.), *Judaisms and Their Messiahs at the Turn of the Christian Era* (Cambridge/New York: Cambridge University Press, 1987).

J. Edward Wright, *The Early History of Heaven* (New York: Oxford University Press, 2000).

Questions to Consider:

1. What are the heirs of apocalyptic writing as a literary genre? Who are today's apocalyptic communities, and how should those who are not members regard them?
2. What motivates some modern readers to adopt radically eschatological, apocalyptic worldviews?

Lecture Twenty-Four—Transcript
Apocalyptic Literature
(Isaiah 24-27, 56-66; Zechariah 9-14; Daniel 7-12)

Biblical wisdom literature seeks to convey information on how to live the good life and to establish at least the question, if not the answers, of the justice of God. Prophetic literature seeks to communicate divine will to human beings and to mediate back to God humans' concerns. The tales of the Jew in the court of the foreign king that we just visited in the last lecture seek to provide advice to people on how to live in the world even when the world is not responding appropriately. But there are times when answers are not forthcoming and, indeed, when the world seems to be caving in on people, as if that genocide that the Book of Esther suggested might happen would really come, as if we were really dealing with history and not simply with folktale or farce.

The difficulties in negotiating the world when bad things continue to happen and when it appears to the people that there is no way that they on their own can provide any sort of rectification—when all these bad things continue, a new genre proceeds to develop in biblical literature. We find it both in Old Testament and in New Testament materials, and this is known as apocalyptic.

The term "apocalyptic" comes from a Greek word meaning "uncovering" or "revelation." You might have heard of the New Testament book, the Book of Revelation—no "s" on the end, by the way. It's also called the Apocalypse of John. Apocalyptic literature is a combination of a variety of other literatures we've already seen. From the prophets it takes the idea of the concern to inculcate moral values and that God is active in history. From wisdom literature it takes speculation on the universe. It raises questions of theodicy. From novels it pulls from characters who are put in awkward, difficult, dangerous positions and then somehow they have to come to terms with their existence, often through the help of a divine mediary. Apocalyptic is, in effect, a combination of the breakdown of prophecy with a little bit of wisdom thrown in and then with influences from Persian thought and then Greek thought.

Let's take a look, then, at some of the influences on the development of apocalyptic, and then we'll look at the Bible's one full-blown—and here "full-blown" is actually a technical term in biblical literature—apocalypse, the last several chapters of the Book of Daniel. In terms of the origins here, it's actually very difficult to define early apocalyptic. People have described apocalyptic much as folks have described pornography—in the sense of, "Well, I can't really describe it but I know it when I see it." Therefore, some earlier texts that many consider to be apocalyptic others will look at as proto-apocalyptic, or moving toward apocalyptic. These would include materials such as the prophet Zechariah, Chapters 9 through 14, where we begin to find unmediated visions, visions not explained fully; symbols; odd angels suddenly showing up and providing information; and mysterious beings flying through the heavens.

Others have looked at the last piece of information that we get from the prophet Isaiah, fourth Isaiah, if you will, Chapters 24–27, where we start getting information about resurrection of the dead, which, as you know, we've not seen much of before. We might want to consider this proto-apocalyptic.

We also have the problem of apocalyptic materials showing up in literature that is not in itself apocalyptic. Sometimes apocalyptic literature is tacked on to other materials. For example, the apocalypse of Daniel is tacked on to those folktales. When we go to the New Testament, the apocalyptic material in the Book of Revelation is actually tacked on to seven letters, so you have an epistolary opening and then you have an apocalypse. And we actually find this non-canonical literature of the early Roman period (the first century Common Era), texts like the Apocalypse of Baruch, Second Baruch, or Fourth Ezra, or even the Apocalypse of Abraham. They begin with letters or folktales, and then suddenly these apocalyptic visions take over.

What does apocalyptic do? Well, it raises questions of universalistic import. Whereas the prophets are interested in the covenant community's history, apocalyptic, like wisdom literature, is interested in all history. It frequently uses a motif referred to in German as *Urzeit*, *Endzeit*. In other words it takes the ur-time, that original time, the Garden of Eden, and then looks at the *Endzeit*, that end time when the covenant community will finally be redeemed, when there will be a general resurrection of the dead, when the wicked will finally be punished and the good rewarded. It matches up the two as if we started in the Garden of Eden and sometime, when history comes to its *telos*—when it comes to its goal—we will regain that Garden of Eden. Apocalyptic is therefore interested in universal history, not just in terms of Israelite history.

We can see some of that cosmogonic opening even at the beginning of Daniel. Daniel 7 talks about the four winds of heaven stirring up the great sea, evoking here that image from Genesis, Chapter 1, about the spirit of God hovering over the deep. It's an *Urzeit*, or first-time, image coming back up, the wind in the sea recollecting the first chapter of Genesis. And the beasts Daniel describes give us another example of apocalyptic imagery. When the prophets use allegory or metaphor, they tell us what they mean. Amos's basket of summer fruit clearly signifies the end time coming—we know that. Apocalyptic literature often leaves its symbols unmediated, unexplained, because apocalyptic is less literature for the public than it is literature for an in-house community, a group of people who already know the codes, already know the symbols.

Here is an example of an image that is not fully described in the Book of Daniel. "After the four winds of heaven stir up the great sea," Daniel tells us, "he sees four beasts coming out from the sea." The beasts—the lion, the bear, this four-winged leopard, and some sort of creature with great iron teeth and 10 horns—actually represent empires such that the lion is Babylon, the bear is the kingdom of the Medes, Persia is the leopard, and this odd beast with its teeth and its horns, that's the empire of Greece—Alexander the Great and those who succeeded him. But Daniel doesn't spell out in detail what all these visions mean.

Apocalyptic is primarily a written genre rather than an oral genre. People would speculate over the texts themselves, and I suspect that, when the apocalyptic material of the Book of Daniel was first being studied, people would look at it and then teachers would tell students, this refers to this and this refers to that. The benefit of this type of literature is that, because the symbols are not always described, the literature is ever new, so a particular beast does not necessarily have to represent Babylon. Two or three hundred years later it could represent Rome or Germany or Iraq or the United States. With the symbols unmediated, apocalyptic becomes a universal literature not only across space but also across time.

Apocalyptic literature also frequently, somewhat like the Book of Ecclesiastes here, offers a very pessimistic view of history, as if history is going on toward something so totally negative that only an act of God can come in and rectify the situation. This is not upbeat material in the least, but at the same time that it shows this pessimistic view of history, apocalyptic is frequently deterministic. That means that God has everything under control, that history is following out a set plan God has established. God had predetermined things were going to go from bad to worse to worst, but ultimately there will be a redemption, a vindication. That allows people living in a state of hopelessness (either a real state of hopelessness, where they really are being persecuted, or in a perceived state of hopelessness, because there are people who are convinced that the world is bad who are actually living relatively the good life), people who are convinced that they have no power, that things are bad, that ultimately God is in control—the literature, by telling them that everything is predetermined, allows them to have hope. It encourages them in perseverance.

My own sense of this, and it comes from the New Testament expression that hell is a place of "wailing and gnashing of teeth," is that apocalyptic literature is somewhat like going to the dentist's office. You know it's going to hurt, and you're told exactly how much it's going to hurt, but at the end there is redemption. You have peace. There is no longer any pain. And you can begin to smile.

Popular in apocalyptic literature are symbolic overviews of time, therefore, with a sense of de-evolution. Daniel actually presents this model in the folktale rather than in the apocalypse. Chapter 2 of Daniel gives us a dream by Nebuchadnezzar. He dreams of a great statue, its brilliance extraordinary and its appearance exceptionally frightening. The head of the statute is described as being a fine gold, its chest in arms of silver, its middle and thighs of bronze, its legs of iron, and its feet partly of iron and partly of clay. The interpretation of the dream is basically an apocalyptic worldview, where you start out with a golden age, and things go to silver, and then they go to bronze, and then, in effect, they go to pot. That's the way apocalyptic literature describes history. But, when things get really bad, that's when God breaks in.

Apocalyptic, given this very negative view of history, and given the fact that the authors and communities that support this view consider themselves to be oppressed, is, as you might expect, dualistic. There are good guys and there are bad guys, and it's very, very easy to tell the difference between them. Apocalyptic is the sort of literature that will proclaim, "I'm saved and you're not," or "I am predetermined to be rewarded at the end, and you are so wicked there is no way you will ever succeed." This is known as dualism.

Frequently we find in apocalyptic a cosmic war pitting the hosts of heaven, often led by angels like the angel Michael, over against the hosts of hell, often led by the developing Satan figure or other demons named Mastema or Belial, figures, supernatural figures, who fight against God. On earth we find in the Qumran community, the Dead Sea Scrolls, a text describing the war of the Sons of Light against the Sons of Darkness. Daniel has the same thing. There are bad guys and there are good guys, and Daniel tells us that the righteous will be raised to everlasting life and the wicked do not get that benefit. Here is an example from Daniel, "Many shall be purified, cleansed, and refined, but the wicked shall continue to act wickedly. None of the wicked shall understand, but those who are wise shall understand." That's Daniel, Chapter 12.

With all these various visions, many of them unmediated, simply symbols without interpretation, apocalyptic, in order to get its message across, actually needs a little bit of interpretation. We find in the Book of Daniel, in the first part, the folktales, that Daniel is an interpreter of dreams. Nebuchadnezzar has a dream; Daniel tells us what it means. When we get to the apocalyptic section, Daniel himself is the dreamer or the visionary, and he needs heavenly figures like angels to come and explain to him what he has dreamed. Here Daniel is the apocalyptic visionary, and he needs heavenly interpretation.

Daniel, for example, has a vision—it's a very famous vision for both Jewish and Christian traditions—in which he sees one like a son of man coming with the clouds of heaven. "He came to the Ancient of Days [this is the idea of God on the royal throne in heaven, envisioned as an old man, old as time] and was presented to him, and to him was given dominion and glory and kingship, that all peoples and nations and languages should serve him." Daniel goes on to say that "The son of man's dominion is an everlasting dominion that shall not pass away, and his kingship is one that shall not be destroyed." This is quite a vision. Daniel then tells us, "My spirit was troubled within me, and the visions of my head terrified me. So I approached one of the attendants to ask him the truth concerning all of this." Daniel knows what he sees; he simply doesn't know what it meant. Therefore he needs the angel's explanation, which he gets in the latter part of Chapter 7.

At times these visions are not interpreted, and you notice I'm not going to give you the interpretation of that one. Sometimes they are simply left up to speculation. It may be, as these stories are told within covenant communities, that the teller of the tale will know what the answer is. The text simply does not provide us that.

In terms of the secrecy motif, I suspect that that secrecy motif is also part of the literary artistry of apocalyptic. Apocalyptic can't simply be bizarre symbols that no one understands because then why would anybody read it? There has got to be a little bit that we can relate to and then we want more, as if we're reading a mystery novel but we don't have all the pieces. Or we find out about a secret society or a fraternity and we know a little bit about what they do and we want to know more. The apocalyptic literature actually provides us hints that draw us in. For example, in Daniel, Chapter 12, an angel tells Daniel, "You, Daniel, keep the words secret and this book sealed until the end of time," as if here is something we wait for. Indeed, what apocalyptic frequently does is provide itself a false author or a pseudonymous author.

Apocalyptic is frequently written during a time of particular stress, but the author, the narrative author is himself—and it's usually a him—frequently backdated 500 years earlier, 1,000 years earlier. A first-century book from the Common Era, called Fourth Ezra, is actually attributed to Ezra, who lived right after the Babylonian exile. If Daniel is a figure of the Babylonian period, as he is in the folktales, and he's presenting these visions, isn't it amazing that all of his visions takes us down to about the year 168-167 B.C.E. of the time of the Greek period, the reign of Antiochus IV Epiphanes of Syria? It is as if Daniel, looking forward from the Babylonian exile, can predict the rise of Persia and the rise of Greece; the rise of the Seleucid dynasty, the inheritors of Alexander; and ultimately the outrages of Antiochus IV Epiphanes. Here is the way apocalyptic can grab you. It can predict time, and, since it looks like that ancient author got it right from the past, perhaps what that ancient author is saying about contemporary times might also be correct.

The Book of Daniel itself, at least the apocalyptic material, was probably written around 168-167 Before the Common Era. Here is the social situation. The empire of Alexander the Great splits up after his death and gets divided among his generals. Judea passes into the hands of his general Ptolemy, who was basically in charge of Egypt. So if you've ever heard of the Ptolemaic empire, that's where it comes from. There is another general whose name is Seleucis who gets the area around Syria, and he founds the Seleucid dynasty.

Then, like any two kingdoms next to each other, they proceed to fight back and forth and back and forth. In the year 198, at the Battle of Paneas, Judea—or Palestine, if you will—at this time passes from Egyptian to Syrian control, and, other than the fact that the Jews are now paying their taxes to a different empire, nothing much changes. But in the middle of the century a new Seleucid king comes to the throne. His name is Antiochus IV, and he calls himself Epiphanes, which means "God made manifest." At the same time as well, some of the high priests, the elite members of the community in Jerusalem, decide that the covenant community should no longer be removed, distinct, from the other nations of the world, that it should become a Greek polis and take its place among the other empires, other cities, that Alexander the Great had founded.

Innovations began to take place in Jerusalem at that time. We have, from the Books of the Maccabees, information that circumcision was becoming outlawed. Kosher food was becoming difficult to find, if not impossible. Sabbath observance was no longer permitted. Indeed, Maccabees even tells us that, for women who circumcised their babies, the Greek soldiers would come and kill those babies and hang the corpses of the infants around their mothers' necks and force the mothers to walk the parapet at the temple.

This is a time of desperation, and it's that time of desperation that prompts an apocalypse like the Book of Daniel. Daniel even notes that the Greeks had so much come into the country and so taken over the temple that a pig—totally non-kosher, horrible in Jewish eyes—had been sacrificed on God's altar in the temple of Jerusalem. Daniel refers to this as "the abomination of desolation," or "the desolating sacrilege." This is a comment from Daniel 12. He says, "From the time that the regular burnt offering is taken away [because kosher sacrifices by appropriate priests are no longer permitted; indeed, the official high priest has been removed from office and executed] and the abomination of desolation is set up, then the end time must come."

And here is another aspect of apocalyptic literature. Daniel says, "There shall be 1,290 days. Happy are those who persevere and attain the 3,335 days." It's as if, perhaps—in fact, quite likely—another editor, another author, had come in and updated the Book of Daniel. He's gotten history right, up to the abomination of desolation, but Daniel himself does not write or even perhaps live long enough to see the end of the Seleucid outrages, the replacement of these assimilationist Jews by more traditional people, by, in fact, the Hasmonean family, who are also known as Maccabees. But that material, in fact, moves us past what the Old Testament covers and into what's known as the Old Testament Apocrypha.

Daniel ultimately has a vision of universal redemption, at least for the good people. This is Daniel 12:2 through 3: "Many of those who sleep in the dust of the earth to the end shall awake: some to everlasting life and some to shame and everlasting contempt. Those who are wise shall shine like the brightness of the dome, and those who lead many to righteousness like the stars forever and ever." We have similar imagery in Isaiah 24 through 27. Daniel does not record the ultimate vindication of the Jews, the faithful Jews in Jerusalem, but at least he expects, in part of his apocalyptic vision, that vindication, in fact, will come by God and it will have a heavenly focus.

In this sense, Daniel's apocalypse might be considered eschatological, from a Greek term meaning "concerning the end time"—when time itself stops and God actually breaks into history. We've already seen hints of that with the third Isaiah predicting new heavens and a new earth. Eschatological literature is, in fact, one of the major forms that apocalyptic takes, and we can see this type of material continuing through history into the New Testament, into medieval speculation about the end of time, and even into contemporary groups seeing signs—with nuclear war or perhaps the foundation of the state of Israel—that the end-time must be coming.

But the point of apocalyptic literature is not so much to predict the end; it is to give people at a specific time hope, indeed, that God will bring about an end. So to take some of those apocalyptic symbols from antiquity and say that they apply today—it's certainly something one can do, but I think the authors of those ancient apocalypses would have been quite surprised because that's by no means what they intended.

A problem here that I have is that, with all this apocalyptic material with its influence of, say, Persian dualistic thought and Greek speculation of heaven and hell and wisdom's concern for nature and prophecy's concern for the divine word, all of this creates for us an *eschaton* because we're at the end of this course, and there is so much more we can do, and it's so frustrating for me that we simply don't have the opportunity. We're not at the end of biblical studies; there is no way we ever could be. We have only scratched the surface. There is so much more to do.

Among the materials that we've only briefly mentioned, it needs so much more: the court histories of David; his war with Absalom. The court histories of everyone else, for that matter—what happens in the northern kingdom and the southern kingdom? What does happen, say, to Jezebel's daughter, Athalia, who becomes queen down in the south? What were the abuses and benefits of Jehu's dynasty? What about the Elisha story, Elijah's successor who creates great miracles and engages in bloodbaths? What about the promise of the prophet Micah, one who, along with the first Isaiah, notes that there will be a day coming when *lo yisa goy el goy herev*, when nation will not lift up sword against nation and study war no longer?

We miss the beauty of so many prophets because there are too many to cover, and we miss the beauty of all of the Psalms and of Lamentations, each with its own aesthetic value and its striking imagery, each with its heartfelt liturgical application.

We miss the artistry of Jonah, which is one of the best short stories ever written, from pathos to humor, from righteous Gentiles to a Hebrew prophet who doesn't want the people to whom he prophesied to repent.

We missed the post-exilic enmity between the returnees from exile and the kingdom of Samaria. When we talk in the New Testament about the Good Samaritan, it's not just the fall of the northern kingdom that causes that problem, it's ongoing political and social difficulties from the edict of Cyrus on down to the first century, and this is, in fact, recorded in Old Testament material.

We missed the development of the worship system. We know that the priests have organized sacrifice, but of what sort and why? And how do all those laws function? What are the laws of family purity?

Why are they there? Did people actually keep them? What do people do with them even today?

We missed to a great extent the change in community self-definition from a tribal organization, which we've seen, but then to a kingdom. What was it like to be a member of the kingdom at the time of Jehu, the northern kingdom? How does this kingdom, this ethnic group, ultimately become a religion? Originally this is a tradition in which one could join as, say, a resident alien, a stranger within the gates, but, ultimately, close to the time probably of the composition of Esther, and certainly by the time of Daniel, this is a community into which one can convert. It's not just an ethnic group; it's also a religion. What prompts that change, and how does that change affect how people would have thought of themselves, as you move from ethnic group to religion?

We missed the canonical process. How finally were these texts put together and at what time? Is it true, as many, perhaps most, Old Testament specialists think, that Ezra really did have an inchoate Pentateuch there that Nehemiah, Chapter 8, records? Or was most of this material put together even in the Greek age? How late is it? Because we don't have any manuscripts earlier than the Dead Sea Scrolls. Could some of this material be Hellenistic—late Hellenistic, even—besides just the Book of Daniel? And who put it together and where? How do we wind up with a standardized text? As you know, the original Hebrew doesn't have any vowels. That's why we have that verse in Job that can be translated in so many different ways. Who finally standardized the texts—put in the vowels, put in the punctuation—and are they correct? How did Jews and Christians decide whether to read from the Greek or whether to read from the Hebrew?

We miss a part that I absolutely love, which are all the ancient Near Eastern parallels to this material, and not just ancient Near Eastern in terms of Sumer, but Egypt and Babylon and Persia and Greece and even some little hints of Rome coming in. We've looked at a little bit of this—you can't really understand what's going on in Genesis 1 without knowing about the Babylon cosmogony—but there is so much more.

The tale of Joseph and Mrs. Potiphar, which we've only mentioned but not gone into detail with, actually has an Egyptian match called "The Tale of the Two Brothers."

We've talked about the relationship between the Mosaic law code and the code of Hammurabi, but we haven't looked at how sacrifice functions in other Near Eastern cultures. We haven't looked at how laws of family purity—who can sleep with whom under what circumstances and at what times—function throughout the rest of the ancient Near East. At the very least this shows us that the Hebrew culture is not anomalous.

What about the Philistines? We've mentioned them, and they've always come off in quite a negative manner. I've often thought that what the Philistines need is some sort of Anti-Defamation League because they are probably not as bad as the Bible portrays them, and from their records, I suspect, if we had enough of them, their views of ancient Israel would be quite as negative as Israel's views of ancient Philistines.

Archaeological remains: the Moabite inscriptions, the Moabite stone in which King Meisha of Moab describes his victory over Israelite kings, or the black obelisk of Shalmaneser III of Assyria, which you can see today, showing, among other figures, King Jehu of the northern kingdom, actually paying him tribute. He's actually a king whose face we can see in an archaeological remain.

The ancient Near Eastern background to wisdom literature—I've mentioned it, but there is so much more there that makes Israelite wisdom richer.

In terms of the stories themselves, some of the tragedies we haven't looked at: the rape of Jacob's daughter, Dinah, and how that affects community self-definition and, indeed, ultimately plays out to describe why Levi and Simeon lose their land, a story which ultimately finds its culmination in the Book of Judith in the Old Testament Apocrypha. The development of biblical material thereby. Midrashim develop stories on Abraham's childhood, on Moses' marriage. The stories of Melchizedek, and we haven't even talked about him. Melchizedek is a wonderful figure who, in Genesis, is a king of a place called Salem, and that becomes Jerusalem, and we find out that Abraham pays tithes to him. But Melchizedek, this mysterious figure, also shows up in the Psalms. He shows up in the Dead Sea Scrolls, and, by the first century, he is a major figure of speculation in both Jewish tradition and even in the New Testament epistle to the Hebrews. We haven't even been able to touch on him.

And finally, messianic speculation. We have all those promises to David of Jerusalem the golden, of the royal grant, of Davidic heirs, promises from the prophets about a wonderful king, a mighty counselor, who will bring about divine redemption. Promises in Daniel to the son of man who, in Daniel, really does represent the corporate community but in later speculation becomes an individual figure who will somehow redeem humankind. How do all those speculations cohere and come together and give us the various messianic portraits and, indeed, job descriptions that we find in Judaism and Christianity?

Obviously, I could go on and on. I won't. I simply want to give you a sense of what else is left both in terms of developing material that we've already looked at and in looking at material we have not even had time to touch.

I can sense that this eschatological moment is approaching, and when I look back *Urzeit* to *Endzeit*, I can find at the beginning of time, or at least at the beginning of our time together, a move from myth to saga to history, from tragedy to comedy to farce. Economic and political pronouncements and beautiful literature and poetry, court intrigue and prophetic morality, heavenly miracles, and sometimes heavenly silence. Questions of theodicy. Answers that satisfy and answers that don't. Destruction and re-building, despair and hope. There is everything in this text to explore.

If I've done my job right, and I hope that I have, at least you've got some sense of how wonderful and how rich this material is. And perhaps some day we'll be able to talk about this in person. I hope you enjoy, and thanks for being with me.

Timeline

Notes: All rounded numbers are approximate. All dates are B.C.E.

1800–1700 (Middle Bronze Age)	Patriarchs and matriarchs
1700–1300	Israel in Egypt
1300	Exodus from Egypt
1280	Reign of Ramses II (1290–1224)
1250–1200	The "conquest"
1200–1000	Period of the Judges
1000–922	Davidic monarchy; time of the (hypothetical) "J" writer
922–722	The Divided Kingdom; time of the (hypothetical) "E" writer
850	Elijah, Jezebel, and Ahab
ca. 750	Amos
ca. 740	Hosea
724–722	Siege of Samaria
722	Assyrian conquest of Israel; dispersal of the ten northern tribes.
715–687	Hezekiah rules the Southern Kingdom
701	Sennacherib's unsuccessful siege of Jerusalem.
700	The first Isaiah
640–609	Josiah
622	Josiah finds the Book of Deuteronomy and implements the Deuteronimic Reforms
612	Nineveh (the Assyrian capital) falls to Babylon

609 ....Josiah is killed and the Deuteronomic Reform ends

ca. 620–597................................Jeremiah

597 ....First deportation to Babylon

587 ....Nebuchadnezzar destroys Jerusalem; second deportation

587–539/8 ....Ezekiel; the second Isaiah; the priestly writers edit J and E

539/8 ....Edict of Cyrus

522–486 ....Darius I; work on rebuilding the Temple begins

ca. 515.......................................Haggai, Zech. 1–8

465–424 ....Ezra (Ruth? Jonah?); editing of Proverbs

423 ....Nehemiah

400–300 ....Early versions of the Book of Esther and Dan. 1–6

331 ....Battle of Issus: Alexander the Great conquers the Persian empire

323–198 ....Judah under Ptolemaic rule

198 ....Battle of Paneas: Seleucids gain Palestine

175–163 ....Antiochus IV Epiphanes

167 ....Maccabean revolt; Daniel 7–12

165 ....Rededication of the Temple

Glossary

A.D.: Anno Domini, in the year of our Lord (see **C.E.**).

Aaronides: Descendants of Aaron and a subset of the Levites who came to power during and after the Babylonian Exile.

Amarna Letters: Cache of letters found in el-Amarna in Egypt, dating to the fifteenth century and testifying to the political turmoil in Palestine involving the Habiru.

Ammonites: Descendants of the son conceived by Lot and his older daughter (see **Moabites**).

Anthropomorphism: Describing the non-human (God, the divine presence, Wisdom) by means of human characteristics.

Apocalyptic: From the Greek for "revelation" or "uncovering"; a type of literature, often ascribed to an ancient worthy, with a concern for heavenly secrets, substantial use of symbolism, and frequently an eschatological focus (e.g., Dan. 7–12).

Apocrypha: From the Greek for "hidden," a term designating the books written by Jews during Hellenistic and Roman times (ca. 200 B.C.E.–100 C.E.), included in the LXX, that became canonical for Catholic and Orthodox Christianity (see **Deutero-Canonical Texts**).

Apodictic Law: Absolute or unconditional law (as in the Decalogue); a characteristic of Israelite law but rare elsewhere in the ancient Near East (see also **Casuistic Law**).

Aramaic: A Semitic language closely related to Hebrew and Syriac (see **Peshitta**); parts of the books of Daniel and Ezra are in Aramaic.

Asherah: The Canaanite mother goddess, as well as the trees or groves dedicated to her.

Atrahasis: Hero of a Babylonian flood myth whose story is preserved on clay tablets dating to the seventeenth century B.C.E.

B.C.: Before Christ (see **B.C.E.**).

B.C.E.: Before the Common Era; a non-confessional expression for B.C.

Baal: The Canaanite god of thunder and rain and, hence, of fertility; the popularity of his cult motivated both polemic from the prophets and the co-optation of his imagery by the psalmist. When not used as a proper name, the noun means "master" or "husband."

C.E.: Common Era; a non-confessional expression for A.D.

Canaan: The geographical area between the Jordan River and the Mediterranean Sea; in Genesis, God promises it to Abraham and his descendants. The region was later called "Palestine."

Canon: From the Greek for "reed, measuring stick, plumb line," the list of books considered inspired or official; the foundation documents of a community.

Casuistic Law: Standard ancient Near Eastern legal formulation that lists prohibitions and consequences for violation.

Cherubim (sing. **Cherub**): half-human, half-animal creatures, often depicted with wings, who guard the divine throne.

Circumcision: The removal of the foreskin; the initiation ritual (for men) into the covenant community and the sign of the covenant.

Codex (pl. **Codices**): The book form as opposed to a scroll.

Corvée: State-mandated forced labor.

Cosmology: A myth describing the ordered origin of the universe.

Cyrus Cylinder: Artifact from 528 B.C.E. reporting the Persian policy of repatriating exilic communities and promoting their cultic practices.

D (Deuteronomic) Source: One of the four (hypothetical) sources contributing to the composition of the Pentateuch; represented in the Book of Deuteronomy and likely composed in the late seventh century B.C.E. (See also **Deuteronomic History**.)

Dead Sea Scrolls: Manuscripts found in 1948 and subsequently on the shores of the Dead Sea (see **Qumran**), including numerous copies of biblical books; extremely helpful for text criticism.

Decalogue: Literally "ten words"; a term designating the "ten commandments" (Exod. 20:1–17 [see also Exod. 34]; Deut. 5:6–21).

Deutero-Canonical Texts: The "second part" of the canon of the Old Testament; an alternative designation by Catholic and (Christian) Orthodox churches for the (Old Testament) Apocrypha. (See **Apocrypha**.)

Deutero-Isaiah: The "second Isaiah" who wrote to comfort the exiled community in Babylon (Isa. 40–55).

Deuteronomic History: The Book of Joshua through Second Kings; likely redacted in the early Second Temple period, the narrative displays the Deuteronomic view that righteousness is rewarded and evil, punished.

Deuteronomic Reform: See **Josianic Reform**.

Diaspora: Greek for "dispersion"; from the Babylonian Exile to the present, any place outside of Israel where Jews live.

Divination: Attempts to determine divine will or predict the future through omens, dreams, and the like.

Documentary Hypothesis: Also called the Graf-Wellhausen Hypothesis; the theory that four sources, J, E, D, and P, were combined to create the Pentateuch.

E (Elohist) Source: Hypothetical source marked by the use of "Elohim" for the Deity; likely composed in the Northern Kingdom ca. 800.

Edomites: From the Hebrew for "red"; descendants of Esau who settled south of the Dead Sea; one of Israel's enemies.

El: Generic word for a god; sometimes used as a proper name, for example, the head of the Canaanite pantheon.

Elohim: Grammatically the plural of El; when used as a designation of the biblical God, it takes singular verbs.

Enumah Elish: "When on high"; the Babylonian creation myth that shares striking similarities to the Genesis cosmogony (Gen. 1).

Ephraim: A son of Joseph and one of the twelve tribes; a (poetic) name for the Northern Kingdom.

Eponymous Ancestor: Figure who gives his or her name to a group of descendants, e.g., Israel, Moab.

Eschatology: Literally, "words concerning the end"; material describing the end of an age or of time and often involving the in-breaking of divine rule.

Etiology: A story of origins.

Exegesis: From the Greek for "to lead out," critical interpretation of biblical material.

Form Criticism: Analytical approach to the structure of a pericope that seeks to determine genre, function, and *Sitz im Leben*.

Gemorah (Gemara): Section of the Talmud containing both legal and narrative materials; a commentary on the Mishnah that links it to the *Tanakh*.

Gilgamesh Epic: Ancient Near Eastern epic, preserved on clay tablets from ca. 1750 B.C.E., with parallels to the Garden of Eden and Flood stories.

Graf-Wellhausen Hypothesis: See **Documentary Hypothesis**.

Habiru: A group, comprised of various ethnicities, whose presence is attested in Canaan in texts from the second millennium B.C.E. (see **Amarna Letters**); this apparently wandering band may have some connection to the Hebrews.

Hannukah: Hebrew for "dedication"; festival celebrating the rededication of the Jerusalem Temple by the Maccabees after their defeat of Seleucid forces.

Hasidim: "Pious ones" who resisted the assimilationist mandates of Antiochus IV Epiphanes.

Hasmoneans: From Hasmon, the grandfather of Judah Maccabee; another name for the Macabees, usually used in reference to the dynasty they founded.

Hebrew: A Semitic language in which most of the Old Testament/*Tanakh* is written; a Semitic population group descended from Eber (an eponymous ancestor, Gen. 10:24); a designation for the covenant community from the patriarchal period until the Babylonian exile, perhaps derived from the Hebrew "to cross over."

Hellenism: Greek thought and culture brought to the East by the conquests of Alexander the Great.

Henotheism: Belief in one supreme god among many divine beings.

Hermeneutics: Term derived from the Greek god Hermes; biblical interpretation related to Exegesis but often with the connotation of involving the presuppositions and goals of the interpreter.

Hexateuch: The first six scrolls (Genesis–Joshua); a theory that the first part of Israel's story ends with the "conquering" of the Promised Land.

Hittites: Non-Semitic people, centered in the second millennium B.C.E. in Syria and Asia Minor.

Horeb: E's name for Sinai; location of Elijah's theophany.

Hyksos: Asiatic group who ruled Egypt from ca. 1710 until being expelled by Pharaoh Ahmose ca. 1570; sometimes associated with the stories of Joseph and the Exodus.

J (Yahwist [German: Jahweh] Source): Hypothetical source beginning with Gen. 2:4b and extending perhaps as far as 2 Sam. 7; marked by anthropomorphic descriptions of God, the use of the name YHWH before the Exodus, the reiteration of the promises of descendants, land, and blessing; usually dated to the Southern Kingdom (Judah) ca. 900 B.C.E.

Jehovah: See **YHWH**.

Josianic Reform: Sponsored by King Josiah in Judah ca. 622 B.C.E. and supported by the discovery of a version of what became the Book of Deuteronomy; its major action was the centralization of the cult in Jerusalem.

Judah: Son of Jacob; tribe of Israel; Southern Kingdom (following the cessation of the northern tribes under Jereboam I).

Judea: Name for and geographical location of the Post-Exilic state; attested in Ezra and Nehemiah; its inhabitants became known as "Jews."

Kenites: Midianites who affiliate with Israel in the wilderness and join the settlement of Canaan.

Kenite Hypothesis: Proposal that Yahwism stems from the Kenites—perhaps through the priest of Midian, Jethro, Moses's father-in-law.

Ketuvim: Hebrew for "writings"; the third division of the *Tanakh*

Levites: Priestly group descended from Levi; disenfranchised from local shrines by the Josianic Reform. Following the Babylonian exile, those who are not also Aaronides become Temple workers.

LXX: Abbreviation for the Septuagint, the Greek translation of the *Tanakh*; the designation "seventy" comes from the legend that the translation was produced by seventy scribes from Jerusalem.

Maccabees: Jewish family who led the rebellion against Antiochus IV Epiphanes in 167 B.C.E.

Marduk: Patron god of Babylon and hero of the Enumah Elish.

Masoretic Text (MT): The received form of the *Tanakh*; edited and standardized by the Masoretes, Jewish scholars who added "points" (i.e., vowels), ca. seventh through ninth centuries C.E.

Megillot (sing. **Megillah**): Hebrew for "scrolls"; traditional designation for the Books of Lamentations, Ecclesiastes, Ruth, Esther, and the Song of Songs.

Merneptah Stele: Egyptian inscription erected by Pharaoh Merneptah (ca. 1210) that contains the first extra-biblical reference to Israel.

Messiah: Hebrew for "anointed" (Greek: Christos).

Mezuzah: Hebrew for "doorpost" and, hence, for the receptacle affixed thereon that contains passages from Deuteronomy (see Deut. 6:9).

Midrash: Jewish stories that expand and/or explain biblical texts.

Mishnah: Collection of Jewish laws codified ca. 200; part of the Talmud.

Moabites: Descendants of the son conceived by Lot and his younger daughter (see **Ammonites**); traditional enemies of Israel; Ruth's ethnic origin.

Monotheism: Belief that there is only one God.

Myth: A story of origins, often featuring divine beings, that expresses a society's self-identity.

Nazirite: An individual consecrated to God, usually for a specific period, whose practices include abstaining from wine and alcohol, avoiding corpses, and eschewing haircuts.

Nevi'im: Hebrew for "Prophets"; the second division of the *Tanakh*.

Noachide Laws: Jewish legend positing that seven laws were given to Noah to provide gentile nations with a moral code.

P (Priestly) Source: Marked by attention to law, Aaron, and genealogies, this (hypothetical) source redacted J, E, and D sometime during or soon after the Babylonian Exile.

Palestine: See **Canaan**; the name derives from the Philistines.

Pentateuch: From the Greek for "five scrolls," the first five biblical books, the Torah.

Pericope: From the Greek for "to cut around," a narrative unit that can be analyzed apart from its literary context (e.g., story, poem, saying).

Peshitta: Syriac translation of the *Tanakh* especially useful for text criticism. Syriac was a dialect of Aramaic that flourished in the early years of the common era, especially among Christians in the eastern part of the Roman empire.

Philistines: Non-Semitic, probably Mediterranean people who settled the coastal areas of Canaan in the early Iron Age (ca. 1200); often enemies of Israel (Jdg.–1 Sam.) until the Davidic monarchy.

Pilgrimage Festivals: Three feasts for which it was traditional to visit the Jerusalem Temple: Passover/Feast of Unleavened bread (Hebrew, Pesach), commemorating the Exodus and the winter harvest; Weeks (Hebrew, Shavuoth; Greek, Pentecost), commemorating the giving of the Torah at Sinai fifty days later and the spring harvest; and Booths/Tabernacles (Hebrew: Sukkoth), commemorating the Exodus, the wilderness period, and the fall harvest.

Prophecy ex Eventu: Prophecy after the fact; the attribution of a text to an ancient worthy such that its description of history appears as prophecy rather than as reflection.

Prophets: The second section of the *Tanakh*.

Pseudepigrapha: Literally "false writings"; Jewish texts from Hellenistic and Roman times ascribed to ancient worthies (e.g., 4 Ezra, 2 Baruch).

Ptolemies: Heirs of Alexander the Great's general, the dynasty that governed Egypt and, from 323–198, ruled Judea.

Purim: Persian for "lots"; festival for which the etiology appears in the Book of Esther.

Qoheleth: A derivation from the Hebrew for "to assemble" (Greek: Ecclesiastes, from Ecclesia, "assembly"); a title for the book and the author.

Qumran: Area where the Dead Sea Scrolls were found.

Ras Shamra: Northern Syrian location where a cache of Canaanite religious texts, including Baal myths, was discovered in 1929.

Redaction Criticism: An analysis of concerns of the editor (redactor) of a text as determined by editorial expansion, arrangement, and comment.

Royal Grant: Covenant granted by a suzerain, sometimes as a reward for past service, and in guarantee of future aid and protection; this covenantal formulation, as opposed to the **suzerainty/vassal model**, is associated with Noah, Abraham, and especially David (2 Sam. 7; Pss. 89, 132).

Samaria: Capital of the Northern Kingdom.

Samaritans: The population of the former Northern Kingdom of Israel following the deportation by Assyria of many Israelites and the resettling in Samaria of peoples from elsewhere in the Assyrian empire.

Second Isaiah: See **Deutero-Isaiah**.

Second Temple Period: Judaism from the beginning of Persian rule to the destruction of the Temple by Rome in 70 C.E.

Seleucids: Heirs of Alexander the Great's general, the dynasty that governed Syria and, in 198, obtained Judea from the Ptolemies.

Septuagint: See **LXX**.

Shekinah: The feminine presence of the Divine.

***Sh'ma* (Shema)**: From the Hebrew for the imperative "Hear!"; the Jewish statement of faith beginning with Deut. 6:4–9.

Sheol: The home of the dead, a shadowy place below the earth; early references display no conception of punishment or reward.

Sinai: Today called Jebel Musa, the "Mountain of Moses"; J's expression for the traditional site of the giving of the Torah to Moses.

Sitz im Leben: German for "setting in life"; the cultural and historical context of a book or pericope.

Son of Man: A human being (Ezek., Pss.); in Dan. 7:13, the symbol of the covenant community who appears in the heavenly throne room and who is given earthly rule.

Sons of the Prophets: Bands or guilds of prophets, sometimes traveling with a prophetic leader, such as Elijah or Elisha.

Sophia: Greek for "Wisdom"; the personification of Wisdom in female form.

Stele: A free-standing pillar with inscriptions.

Suzerainty/Vassal Treaty: Covenant formulation between unequal parties guaranteeing protection on the part of the suzerain and fidelity on the part of the vassal; the form of the Mosaic covenant (see **Royal Grant**).

Tabernacle: The wilderness shrine that housed the Ark (see Exod. 25–40).

Talmud: A compendium of Jewish law and lore consisting of the Mishnah and the Gemorah; the Babylonian Talmud was codified ca. 700 C.E. and the Palestinian, ca. 400 C.E.

***Tanakh* (Tanak, Tanach)**: Acronym for "Torah, Nevi'im, Ketuvim"; a way of designating the canon used by the synagogue.

Targum: An Aramaic translation/paraphrase of a biblical book.

Tefillin (Greek: phylacteries): Small boxes containing scriptural passages that are worn on the left hand and forehead for worship and kept in place by straps wrapped, respectively, seven times around the left arm and around the head.

***Tel* (*Tell*)**: From the Hebrew/Arabic for "hill," an artificial mound created by the layers of habitation debris.

Tetragrammaton: Expression for the "four letters" (consonants) that stand for the personal name of the Deity (see **YHWH**).

Text (Textual) Criticism (Low Criticism): Method for determining the original wording of a text.

Theodicy: From the Greek for "justice of god," the question of why the wicked prosper and the righteous suffer.

Theophany: From the Greek for "god's appearance," a manifestation of the Divine.

Torah: Hebrew for "instruction" or "law"; the first five books of the Bible.

Twelve, Book of the: The collection also known as the "Minor Prophets": Hosea, Joel, Amos, Obadiah, Jonah, Micah, Nahum, Habakkuk, Zephaniah, Haggai, Zechariah, and Malachi.

Type Scene: A literary convention; manipulation of the conventional elements entertainingly reveals character development; examples include the "ancestress in danger," the "woman at the well," "annunciations," and "rival wives."

Ugarit: Canaanite city in modern Syria; location of a major cache of Canaanite myths.

Vulgate: From the Latin for "common," St. Jerome's translation of the Hebrew canon into Latin in 405 C.E.

Wisdom Literature: An international genre addressing questions of theodicy and nature and how to live the good life. Biblical examples are Proverbs, Ecclesiastes (Qoheleth), and Job; the Old Testament Apocrypha/Deutero-canonical collection offers Wisdom of Solomon and the Wisdom of Jesus Ben Sirach (Sirach, Ecclesiasticus).

YHWH: The personal name of God, likely meaning "he will be what he will be"; it is not pronounced in Jewish liturgical settings. English translations usually render this term as "Lord" (the four letters in each facilitate remembering the connection).

***Ziggurat* (*Ziqqurat*)**: Mesopotamian temple in the form of a terraced mountain or pyramid erected to serve as a symbolic bridge between heaven and earth.

Zion: Another name for Jerusalem; the Temple mount.

Bibliography

Essential Reading: The Old Testament/the *Tanakh*.

Note: The Hebrew is to be preferred in all cases. No translation can capture the riches of the original: the puns, the polyvalency, and ambiguity. Should the reader not be fluent in biblical Hebrew (which is not the same as modern Hebrew), several very good translations are available. These include, but are not limited to, the ones listed below.

The Jewish Publication Society (JPS) version: *Tanakh: A New Translation of the Holy Scripture According to the Traditional Hebrew Text*.

The Revised Standard Version (RSV): An essentially literal translation but with updated language.

The New Revised Standard Version (NRSV): Substantially the same as the RSV, but gender inclusive (which sometimes skews the connotations of the Hebrew). Several editions with critical notes from interfaith scholarly contributors are available, for example, Gail R. O'Day and David Petersen (gen. eds.), *The Access Bible: New Revised Standard Version, with the Apocryphal/Deuterocanonical Books* (New York: Oxford University Press, 1999).

The New American Bible (NAB): Translation produced by and for Roman Catholics.

The New International Version (NIV): Produced by and for Protestant Evangelicals.

Everett Fox, *The Five Books of Moses: Genesis, Exodus, Leviticus, Numbers, Deuteronomy: A New Translation with Introductions, Commentary, and Notes* (New York, Schocken Books, 1995): An attempt to preserve the sense of the Hebrew (better when read aloud). See also Fox's *Give us a King! Samuel, Saul, and David: A New Translation of Samuel I and II* (New York: Schocken Books, 1999).

The King James Version (KJV) or "Authorized Version" is the one with language most familiar to English speakers. The volume was commissioned by King James I of England for use in the Anglican Church. It is, however, often difficult to understand, and its renditions of the Hebrew do not have the advantage of more recent manuscript discoveries, linguistic study, or the witness of the Dead

Sea Scrolls. It also occasionally adapts the Hebrew to the Christological concerns of the New Testament.

I encourage students to avoid modern paraphrases, such as *Good News for Modern Man* and *Today's English Version* (TEV).

Supplementary Reading:

Note: Studies of the Old Testament/*Tanakh* have been produced since the Hellenistic period; written by Jews, Christians, and Unitarians, as well as atheists, agnostics, and members of other traditions, they are found in synagogues and churches, seminary libraries and secular bookstores, in private homes and in museums. The bibliographic items listed after each chapter and below offer only a small representation of the academic study of the Bible. I have attempted to avoid works requiring knowledge of ancient languages, works requiring a nearby divinity school or seminary library (including articles in professional journals), and works with a relatively narrow denominational or confessional focus. I have attempted to include works that present a variety of opinions and approaches and to list primarily recent studies (in almost all cases, the sources listed below have their own bibliographical references to earlier scholarship). I also list several encyclopedias and dictionaries.

Resources

Achtemeier, Paul J. (gen. ed.), *The HarperCollins Bible Dictionary* (San Francisco: Harper San Francisco, 1996): Dictionary produced in cooperation with the Society of Biblical Literature (a major professional society of biblical scholars).

Aharoni, Yohanan, and Michael Avi-Yonah, *The Macmillan Bible Atlas* (New York: Macmillan, 1977).

Brown, Raymond, Joseph A. Fitzmyer, and Roland E. Murphy (eds.), *The New Jerome Biblical Commentary* (Englewood Cliffs, NJ: Prentice Hall, 1999).

Coogan, Michael D. (ed.), *The Oxford History of the Biblical World* (New York: Oxford University Press, 1998): Articles by leading scholars on the historical and cultural periods in which biblical events took shape.

Farmer, William R. (ed.), *The International Bible Commentary: A Catholic and Ecumenical Commentary for the Twenty-First Century* (Collegeville, MN: Liturgical Press, 1998).

Freedman, D. N., et al., *The Anchor Bible Dictionary*, six vols. (New York: Doubleday, 1992; available on CD-ROM): Signed articles by leading scholars; inclusive bibliographies; a major resource for scholar and lay reader alike.

Hayes, John H. (gen. ed.), *Dictionary of Biblical Interpretation*, 2 vols. (Nashville: Abingdon, 1999): Major scholars and methods.

Knight, Douglas A., and Gene M. Tucker (eds.), *The Hebrew Bible and Its Modern Interpreters* (Philadelphia: Fortress Press, 1985): Excellent collection of essays on the major issues and theories in academic biblical study.

Matthews, Victor H., and Don C. Benjamin, *Old Testament Parallels: Laws and Stories from the Ancient Near East* (New York: Paulist Press, 1991).

Metzger, Bruce M., and Michael D. Coogan (eds.), *The Oxford Companion to the Bible* (New York: Oxford University Press, 1993): Short articles on major figures, events, locations, and other topics in dictionary format.

Newsom, Carol A., and Sharon H. Ringe (eds.), *The Women's Bible Commentary* (Louisville: Westminster/John Knox, 1992): Essays by women academics that combine more traditional approaches with attention to gender roles, women's history, and hermeneutical implications.

Shanks, Herschel (ed.), *Bible Review* (as well its sister publication, *Biblical Archaeology Review*): An often original, sometimes irreverent magazine written by scholars but designed for the general public; the illustrations are superb.

Series (commentaries on individual books, as well as major subject areas):

Anchor Bible (New York: Doubleday).

Anchor Bible Reference Library (New York: Doubleday).

Berit Olam (Collegeville, MN: Liturgical Press).

Feminist Companions, edited by Athalya Brenner (Sheffield: University Press).

Hermeneia (Philadelphia: Fortress Press).

New Interpreter's Bible (Nashville: Abingdon).

The Old Testament Library (Louisville: Westminster/John Knox).

Introductions (a few among many):

Anderson, Bernard, *Understanding the Old Testament*, 4th ed. (Englewood Cliffs: Prentice Hall, 1986).

Flanders, Henry Jackson, Jr., Robert Wilson Crapps, and David Anthony Smith, *People of the Covenant: An Introduction to the Hebrew Bible*, 4th ed. (New York: Oxford University Press, 1996).

Frick, Frank S., *A Journey through the Hebrew Scriptures* (Fort Worth: Harcourt Brace College Publishers, 1995).

Gottwald, Norman K., *The Hebrew Bible: A Socio-Literary Introduction* (Philadelphia: Fortress Press, 1985).

Levenson, Jon D., *Sinai and Zion: An Entry into the Jewish Bible* (Minneapolis: Winston, 1985).

Individual Studies:

Ackerman, Susan, *Warrior, Dancer, Seductress, Queen: Women in Judges and Biblical Israel*, Anchor Bible Reference Library (New York: Doubleday, 1998).

Alter, Robert, *The Art of Biblical Narrative* (New York: Basic Books, 1981): A prize-winning literary critical study that popularized the study of type scenes, traced the impact of themes and even key words throughout different books, and explored the importance of the juxtaposition of stories for mutual interpretation.

Anderson, Gary, Michael Stone, and Johannes Tromp (eds.), *Literature on Adam and Eve: Collected Essays*, Studies in Veteris Testamenti Pseudepigrapa (Leiden and Boston: E. J. Brill, 2000).

Bailey, Lloyd R., *Noah: The Person and the Story in History and Tradition* (Columbia, SC: University of South Carolina Press, 1989).

Bal, Mieke, *Death and Dissymmetry: The Politics of Coherence in the Book of Judges* (Chicago: University of Chicago Press, 1988).

Ballentine, Samuel E., *Prayer in the Hebrew Bible* (Philadelphia: Fortress, 1993).

———, *The Torah's Vision of Worship* (Minneapolis: Fortress, 1999).

Barr, James, *The Garden of Eden and the Hope of Immortality* (Philadelphia: Fortress, 1993).

Blenkinsopp, Joseph, *The Pentateuch: An Introduction to the First Five Books of the Bible*, Anchor Bible Reference Library (New

York: Doubleday, 1992): A good overview of approaches, with a helpful description of the Documentary Hypothesis.

Brueggemann, Walter, *Theology of the Old Testament: Testimony, Dispute, Advocacy* (Minneapolis: Fortress Press, 1997).

Collins, John J., *The Apocalyptic Imagination: An Introduction to Jewish Apocalyptic Literature*, 2nd ed. (Grand Rapids, MI: William B. Eerdmans, 1998).

Craig, Kenneth M., *The Poetics of Jonah: Art in the Service of Ideology*, 2nd ed. (Macon, GA: Mercer University Press, 1999).

Delaney, Carol Lowery, *Abraham on Trial: The Social Legacy of Biblical Myth* (Princeton, NJ: Princeton University Press, 1998).

Dever, William G., *Recent Archaeological Discoveries and Biblical Research* (Seattle: University of Washington Press, 1990).

Douglas, Mary, *Purity and Danger: An Analysis of Concepts of Pollution and Taboo* (London/Boston: Ark Paperbacks, 1966, 1984).

Dundes, Alan (ed.), *The Flood Myth* (Berkeley: University of California Press, 1988).

Dundes, Alan, *Holy Writ as Oral Lit: The Bible as Folklore* (Lanham, MD: Rowan and Littlefield, 1999).

Eilberg-Schwartz, Howard, *The Savage in Judaism: An Anthropology of Israelite Religion and Judaism* (Bloomington: Indiana University Press, 1990): Prize-winning, controversial study of ritual practice and the use of metaphor.

Exum, J. Cheryl, *Fragmented Women: Feminist Subversions of Biblical Narratives* (Sheffield: JSOT Press, 1993).

Falk, Marcia, *Love Lyrics from the Bible, The Song of Sons: A New Translation and Interpretation* (San Francisco: HarperCollins, 1990): Poet and linguist happily meet.

Fewell, Danna Nolan, *Circle of Sovereignty: A Story of Stories in Daniel 1–6* (Sheffield: Almond Press, 1988).

Fox, Michael, *Character and Ideology in the Book of Esther* (Columbia, SC: University of South Carolina Press, 1991).

Friedman, Richard Elliott, *Who Wrote the Bible?* (Englewood Cliffs: Prentice-Hall, 1987). Idiosyncratic but extremely engaging study.

Harrelson, Walter, *The Ten Commandments and Human Rights* (Philadelphia: Fortress Press, 1981): A study by a leading Old

Testament scholar of how the Bible has been, and can be, used for purposes of social justice.

Humphries, W. Lee, *Joseph and his Family: A Literary Study* (Columbia, SC: University of South Carolina Press, 1988).

Jobling, David, *First Samuel* (Collegeville, MN: Liturgical Press, 1998).

Kirsch, Jonathan, *Moses: A Life* (New York: Bantam Books, 1998).

Kugel, James L., *In Potiphar's House: The Interpretive Life of Biblical Texts* (San Francisco: HarperCollins, 1990).

———, *Traditions of the Bible: A Guide to the Bible as It Was at the Start of the Common Era* (Cambridge, MA: Harvard University Press, 1998).

Kvam, Kristen, Linda S. Schearing, and Valarie H. Ziegler, *Eve and Adam: Jewish, Christian and Muslim Readings on Genesis and Gender* (Bloomington: Indiana University Press, 1999).

Larsson, Göran, *Bound for Freedom: The Book of Exodus in Jewish and Christian Traditions* (Peabody, MA: Hendrikson, 1999).

Lemche, Niels Peter, *Early Israel: Anthropological and Historical Studies on the Israelite Society before the Monarchy* (Leiden: E.J. Brill, 1985).

Levenson, Jon D., *Death and Resurrection of the Beloved Son: The Transformation of Child Sacrifice in Judaism and Christianity* (New Haven: Yale University Press, 1993).

Matthews, Victor H., Bernard Levinson, and Tikva Frymer-Kensky, *Gender and Law in the Hebrew Bible and the Ancient Near East* (Sheffield: Sheffield Academic Press, 1998).

Mazar, Amihai, *Archaeology of the Land of the Bible: 10,000–586 B.C.E.* (New York: Bantam Doubleday Dell, 1990).

McKenzie, Stephen L., *King David: A Biography* (Oxford and New York: Oxford University Press, 2000).

Meyers, Carol, *Discovering Eve: Ancient Israelite Women in Context* (New York: Oxford University Press, 1988): Prize-winning, innovative study combining sociology, archaeology, and linguistics.

Murphy, Roland E., *The Tree of Life: An Exploration of Biblical Wisdom Literature* (New York: Doubleday, 1990).

Neusner, Jacob, William Scott Green, and Ernest S. Frerichs (eds.), *Judaisms and Their Messiahs at the Turn of the Christian Era* (Cambridge/New York: Cambridge University Press, 1987).

Niditch, Susan, *Ancient Israelite Religion* (New York: Oxford University Press, 1997).

———, *Folklore and the Hebrew Bible* (Philadelphia: Fortress Press, 1993).

———, *War in the Hebrew Bible: A Study in the Ethics of Violence* (New York: Oxford University Press, 1997).

Olyan, Saul, *Rites and Rank: Hierarchy in Biblical Representations of Cult* (Princeton, NJ: Princeton University Press, 2000.

Perdue, Leo, and Clark Gilpin (eds.), *The Voice from the Whirlwind: Interpreting the Book of Job* (Nashville: Abingdon, 1992): Studies addressing historical, literary, and theological issues edited by a professor of biblical studies and a theologian.

Rendtorff, Rolf, *The Covenant Formula: An Exegetical and Theological Investigation*, Margaret Kohl, trans. (Edinburgh: T&T Clark, 1998).

Rogerson, John, and Philip Davies, *The Old Testament World* (Englewood Cliffs, NJ: Prentice-Hall, 1989).

Sawyer, John F. A. (ed.), *Reading Leviticus: A Conversation with Mary Douglas* (Sheffield: Sheffield Academic Press, 1996).

Smith, Mark, *The Early History of God: Yahweh and Other Deities in Ancient Israel* (San Francisco: Harper, 1990).

Spiegel, Shalom, *The Last Trial*, Judah Golden, trans. (New York: Schocken, 1969): Fascinating study of the history of the interpretation of the *Akedah* (Gen. 22).

Steussy, Marti J., *David: Biblical Portraits of Power* (Columbia, SC: University of South Carolina Press, 1999).

Trible, Phyllis, *Texts of Terror: Literary-Feminist Readings of Biblical Narratives* (Philadelphia: Fortress Press, 1984).

Wills, Lawrence, *The Jew in the Court of the Foreign King: Ancient Jewish Court Legends* (Minneapolis, MN: Fortress Press, 1990).

Wright, J. Edward, *The Early History of Heaven* (New York: Oxford University Press, 2000).

Yee, Gail (ed.), *Judges and Method: New Approaches in Biblical Studies* (Minneapolis: Fortress Press, 1995).

